KU-153-941

From East to West by Saddle is Best

A horseback journey across
the Scottish Highlands

Written by
Claire Alldritt

From East to West by Saddle is Best

Text copyright © 2020 Claire Alldritt

Photographs copyright © 2020 Claire Alldritt

Illustrations copyright © 2020 Leandra Sutherland

Map by Claire Alldritt
Copy-edited by Sari Mayhew
Text design by www.georginatalfana.com
Cover design by www.georginatalfana.com
Cover Image: Glen Tilt, photo by Fiona Duniam

ISBN number 9798698092957

All rights reserved.
No part of this publication may be reproduced
or used in any form without the prior written
consent by the author.

Horse Trails with a Bear and a Spotty Bum

www.bearandspottybum.com

Illustrations by Leandra Sutherland

The Author
Claire Alldritt

Photo by Ellen Klaveness

Claire has always had a passion for outdoor adventure. This started at a young age, with both parents being involved in the Scout and Guide movements resulting in many weekends spent under canvas, whittling sticks, peeling spuds, and cooking over an open fire. In adulthood, this led to adventure travel in many different countries and wild places around the world.

Closer to home in Scotland, the adventure is constant; when Claire says she is just 'popping out' with a rucksack over her shoulder, don't expect to see her for a while. Her fascination to see where a trail leads to, or what's just around the next corner, feeds her constant desire to explore.

Recognising the importance of adventure for all, Claire runs a charity (Outfit Moray) in her spare-time that provides the opportunity of outdoor activities to disadvantaged and vulnerable young people near where she lives.

Horses have always featured in Claire's life, but work commitments as a petrophysicist (someone who studies rock properties for the oil industry) and then as an outdoor sports instructor required a different focus for a while. A better work-life balance as a paramedic, enabled a return to all things equine and the realisation of her childhood dream to own horses.

Mixing a love of the hills with owning horses, plus a craving for exploration, challenge, and adventure - led to a sport she likes to call dobbineering. She regularly carries out this gentle kind of mountaineering with horses in the Scottish Highlands, exploring the glens and an occasional hilltop but especially the history of the places and routes travelled through.

Acknowledgements

Much gratitude to those who encouraged me to write: my parents and my wonderful friend Jo Keen. There was a long gap between starting it and continuing the project to completion, a gap where I struggled to find spoken words let alone any written ones. I would not have started writing again if it wasn't for you.

My parents and the Scout/Guide movements need appreciation for initiating a need for adventure that I just can't shake. It really all started with 'expeditions' to discover 'gold' near the closed mines of Wales.

There are two main journeys within this book, the one to my horses (the forming of deep understanding and a cohesive bond) and the one with my horses (the physical east to west ride). I could not have travelled along either journey without help. Thank you Yvonne, Leaf, Alice, Ellen, Holly, Dave, Fiona, Adrian, and Sal. I also very much appreciate the generosity from strangers I have met and continue to meet along the way.

Thank you to Leandra Enstone for her wonderful illustrations. Sketches she prefers to call "doodles", but many of us think they are much more than that.

Most thanks (and undying love) must go to my biggest supporter, my rock, my confidant and long-suffering husband, Dave. I have no idea how he stuck with me through the worst of my Lyme disease days, but I am thoroughly indebted. I could not have pulled myself out of the dark depths without him. I am also truly blessed to have found someone who understands my deep-rooted need to adventure.

Claire Alldritt 2020.

Contents

The Game of Maps from east to west

The Game of Maps

Maps have always held a fascination for me. Any type will do, but there is nothing quite like the comforting familiarity of an Ordnance Survey 1:50,000. I love following the contours, bringing an image of the solid reality of the hills and glens to my mind. Visions as full of colour as the maps themselves, creating a sense of movement and motion as you travel so quickly through the dream. Flying over undulations with the wind through your hair, blowing leaves off trees, and rustling the grass or heather at your feet.

The tinkle of rivers, their tributaries, sources and ends, quirky place names, old settlements, and the placement of lochs. The strange shapes of rocky crags, huts positioned in far-away places, and ruins presented in 𝔬𝔩𝔡 𝔰𝔱𝔶𝔩𝔢 𝔱𝔢𝔵𝔱 to entice you into exploring their past. Nothing, however, beats following marked trails, seeing how far you could travel before a barrier brings you to a halt.

Like a game of snakes and ladders but with a main road, an expanse of water, or a boundary fence to slide you back down to the start. When that barrier is reached, you play the trump card of the game, by zooming into a 1:25,000 view to discover a tiny path that might allow play to continue. How far can you go, what circuits exist, which labelled curiosities to explore, what discoveries or treasures might you unearth on your way?

In the past, as the winner of the game, I would have collected hill tops as point-scoring prizes. Now the trophy is acquired by continual travel, connections, historical context, and long-distance resilience. A gentler but by no means easier win. The reasons for the change of tactics unfold; first two legs, to six, and now ten involved.

Horses have been a part of my life since childhood, but I never thought I'd realise the dream of having one of my own. I certainly never thought I'd end up with two. Unplanned, the second addition was the beginning of a new addiction; long-distance travel, self-supported by horse. I am happiest remote, with wilderness as my companion, but that doesn't mean it has to be a lonesome experience. With a horse by your side, there can be no one more amicable with whom to travel than this gentle giant, willing to please, content to just be, and of the most forgiving nature.

To create that standard of companion is a journey itself of character exploration, training, mistakes, and hard lessons learnt. Thankfully, the horse is a patient teacher, and waits until you understand their language, develop your inner self-control, and earn their loyal trust.

Playing the Game of Maps on paper is only the start of the process. You may have avoided the snakes in the game but with eight hooves to manage along the trails, those routes may be more difficult to negotiate than first imagined. I guess I learnt the hard way at times, about what constitutes a suitable trail; it might look fine on the map, might sound good in recommendation, but would materialise as a risky reality.

Guidebooks are few and far between for this sort of thing. Those that exist could inspire, plant seeds and motivate, however, none could be specific enough for you and your unique team, to become an essential reference on the trail. Traffic light systems commonly used to grade other modes of outdoor adventure; of easy, moderate, or severe, just don't apply to this kind of game. The grade can't be defined by one person's ability or experience as the complexity of the relationship between specific humans and horses must be considered - and this alliance developed to create a unified team.

Defining what suitable means to you and your team is an individual process and each must find their own sense of purpose and level of play. What is suitable with one horse might not be with two to pilot. What is reasonable for one person with their unique horse (or horses) might be completely inappropriate for you with yours. Only the player knows the current level of trust and cohesion achieved, to judge what constitutes a reasonable and safe challenge to accept. The more you travel and face together, the more understanding is gained and the more accurate the estimate of 'suitable' becomes. Boundaries and comfort zones carefully explored over time provide this clarification.

One day I mastered the Game of Maps, and the dashes and dots joined Scotland from the east to the west. I spent a long time flying over the undulations before preparation began, to step up to the mark, to play the game for real. On paper, it looked achievable, but would the reality on the ground provide the right kind, the 'our kind', of suitable trails? After weeks of reconnaissance by vehicle, bike and foot, I felt that this game of east to west was on. Numerous obstacles to overcome, some on the edge of our current comfort zones, but none that should slide us back down to the start. We'd need some support along the way, but the challenge was established, it was accepted, and it was about to begin.

Day 1:
St Cyrus to Edzell
(Distance 28km, Ascent 306m)

After a restless night's sleep in our converted campervan parked by the beach, I awoke to high winds and heavy rain. Not exactly the start I was hoping for. This was going to be a big challenge for myself and my two horses and it would have been nice to set off in more clement weather. Still, there's not a lot you can do about the weather. As Billy Connolly once said, "There's no such thing as bad weather - only the wrong clothes" so I togged up in double waterproofs, one to keep out the rain and one in psychedelic colours to alert any traffic to our presence. I then found some determination to just get on with it.

'It' was a plan to ride one horse across Scotland from the east coast to the west coast whilst leading a second horse who would carry all our equipment. The type of equipment needed for the route I had planned not only included camping gear for me, but a collapsible corral system complete with electric unit to keep the horses enclosed at night and enough food for us all to last several days. I had christened this type of activity dobbineering: a gentle mountaineering with horses.

This was no direct A to B route; I planned to do this as self-supported as possible, exploring the hills and glens and avoiding as much tarmac as I possibly could. This meant that the route wove a winding trail and would take nearly three weeks to complete. The Game of Maps had linked up the trails from St Cyrus in the east, which offered a short route into the mountains from the North Sea, through familiar ground in the middle, to Glen Elg

4

in the west and the Atlantic Ocean. The middle of the proposed route would pass near where I lived and where I learnt the art of dobbineering by self-taught means.

Glen Elg was deemed a suitable end point to this marathon due to its historical links to droving. Drovers of times gone by, who often used horses and ponies, herded their cattle from this small town in the west to market towns further south. Since I was also travelling by horse and would be using some of their old ways through the hills, it seemed a fitting place to finish.

According to Thomas Gisbourne (an English essayist writing in 1849), "The Scottish drivers are for the most part mounted on small, shaggy, spirited ponies." Now, neither of my mounts could be described as particularly small, but they did have spirit and would probably look shaggy (as would I) by the time we finished the trek. My equine companions on this adventure would consist of Yogi (a chestnut Highland Pony cross Thoroughbred) known affectionately as 'The Bear', and Swift (a lanky Appaloosa cross American Quarter Horse), known just as affectionately as 'Spotty Bum'.

I had spent several days packing, trying to get everything I thought I would need as small and as light as I could but despite my careful preparation, I had a considerable amount of first-day bag faff. Getting everything to sit just right on the spotty bum packhorse was going to take a few days to get used to. By the time I was organised and ready to start out on my big adventure, both wind and rain had fortunately eased off a little. Finally, I felt I was all packed up and ready to go.

"Have you packed your torch?" asked my husband helpfully.

"No - it's still in the van."

Now, surely, I was all packed up and ready to go...

As I had prepared the horses and myself to leave I had been feeling generally calm, but now the start line approached I unexpectedly felt extremely nauseous and nervous. I relish challenge and adventure, but this one was suddenly scaring the life out of me. The west coast, all at once, felt like the other side of the world and questions were spinning round my head. Why on earth was I doing this and what planet was I orbiting when I came up with this insane plan? Would I remember how to get there? Had I packed my maps? What kind of danger was I heading into? Would I be able to keep my horses safe?

I pulled myself together, pulled on my riding hat, and jumped up onto Yogi's saddle. Looking and feeling a rather peculiar shade of green, I picked up the lead rope attached to Swift and set off. I was sure once I grew into my stride, the nerves in my stomach would settle down. Although I would be spending many days and nights on the trail alone, I had arranged some help at certain points along the way. Today at least, my faithful hubby, Dave, was here for support to begin my journey. With Dave holding my hand a little at the start, I told myself that I just needed to get on with the first few kilometres; then I was sure I'd feel just fine.

I didn't get very far at all (maybe five hundred metres) before I was stopped in my tracks by a woman who wanted to know all about Swift and where her spotty bum came from. Perhaps this woman was right, and despite my knotted stomach, the 'Spotty Bum' nickname required a moment of contemplation. Due to Swift's particular Appaloosa breeding (Appy for short), she had the potential to have spots in a variety of different colours, shapes and sizes and could have these arranged in any form of pattern.

Swift's coat arrangement is mostly bay (brown) in colour with white spots over her rear and a striking, silver mane and tail. This wouldn't be considered a standard format where Appy's are concerned and I have my own suspicions as to why Swift has such unusual markings. My theory being, that whilst standing in the spot distribution queue, she must have taken offence at the design artist, turned her back, and as a result, the spots were only sprinkled over a patch of her bottom. The artist then hurriedly swept with his brush (as she left the queue in a huff) only catching her mane and tail.

"Wasn't my fault," sniffed Swift, "the guy with the paint brush was rude, he said I had ears like a mule!"

She gave her head a shake, flopping them from side to side. "I love my long ears - they are useful for keeping the flies away."

"I love them too, Swift," I said, and gave her right ear a gentle pull for reassurance.

The woman who had stopped me was a true Appy enthusiast. The questions about what I was doing and why, only followed after a very long discussion about Swift and the woman's Appaloosa horses who were in the field behind her. She didn't seem to realise that my horses and I were 'not from round here' and were looking rather unusual decked out in our full expedition gear. Our appearance in general seemed to be of a secondary concern to her, fascinated as she was about the distribution of spots. Her horses appeared to have a very even covering of spots all over their bodies, and she seemed immensely proud of their perfect behaviour in the spot painting queue.

Eventually when the conversation moved on, I tried to explain our plan, our reasons, and our methods as best I could. However, since I'd only been asking myself the why, when, and where questions some five minutes previously, I struggled a little to form the answers the woman was looking for. Yogi was also struggling a little as he was feeling somewhat left out with all this talk about spots.

Any inequalities, however, were soon righted as we continued down the road only a short distance further and were once again halted in our tracks. This time by a woman who came rushing over, threw her arms around Yogi's neck and disappeared under his mane, much to all our surprise! There was an awkward pause while Swift and I shuffled our feet and exchanged confused glances, Yogi's eyes stood out on stalks, and we all wondered what on earth was happening. During this pause, the woman took a huge sniff of Yogi's neck.

The woman eventually emerged from under Yogi's mane exclaiming, "I love the smell of horses." Now this is a sentiment that I totally understand and absolutely share. However, I'd usually be polite enough to ask if I could possibly have a sniff of someone else's equine before throwing myself around their neck - especially if they appeared (as I hoped we did) as though they were on a mission to get somewhere and that stopping them may cause a delay.

"That was kind of nice," mumbled Yogi, as he started to blush.

"It was actually a little strange but I'm glad you enjoyed it!" I replied.

"What was that all about?" asked Swift, looking all confused with her long ears flopped out to the sides of her head.

Yogi's ego restored (as he'd been the chosen horse to sniff), we continued on our journey. These early and strange interruptions had worked some kind of magic to settle the nerves, so I didn't mind too much when Dave declared that it was time to pause again and take some photos to prove we were leaving from the very edge of the east. Fair point, I suppose. The fanatical Appaloosa woman and the strange sniffing woman weren't exactly going to be the most reliable witnesses.

Photo session complete, where Yogi and I posed for the camera and Swift pulled her usual goofy faces as soon as the lens was pointed in her direction, we set off up the steep road climbing out of St Cyrus to face the first major road of the journey. I really do dislike riding on roads, as many drivers these days show such lack of patience and understanding towards animals using them. Luckily, we didn't have far to go on the main road and Dave protected us from any fast traffic by driving the van and trailer in the middle of the road a little way behind the spotty bum.

My route, if I could remember it correctly, was a course of zig-zags to stay on the smallest roads found on the map in an effort to avoid larger and faster vehicles. Dave would be dipping in and out of this route, by the way of support crew, in locations where we considered the worst of the traffic might be. I waved goodbye to Dave as I rode away from the main road, knowing we were to meet up again soon and as planned, we didn't encounter any traffic for a while. This allowed us to concentrate on finding our travel rhythm - something that can take a few days to develop. It's hard to explain to someone who hasn't travelled by horseback, what this rhythm is exactly but when you don't have it, you just feel out of sync with your companions, out of sync with your equipment, out of sync with all the bags you've packed, and just a bit awkward and frustrated in general. It usually takes a day or two to iron out the wrinkles and have everything feeling smooth within the team. We weren't working truly as a team nor enjoying any smoothies just yet.

I was, however, enjoying the colours of the crops in the fields, as the contrast of the bright yellow rape against the lush green grass was reminding me of my childhood days in Cheshire. The sweet scent from the field, mixed with the odour of horse and the air of anticipation, showered my sense of smell from every possible angle. The gentle rolling hills of green and yellow were unbroken in their poise. With no hedgerows and few fence lines for separation or interruption, the vegetation butted up against the tarmac on either side of the road. I'd initially found this arrangement so very strange when settling in North-East Scotland after a childhood in Cheshire.

Both areas are renowned for agricultural prominence; the only distinction between them is a bias toward production of dairy in one and meat in the other, but they are fundamentally the same. In England each field is bounded by thick hedges interspersed with tall, strong trees. This shrubbery, teeming with bird song and wildlife, is a sight so rarely seen in the North-East of Scotland where one field rolls into the next without any demarcation. Perhaps it's too bleak for the hedges to establish their roots so far north, rather than any preference expressed by those that tend the land.

Winding through the level expanse of green and yellow, we rode without incident for eight kilometres or so, to a junction with the A90 Dual Carriageway. With no underpass or overpass to be found during a recce of the route, Dave met me at the agreed location with the horsebox to untack, load, drive over the dual carriageway, unload, and re-tack. A necessary inconvenience to keep the whole team safe. We found a break long enough in the traffic to drive a vehicle over, but I was glad I hadn't attempted this on foot. The horses would have been stuck in the feeder lane in the middle of the carriageway with vehicles zooming past in front and behind. It would have been an uncomfortable period of time caught there, waiting nervously for a second pause in the otherwise constant fast stream of traffic.

Over safely and all tacked up, we set off again and met face to face with a strange wifie (local dialect for woman) on a bike. She was wearing a riding hat, a lot of high-vis clothing, and was armed with a big camera. I was relieved to discover that she may be strange, but only as strange as me, and that this was my friend Leaf who had decided to come and join us for the rest of the day. Leaf had figured that the first section of my journey would be a stressful one for all three of us, and that she had better step in and give the team a hand as we gathered momentum and rhythm. Both of her hands were most welcome as it made the day much more sociable, easier to manage, and less taxing for us all.

I placed Swift's lead rope into one of Leaf's (most welcome) hands with a confident smile. Leaf and Swift were already well acquainted as Leaf had been her previous owner before Swift came to live with me. I knew that Leaf would be able to cope well with Swift's quirky personality, so as they settled into a familiar companionship, I started to relax and shake out the start-line nerves as I rode Yogi up ahead.

The time passed quickly until we arrived at my carefully planned lunch stop at the Sauchieburn Hotel. According to the internet, it was "a treasure in the Howe O' the Mearns." I was looking forward to a celebratory and calming drink to toast the start of our adventure and had carefully researched the pub opening times online. It was apparently open from twelve until two o'clock every day and served my favourite tipple of real ale. This had sounded rather perfect and I'd planned my timings to be perfect too - to arrive there a little before one o'clock. Well, it just goes to prove that you can't believe everything posted on the internet as the pub was well and truly shut.

Not to put a dampener on an already moist day, we decided to rest up in the carpark for a while with soggy sandwiches for us and humid hay for the horses. Thoughtful husband produced some beers he'd found in the van to wet the whistle too. I was just about to crack open a bottle when the landlady appeared with those words that can always be taken in at least two different ways: "Can I help you at all?" In haste I waffled out my mad plan of adventure. She was so baffled and incredibly relieved that we weren't a bunch of travellers setting up residence in her business carpark, that she kindly made us a huge pot of tea.

While we enjoyed the tea and made ourselves more comfortable by using the pub loo, Swift proceeded to try and drink the pub taps dry. I think that Yogi had been telling her a few tales about some of the 'sessions' he had as a lad and she didn't want to lose face, her being the unruly teenager of the team and all that. I didn't have the heart to tell her I was only bringing her tap water (rather than beer) as she guzzled bucket after bucket to prove to Yogi she could keep up with the best.

As Leaf, the horses and I continued our way along the road, we again waved goodbye to Dave for a while. Unfortunately, the theory I'd had of only using the tiniest roads on the map to avoid heavy traffic, didn't quite work out as planned. The afternoon turned into a game of cat and mouse (or rather, a game of tractor and horse) as our team of four negotiated the single-track roads amongst high-speed tractors towing dung-laden trailers. They rushed to complete their job of muck spreading in a nearby field and judging by their speed, the drivers were being paid per trailer load and not by the hour. Some drivers were more courteous and understanding than others as we tried to quickly get out of their way.

"Those tractors are big and scary," said Yogi.

"The trailers too," replied Swift, nodding her head and swishing her tail in agreement.

"They smell *really* bad," said Yogi, snorting three times in a row.

"We'd best stay on high alert!" exclaimed Swift, as she rushed up behind him bumping her nose into his tail.

In the midst of this game we were stopped by a frightened lady, babbling about travellers being in the area and possibly eyeing up her horses to steal. She told us to be careful about where we stayed for the night. It didn't take long to work out and then explain that Dave was doing nothing of the sort. He *was* driving around in a dodgy-looking transit van with dishevelled horse-trailer attached, but was merely doing this to meet the team at strategic traffic hot spots. Good to know I suppose that Farm Watch has a rapid and effective communication system, but it's a shame that so many feel nervous about travellers being in the area.

As we passed a large farm with a lot of wool in the fields, Leaf proved her place in my heart as she happily listened then participated in my theory about sheep. I can be quite profound at times, and I started thinking as I watched this year's spring lambs race and bounce around the fields together: why aren't adult sheep cute?

Puppies and adult dogs I consider to be cute, kittens

and adult cats are the same, foals and adult horses are both lovely. I would even say that there is something charming about calves and cows and in fact most other adult animals, but not sheep. Lambs are just the cutest fluffiest things, but adult sheep are somewhat lacking in the 'oh-how-sweet' department in my humble opinion.

Woolly depression

My other thought on this matter is why don't you ever see adult sheep play? You see adult dogs, cats, horses, and even cows play with each other and their young. Whereas sheep tend to send their youngsters off to play in a big group together while the adults just stand around ... looking ... well ... depressed! Maybe they are depressed about the fact that they are no longer cute.

Leaf I think enjoyed this discussion and helped take the profoundness to a deeper level. With her experience of growing up in Wales I felt she brought a certain amount of credence to the whole subject matter. This debate whiled away the time and we were soon in Edzell where we located my husband and Leaf's car (luckily where she had left it). They both accompanied me to find the team's digs for the night at The Burn House, Edzell, where I was in for a big surprise.

During the trip preparation phase, I'd been given the number for Sarah and David by the local campsite. They were described as people "who have donkeys and may be able to help you with horse accommodation." When I'd phoned, they had offered Yogi and Swift the donkey's grass for the night and said I would be able to camp in their grounds. Well, to be completely honest, they had said I could have a room in the house if I liked, but since I'd never met them before I felt that it might be a little imposing. It was a very generous offer to extend to a stranger and was absolutely the type of thing I would also offer to a stranger with a shared interest. However, I always feel more comfortable giving than receiving such a thing, so had politely declined and said I'd put up my tent.

With horse care always the main priority - an importance today's support crew understood - I said a hasty goodbye to Leaf and Dave as Sarah and I settled the horses into the field. I also gave the two *very* cute donkeys (both adults, so please refer to previous profound statements) a little cuddle, to thank them for giving up their field for the night. I had asked Swift to thank them, but she was extremely jealous about the length of their ears and so refused to even acknowledge their existence.

Whilst tending to the horses, Sarah had been telling me all about the difference between donkey and horse care - it's not just the length of their ears it seems, but differences in coat weatherability and personality traits too. She again re-offered the room in the house option and insisted on showing me around the house before I pitched my tent. It was becoming rude to refuse and very shortly I was going to be rather glad that I gave in and agreed.

The house turned out to be a massive lodge house used as an academic retreat. It wasn't Sarah and David's personal abode at all, and it had everything you could want. Proper beds, proper bathrooms, warm rooms, fabulous views, lovely grounds for an evening stroll and even a bar with real ale. Needless to say, I no longer required much persuasion and I even imposed further on their hospitality by accepting the offer of a free evening meal.

Over dinner, I reflected that saying goodbye to Dave and Leaf had felt a little rushed. Whilst either would have been happy to help with the horse care that had distracted from a protracted farewell, they perhaps sensed that if they lingered, I might not want them to leave at all. I was a little daunted, to say the least, to think that I was now on my own for the next three days and having done an extensive recce for this trip, I knew that those next three days held a considerable amount of challenge.

I'd obviously experienced solo dobbineering before, getting to a stage where I could contemplate this cross-Scotland adventure with packhorse in tow. However, I still considered myself to be fairly new to it all and although I'd done periods of four days and nights on my own, this trek had nine days alone in total ahead. You could say I'd doubled the challenge stakes. If I was travelling entirely alone with a rucksack on my back, then these challenges would be minimal - but I had two charges to be responsible for. They had four legs each, could sometimes be unpredictable, and had completely

16

different wants and needs to a rucksack. I also love my equine companions much more than any rucksack I have ever owned.

My biggest fear (and guilt) was that they could possibly suffer due to something that was my ambition, not theirs. At the end of the day, it was not their choice to attempt this adventure and the responsibility to keep them safe felt very heavy indeed. I was feeling nervous about the road (or rather trails) ahead and the responsibility of keeping my horses safe and well during our travels. This worry was the main focus, but more than that, I wanted them to enjoy themselves too - even though the task I had set for them would be hard work. Other concerns, therefore, surrounding tasty grass, fresh water, kind weather, and a breeze to keep the midges away, were circling around the core anxiety of good health and safe negotiation of hazards.

My drive to undertake adventure of any kind - despite such nervous reservations - is mainly founded on curiosity about something, somewhere or someone. With dobbineering, this curiosity is about exploring an environment so familiar from years of hill walking but now with different challenges to face and the alternative perspective horse travel presents. It provides an adjusted historical connection and the feeling of stepping back in time, with a recognition that the places travelled through and this mode of transport haven't changed all that much through the years. The mountain landscapes still contain the navigational array of bogs, steep slopes, fierce weather, and rough ground they always had. Horses still have a leg in each corner, they manage the terrain well, thrive on constant movement, and are well-adapted for subsistence in wilderness areas. These aspects haven't significantly changed.

What has changed, however (in a sweeping generalisation based on my own experience), is human expectation. We now seek easier and more comfortable travel, with advanced equipment to keep us warm, dry, and safe. The risk assessment of travel by horse has perhaps transformed with our softer modern values, and it has been forgotten that the perceived 'amazing horse adventures' of today were often a component of everyday life in times gone by.

I have a large amount of curiosity about this aspect too - what routes were used in days gone by and for what purpose or to what end? I also wonder whether those using horses to travel through mountainous terrain in the past worried about their mounts in the same way I do. I'm not sure they would have been as sentimental as me about the comfort felt and/or enjoyment reached by their equine companions, but I struggle to comprehend how they could have achieved the great journeys undertaken without having a solid relationship built on trust, respect, admiration, and - I hope - a little love too.

You could say that this historical mode of transport has 'had its day' (in the UK anyway), with the development of capable all-terrain vehicles. However, if the mountain environment hasn't changed and neither have the horses, then why not still travel in this way?

Although I'm not willing to give up on the luxuries of modern clothing and equipment, I am curious to explore the (largely) lost art of mountainous horse travel to discover what I, they, and us as a team together, are truly capable of. If it could be done before, then it can be done again and I'd like to prove that this wonderful, rewarding mode of transport has *not* had its day. Perhaps even a thought - that dobbineering could become a more popular sport of the future!

So, driven by curiosity to view the familiar from a different perspective and to explore new boundaries of capability with my companions, I found myself feeling tenacious but tense about the days ahead. As I took the moment to scrutinize my fears, I suddenly became aware and surprised to find that the apprehension I was experiencing was held almost entirely for my horses. There appeared to be little fear or regard for myself inside this brewing pot of worry.

Whether I was subconsciously blocking this out or whether I feel genuinely at home in the hills, I don't know, but I was experiencing a strange lack of consideration for my own safety. A lack of self-regard only up to a point, though. That point being - if something disabling happened to me on the trail, then what would become of my horses? Besides this, any discomfort, or bearable hardships I might face ahead, were inconsequential compared to concerns about my horses.

The only other concern spicing up the brew was an (irrational) fear of failure - of having to give up on what I had started for one reason or other. I'm not sure how much pride was involved here; sometimes it's best not to search too deep, but I am very much a finisher in life. Brought up on the mantra of 'if a jobs worth doing, it's worth doing well', and 'well' in my mind implies completed. So, although the anxieties described were mixing nicely in the pot, there was an inner determination and resilience to continue to the finish line. It was clearly shouting "Never give up, never surrender!" accompanied by a whisper of "Unless my horse's comfort or safety was about to be compromised."

This inner determination had become practised over the years at overcoming negative thoughts and anxieties during time as an outdoor instructor in hazardous environments and as a paramedic. My method was to simply pop the doubts back into the pot then muffle the sounds from within by firmly slamming down the lid. I would then resolve to take one small step, and once started, well then! - I had to finish with no white flag in sight.

One way to aid the muffling is by finding a distraction, so after dinner I took a gentle stroll in the grounds full of brightly coloured rhododendrons and big old trees that could tell a story or two if only they could talk. It felt strange that I'd never known this place existed, yet this was an area I'd spent a lot of time in many years ago, when I worked in the oil industry in Aberdeen. If I listened carefully from the grounds of the big house, I could hear the rapids of the North Esk River that used to be my favourite playground most weekends for many years (with kayaking my main hobby then).

It was the perfect way to ease myself into this journey, and upon returning to the house I was entertained by chatting to other guests, which very effectively took my mind off the potentially difficult days and weeks ahead. As I tucked all my worries and fears under a thick duvet, I enjoyed a very comfortable night's sleep and hoped my equine companions were having the same.

Day 2.
Edzell to Invermark
(Distance 26km, Ascent 407m)

I awoke before my alarm to a noisy dawn chorus, but I didn't mind the chirpy awakening because, despite my nerves, I felt refreshed and keen to continue my adventure. I was eager to get going, looking forward to a rather special venue for my next evening's stop. I did, however, vow to return to the Burn House one day as there was so much more to explore here.

I started the morning's packing faff with enthusiasm despite the now familiar knotted feeling in my stomach and the list of (muffled) potential disasters spinning around my brain. It takes a few days to get efficient at balancing the pack bags and I was glad of the advice and encouragement from the long-eared donkeys, peering over the door of their stable as I shuffled dry bags from saddle bag to saddle bag.

After what seemed like far too long, I was ready to wake up Yogi and Swift. Yogi as usual was raring to go and Swift was playing it cool. Catering to their personalities, I started to get them ready and was joined by my hosts, David and Sarah, who were intrigued (or baffled) by my mayhem and equipment. Before succumbing to the charms of donkeys, they had owned horses themselves and so were naturally interested in how I do what I do.

The saddles were poked and prodded, tested for weight, and the questions began. We chatted while I tended to feet, saddled up, and attempted to get the saddle bags up on top of the lanky spotty bum packhorse. I'm roughly 5'2ft which works out around 160cms tall.

Swift is 16'2 hands (measured from floor to top of shoulder/base of neck at the withers) which puts her at around 167cms at her shoulder, not including the height of the saddle. Adding to her looming presence is her long neck and head and, when her head is held high, she towers over me in a giraffe-like fashion.

For someone as vertically challenged as myself, getting the saddle bags up onto her back always involves tip-toes and a balancing act of bags on my head as I slide them on. Despite this taking a certain amount of concentration and the need to pull funny faces by both myself and Swift, I did manage to relay to David and Sarah the story of how I came to be using treeless saddles on both my horses.

I naively bought my first horse Yogi (The Bear) without expert advice and despite having a Stage Five Vetting done at the time, it rapidly became apparent that I had bought a damaged horse. A Stage Five Vetting is a veterinary certificate of fitness, Stage Five being the most in-depth and - incidentally - the most expensive. It wasn't picked up during the high-cost inspection, but it turned out that Yogi had issues with his back due to a previous injury. According to his earliest owners (who I had since contacted), this wasn't a fixable problem.

You may have realised by now that I am a fairly determined person, so undeterred by the 'written off' diagnosis, I set about trying to repair said damaged horse. This involved several years of gentle exercise, lots of in-hand work, pole work, and long reining before moving onto ridden work. It also included many different equine back experts, a lot of patience, and a lot of listening to my horse. Finally, I found a back expert able to visit regularly who found tight muscles that others had missed, and eventually Yogi received a clean bill of health for his now fully recovered self.

Finding the right saddle was a large part of the healing process. I tried several saddles and none of them passed the tacking up sniff test. Yogi is a very sensitive and communicative beast, and if the saddle you are trying to put on him wasn't comfortable the last time he wore it, then he will let you know his disapproval by stepping away. He checks which saddle you are approaching with, by giving it a thorough sniff test.

During my saddle search, Leaf had let me try one of hers. Not only did Yogi move better underneath it but, after a few rides out, it passed the sniff test with flying colours so I bought one. I am happy to report that it was also the most comfortable saddle I have ever sat on and that luckily, I was able to reach that conclusion without having to get my nose anywhere near it.

The saddle just happened to be treeless (and of Western style like you see in cowboy movies), but the more I read about them the more converted I became to this idea and so Swift has the exact same saddle. This comes in handy when you need to swap ridden horse for packhorse on a trip like this, as both saddles are interchangeable. A treed saddle has a solid frame inside and is carefully measured to fit your horse exactly. A treeless saddle's fit relies more on the padding (or shims) placed underneath the saddle in the pad.

Saddle story told and everything set to go, we had our first proper incident of the trip. Our rhythm not found quite yet, I messed up negotiating the personalities of Mr Enthusiastic Yogi, "Let's go, let's go!" and Miss Laidback Swift, "Can I press the snooze button one more time?"

through the field gate. Yogi stood on his dropped rein, had a minor moment of panic, and the rein became the first casualty of the trip.

Beginning to think I was destined to never leave The Burn (which wouldn't have been all that bad), I kept my calm and quickly came up with a temporary fix. The type of Western split reins I use can simply be turned upside down and, with a spare karabiner to attach it back to the bridle, we were off for our Twitter photo shoot.

Yogi was a little nervous about being 'tweeted' as he didn't really know what it meant and Swift didn't help by teasing him with stories of horse-eating birds with huge beaks who 'preferred the ginger flavoured ones', but I managed to persuade him round to the front of the big house where David was now waiting with his camera. David was quite new to the tweeting too and was excited about having such an unusual tweet to twit.

Amazingly, David somehow managed to charm Swift into not pulling goofy faces and with our second photo shoot of the trip complete, we set off down the huge, tree-lined driveway. Our day's ride today would involve working our way up the length of the beautiful Glen Esk. After a short section of main road, we were onto a track up the south side of the river. It was a quiet and peaceful solitude after the road riding yesterday. The word solitude was on my mind when suddenly that exact word appeared on an old wooden signpost before me.

I was a little freaked out for a few moments - what witchery was in motion here? Then I relaxed and remembered that one of the main rapids on this section of the river was called the Rocks of Solitude. Maybe there weren't mind-reading witches in the woods after all. Yogi however, remained unconvinced and continued to stay on high alert, just in case there were any witches about that might need 'ear of horse' as an ingredient in their cauldron. For the sake of his sanity, I kept quiet about the fact that one of the other rapids was named The Witches' Cauldron. Swift, who I have concluded has a witch-like ability to read my mind (since she always knows which direction I want to take almost before I do), was sniggering quietly to herself.

I had reached a part of the track that I just hadn't had time to recce. It couldn't have been more than a mile in length, and I had checked out the track either side of it. Overall, I think I must have walked, run, or biked about ninety-five percent of my total cross-Scotland route prior to setting off, so this short mile was unusual in its unfamiliarity. I rounded a corner and discovered a cattle grid with a side-gate that appeared to be completely bolted shut. The clue is in the name and cattle grids are designed so that hooves can't walk over them.

This is exactly why I spend so much time running around the hills before any long-distance horse trek, as sometimes humans just don't consider those with hooves. I tried to lift the gate off its hinges on the right-hand side, but even with my determination not to be thwarted at the first hurdle, it wouldn't budge. I pondered on whether I had any tools in my kit bags that could be used to undo the bolts, but since they looked rusted on anyway, I doubted that even my trusty Swiss multi-tool could handle this job. The hacksaw would take me weeks.

While Swift and Yogi happily munched on the grass beside the track in complete oblivion to my frustration and anger, I noticed a couple of pieces of metal sticking out from the bottom of the metal barrier running along the side of the cattle grid. On closer inspection I discovered that if these were lifted, the whole metal barrier plus the bolted on gate could be swung round to create a big enough gap to get the whole team through, albeit one at a time and in single file.

I was obviously very relieved at this discovery but felt a little aggrieved that whoever designed this strange contraption hadn't thought to leave step by step instructions. As we carried on, I hoped I wouldn't meet any more barriers before reaching the area of track I had already checked out on my mountain bike. Thankfully, this was the case and we all enjoyed the ride alongside the River Esk. The track at one point took us close to the banks of the river and I found myself looking down on one of the frothy white rapids I used to paddle. It brought back memories of fun times, good friends and a few wetter than planned moments rushing into my head.

When I'd first moved up to Scotland to live, it had been the end of November and I hadn't appreciated how few day-light hours there would be, during winter, so far north. It was pitch-black in the morning on my way into work, my office happened to be in a basement with little natural light and it was pitch-black late afternoon, prior to my journey home. It also seemed to rain all day, every day and I was rapidly regretting my flit (local dialect for house move) to this dark and depressing place. Then, however, I discovered a local canoe club!

Kayaking was a hobby I'd dabbled with throughout my school days and one I'd tried hard to develop whilst at University, but I'd always struggled with confidence in the water. The structure of a canoe club full of friendly encouraging coaches and many new friends was just what the Doctor ordered - for me to become happy in my new home and to help me develop skills in a sport I had fallen in-love with. I also realised the advantage of that rain every day, with numerous rivers bursting at their seams supplying endless options for entertainment. It suddenly didn't appear to be such a depressing place.

The other thing I began to love about living in Scotland was the abundance of trails, tracks and places to explore. No longer hemmed in by set public routes, 'No Entry' signs and those that stated clearly 'Private Keep Out', I enjoyed the freedom to roam that this country had to offer and particularly how welcome you were made to feel in acres upon acres of Forestry Commission plantations. I enjoyed them back then, by foot and mountain bike, but these days, it's the horse riding routes that I so very much appreciate.

Although the Forestry Commission provides miles and miles of good quality tracks for myself and my horses to enjoy, at times, however, I find myself annoyed with them as an organisation. Tracks that you regularly use or had planned to use can become impassable and/or obliterated by timber collections. Beautifully peaceful, creature-filled forests can become apocalyptic scenes overnight, devoid of any life or any way through.

During the recce for my cross-Scotland journey, I had followed this route up Glen Esk as marked on the map and found myself knee-deep in mud as the track had been completely destroyed by the heavy machinery of tree felling works. Only when I arrived at the other end of the Forestry Commission area did I spy a notice on a gate. I was lucky to find this notice as the gate was open, and any information was therefore hidden. The sign suggested that walkers should use the field next to the track while the tree felling was taking place.

The statement 'better late than never' often applies, but I am not sure my boots, socks, and trousers agreed. Neither did my companion - the now filthy and mud-packed Jack Russell (Tully), who knew with certainty that a dreaded bath was coming her way before the end of the day. On my recce return journey, I biked across the field to explore the alternative and rode straight into a herd of lively cows with mothers protecting their young calves from bike, human, and dog. With the track still out of action, I was now worried about what the cows would think of the horses and more crucially how would the horses react to a stampede?

I eventually reached this huge field with the horses and was relieved to find that today there was no sign of any cows, stampeding or otherwise. There were just numerous sheep dotted around the field and, since they mostly mooch around in deep depression due to a lack of hope for achieving cuteness in adulthood, all was calm.

The field stretched for miles, surrounded in a glorious fashion by the foothills of the Cairngorm Mountains. The grassy green expanse extended far into the distance where the blues and greys of the hills started to ascend - hiding as they were in modesty behind a thin veil of haze. The ground was flat and in great condition and I was tempted to canter and possibly even gallop. No sooner had the thought crossed my mind when Swift swiftly reminded me about the heavy, cumbersome burden she carried - "What did you pack, the kitchen sink?" If I asked her to do what I had in mind, she was likely to deposit the load one way or another.

Heeding the threat, we settled for a relaxed pace in the sunshine with a few periods of slow jogs. Reaching the end of the field, I knew I had to divert to avoid another cattle grid without a side-gate and I let the horses munch the rich grass at the alternative gate for twenty minutes while I had a bit of lunch. Having a free hand to eat lunch is rare on this type of journey with only two hands to manage two horses, a drink, and a sandwich. This, however, was an ideal spot, with a fence line and a wall providing a corner to contain the horses without much human management required.

Setting off again, it wasn't long until we had our second and third incidents of the trip in quick succession. I guess we were still searching for that elusive rhythm. At the next gate negotiations, with a slight misunderstanding, we all suddenly became a tangle of reins, lead ropes, and fingers. With three different opinions on how to untangle the mess, a finger lost the debate and also lost a large chunk of skin.

With my line of work as a paramedic I knew just what to do, but my prescribed treatment of at least five swear words followed by placing hurty finger in mouth just wasn't doing the trick. Rather than drip the important red stuff everywhere, I had to gently prise the first aid kit out to find several plasters. As I tottered on into the third incident, I vowed to tell my fanatical health and safety friend Yvonne that she was indeed right about always wearing gloves.

Plasters and gloves in place ('better late than never' really is a stupid statement), we approached the next gate. I recognised it immediately: this gate beside a cattle grid had taken me about half an hour to clear during my recce. One side of the gate had been blocked by a huge fallen tree, and on the other, large branches littered the ground where new trees were growing, blocking the entrance to the gateway. It was now nearly one month further on and I was shocked to see how much the young trees had grown up. I opened the gate as far as it would go and decided that the horses would just be able to squeeze between the cattle grid side-barrier and the young trees.

Distracted by my struggle with the gate, and before I had time to start the delicate process of supervising the squeezing, Mr Enthusiastic Yogi was already on his way through the gate mumbling, "Grass looks greener on the other side and the trail goes this way..." Thankfully, without any guidance he slipped through safely without even catching his widest part - his rather rotund belly. In the blink of an eye, before I could reach her, Swift followed (also unguided) stating, "Where he goes, I go, and I hate to be left behind." I thought she was lined up perfectly, until she took a sudden step sideways and the brand new, ordered in especially from the USA saddle bag, caught the metal barrier and ripped wide open. Sigh!

By this time I was really hoping that the old saying about bad things coming in threes was correct, and that *now* we would achieve our rhythm. I pulled out a few spare straps from another saddle bag and did a temporary repair to hold it all together. I guess I now had a sewing job to do that evening, hurty finger notwithstanding.

The rest of the afternoon progressed in a leisurely manner, despite many more gates to negotiate, and I felt that we were becoming more in tune with each other and starting to work as a team. We arrived at the next identified hazard in a timely fashion: a farm to walk through. Farms aren't generally hazardous, but when I had biked through here on the recce, I had spotted three young horses in the field that the track weaves through and these youngsters were entire colts (young stallions).

Swift is still quite young (only just turned six years old) and often her hormones can bounce about nearly as much as her legs and tail do in the presence of a virile young lad. For the sake of the length of my arms, and for the safety of the colts in the field who might have got more than they bargained for, I had found the owner, Jo, to discuss my route plan and she had offered to move the colts into a different field for the day.

As I approached the field, I could see that Jo had fortunately remembered this arrangement from three weeks ago and as we arrived at the farmhouse, she came out for a chat with an offer of a cup of tea. My horses, however, were a little restless with the other horses about, so with one intact hand as full as the not-so-intact-anymore hand, I politely declined the tea. We did have a chat though about barefoot horses and hoof boots while we offered the horses some water from a trough in a field.

It seemed that my theory about Swift thinking she was drinking beer the day before at the pub was correct. She'd guzzled up the water then but was not interested in even a drop today, despite finding nowhere for the horses to drink since morning. We tested and proved the theory of taking a horse to water before continuing through the farm and back onto the Glen Esk tarmac road, with only a few kilometres to go to the day's special end point.

We had not been on the road for long when a hurrying Land Rover flew past. This gave the horses a heart stopping moment which resulted in the whole team suddenly jumping a metre to the left, landing intact as a complete unit with exactly the same spacing between us as before. Hey ... look at that, we had suddenly found our rhythm!

Despite this revelation, I was still annoyed. The driver had passed us so quickly but had now screeched to a halt immediately in front of us. Since they were going to stop there anyway, why did they not just wait one minute until we had moved out of their way? I didn't have long to think about my poor perception of their decision making, as the three occupants were out of the Land Rover and advancing towards us in a purposeful manner.

Suddenly a large, fluffy microphone was thrust between the two horses and into my face. Pausing during this moment of surprise, I was treated to a perfect demonstration of the personality differences my horses have. Yogi (the rather fearful bear), his eyes wide, immediately thought, "Oh my God – is that *thing* going to eat me?" Swift (the rather curious spotty bum) was on a different train of thought entirely and, giving the microphone an exploratory sniff, she uttered, "Now that looks interesting ... can I eat it?"

I knew exactly what my horses were thinking, but I had absolutely no idea what was going on in my own head. My brain was as fluffy as the microphone. What on earth was happening now? It turned out that I was about to be interviewed for BBC Radio Scotland's *Out of Doors* programme, after the show had received an email from a friend about my journey. They were in the area to cover another feature and had happened upon me during their travels. It appeared we weren't their first choice, but I tried to answer their questions politely anyway.

Finding words to answer the questions was challenging enough considering the nature of the surprise ambush, especially when I had finally relaxed into a rhythm with the horses and had relapsed into a contented daze. However, the whole experience was made even more challenging given that it was taking place in the middle of a road, with not the best line of sight and which, before long, would no doubt contain traffic.

If it wasn't for some clever editing afterwards, you may have heard a nervous giggle or two, some screeching brakes, and some restless hoofsteps on the radio as the interview was suddenly interrupted by the appearance of another Land Rover, towing a rather rattly trailer. We did resume the interview after that, but for some reason it suddenly picked up urgency and seemed to come to an end rather abruptly. I suspect the interviewer and sound person had suddenly become more aware of the vulnerability of their toes.

Interview surprise

We made our way up the glen without further interruption and soon arrived at the Mark House B&B to find nobody home. Nobody home, that is, except for one black Labrador who was very happy to see us and another one who clearly didn't share that sentiment. I found somewhere to tie the horses and set about unloading the saddle bags, untacking and de-booting to the accompanying sounds of barks and growls from the unhappy Labrador and tail-wagging from the happy one.

Swift and Yogi were playing it cool and set about weeding the driveway, but I could tell that they were a little upset by this half-frosty reception. Turning their backs to the unhappy dog, Yogi sneered over his shoulder, "We're celebrities don't you know and will be appearing on BBC Radio!" He rounded this statement up nicely with an irritable flick of his tail and, in support, Swift gave the grumbling dog one of her renowned, blood-curdling mare-glares.

As I waited for the human owners of the B&B to arrive home (although the grumpy dog was adamant HE was in charge around here), I reflected on the last time I was here and how my visit then had turned things around in terms of my mental attitude to my adventurous undertaking. It was this significant mental switch gifted by the B&B owner Ian that made this place so special.

During the planning phase for this trip, I had contacted Ian to see if he knew of anywhere I could park my horses for the night at the head of Glen Esk, and he had offered me one of his fields. I also, somewhat cheekily, requested to camp in the field with the horses rather than be faced with the cost of a room as I was working to a strict budget with a diminished bank account after getting married just a few months previously.

Although I'd chosen not to sleep there, during my miserly online negotiations Ian had offered an evening meal at the B&B. Weighing up the choice of a delicious meal served to me in comfort, against cooking my own over the camping stove whilst fighting off the infamous

Scottish midges, I had agreed. I was confident that, given the circumstances, my bank manager would be sympathetic towards the cost of the food.

With only a few weeks to go before my start date, and with time running out for the planning phase, I'd been frantically checking the route recce gaps I still had to fill. I'd been across to the west coast to investigate what would be the final day of the adventure, and had seen just how challenging that day was going to be. I'd then driven east to check out the route near to the B&B which included the ascent of a Munro (a classification of mountains over 3000 feet high) - another significant undertaking with horses.

This mammoth drive from west to east had seemed incredibly far by van, let alone by horse, and had made the cross-Scotland by saddle proposal appear a little preposterous. The enormity of my challenge was just sinking in as I called into the B&B during the recce, stopping for a cup of tea, a chat with Ian, and a seat outside in the sunshine. Sipping my tea, I was feeling a little overwhelmed and was having serious doubts as to whether I would be capable of completing the proposed trek. As I discussed my worries and fears with Ian, I became completely astounded by the generosity he offered.

Listening to my anxieties and upon hearing that my ride would be raising money for charity, Ian upgraded the future dinner date to include a free room for the night and I was left unusually speechless. This unexpected and generous offer of a free room suddenly seemed to turn all my nerves upside down. If this was the kind of support I was going to get from strangers along the way, then maybe, just maybe, it was possible that I would be able do this after all.

My emotions, like a flick of a switch, changed from doubt and uncertainty to belief and optimism and I suddenly found myself shedding a couple of happy tears. All at once, the start of the journey didn't seem so hard. I had a focus and couldn't wait to get to the head of Glen Esk, not only to stay in such a beautiful spot but to lap up such generous hospitality. The trip was psychologically back on track and I was extremely grateful to Ian, who was possibly oblivious to the effect his generosity had just had.

As though he knew I was thinking about him, Ian's car turned into the driveway. We quickly settled the horses in their field with plenty of water, which Ian helped me carry over to them. The fabulous hospitality I anticipated was certainly not lacking, and I enjoyed a lovely pot of tea in the sunshine while I sorted out my bags and stored everything I didn't need for the night in the shed. The friendly black Labrador received waggy-tailed cuddles during this process, but I didn't manage to win round its grumpy counterpart.

Refreshed with a hot shower and a little dance of delight at the comforts of my room for the night, I descended to the lounge to sort out the issue of the torn saddle bag. Ian quickly equipped me with a box of sewing materials, and I set about trying to make my repair as strong as possible given that the bag still had rather a lot of kit carrying miles to go. As I concentrated on trying to make the repair something my mum would be proud of (despite my sore finger), four other guests arrived, and we all introduced ourselves to each other.

Talking to one of the couples, I discovered that they

had been married here only three weeks previously. They were regulars at the B&B and had wanted to get married in this beautiful spot. A 'different' kind of wedding in an idyllic and remote location, it was a small and personal ceremony with the B&B owners as their witnesses. I shared a joke with the recent bride about us both being on our honeymoon but at least she had the decency to bring her husband with her.

My wedding had been slightly 'different' too. I had only been married nine weeks and already I was off on a three-week adventure without my husband by my side. This might give you a clue as to the relaxed and supportive relationship I am very lucky to have. We had been together for almost fourteen years, and had defended our position against the onslaught from family and friends so successfully that 99.9% of them had given up asking when exactly we were going to tie the knot. It seemed unlikely that my mum, the 0.1%, would ever give up dropping unsubtle hints; but we were happy enough to live with that.

The idea of spending a year or more organising a huge event with the expectations, stress, hassles and expense that it brings, quite frankly put us both off even thinking about it. We had both been married before and had been through all that already. We didn't really think seriously about it ... that is until we started organising my fortieth birthday party.

My boyfriend/partner (what is the appropriate word to call them when you are approaching forty years old?) had put out a massive invite to all friends and family to join us for a weekend of outdoor activities and festivities for my birthday. It soon became apparent that a lot of people were going to turn up and an idea started forming in my head. So, when Dave asked me what I would like as a present for my birthday - I replied, "I'd like to get married."

As he picked himself up off the floor from the shock of this suggestion, I went on to explain that I'd like to keep it a secret from everyone and surprise all of our guests at my party with a sudden change of celebration half way through the weekend. He then surprised me at how quickly he warmed to the idea and checked that important family members had confirmed they were coming. I immediately phoned our registrar friend to see if he was willing to be an ally in the secret mission and to ensure that he was available.

Planning this little secret was a whole heap of fun, and sorting out the details of the plan as a couple, brought us closer together than ever. How many grooms have had to help the bride select a dress? Well mine had to, as I had nobody else I could ask for an opinion. It's not traditional for the groom to have anything to do with the bride's dress (at least until after the ceremony), but the wedding plan wasn't traditional either.

The only person who was given a warning of the plan was my 'adopted dad' from Canada. I had lived out there for a spell when much younger and Art had taken me under his wing and welcomed me into his family. Art was planning his first trip to the UK and I needed to alter the date of his travel plans so that he didn't miss this significant event.

It would be a big surprise for everyone who turned up, not least my mum, who had dropped her usual unsubtle hint only the night before the party weekend: "Would it not be easier if you two just got married?" Then there were those who would end up playing a role in the wedding party, too; the father of the bride obviously, my three step-daughters (Dave's girls from his previous marriage) who would be bridesmaids, and the close friends selected to do the readings, the photography, and be the best man. All given about fifteen minutes notice while I went and changed into a more appropriate dress for a wedding.

At the end of the day we just wanted to get married without all the fuss, and we really had not anticipated the reaction our little secret would have during the moment it was revealed. Dave's public engagement proposal resulted in all the air being sucked out of the room as eighty-plus people simultaneously gasped, only to be followed by tears of joy and disbelief as he explained to the audience what was going to happen next. As in fifteen minutes time, right here, right now, in the room next door.

As I disappeared to go and get changed, followed by three tearful (but extremely happy) bridesmaids to be, my aunt grabbed me and asked, "I need to know ... I really *need* to know ... is this for *real* or is this just one of your elaborate practical jokes?" Even tough guy Adrian, a friend of ours, was seen to shed a tear or two. Actually, he was completely blubbering, but if I wrote that here, he probably would never forgive me for the tarnish of his tough reputation.

It was a fantastically personal ceremony delivered by our registrar friend who knew us well and knew what was important to us. The element of surprise made it into a particularly emotional, uplifting, yet fun and relaxed experience. The party atmosphere took a huge leap into the air, everyone had lights in their eyes, and the revelry continued well into the early hours of the morning. The effects lasted several weeks, and we even ended up with fifteen minutes of fame when the story made the local newspapers and the dizzy heights (hmmm) of the *Daily Mail* and *The Sun*.

Back at the Mark House, the two different wedding tales drawing to a close, Ian called us through for dinner. As the first plate of a three-course meal was laid before me, I knew I was not going to eat this well again for quite some time. It was a delicious meal, complimented perfectly by very pleasant company, good banter, and a lovely glass of wine.

Completely full and feeling sleepy, I excused myself to go check on the horses before bed. As always, they came running over as soon as they saw me, mostly to frisk my pockets for treats or to get me to scratch that itch they couldn't quite reach, but I allowed it to feel good in my heart regardless. They both complained about the number of midges and the depressed sheep they had to share their field with. Knowing that they would be fine until morning, I said my goodnights and climbed into a very comfortable bed.

Day 3:
Invermark to Glen Muick
(Distance 22km, Ascent 930m)

Well rested, I was up early. Today was one of the biggest days in the whole journey. We had miles of rough terrain to cover, including almost one thousand metres of ascent and a boggy section to safely negotiate - bogs are one of Yogi's pet hates, so I had omitted to tell him about this (shhhh!). I made myself a cup of tea in my room while I packed the bags and vowed to eat breakfast on the move, if indeed I could face any food at all, as right now that nervous nausea had firmly established itself in the pit of my stomach again.

It was a beautiful sunny morning and the horses stood dozing as I prepared them to leave. This I did accompanied by one wagging tail and one growling mouth. I took it as a positive sign that the aggressive sounding barks had diminished to a low, grumbling growl. I was definitively making progress in winning the unfriendly Labrador over with my charm.

Getting more efficient with the saddle bag packing system, we were ready to leave before nine o'clock. However, I waited patiently for an extra five minutes while Swogi were fed some organic carrots by the B&B staff.

"Swogi?" I asked, looking at my two horses for clarification.

"Yes, that's us!" said Swift and Yogi, in between mouthfuls of delicious carrots.

The horses had decided (apparently) to come up with a collective celebrity name overnight. They figured that now they were famous it would be easier all round if they modelled their image on the likes of 'Brangelina', a Brad Pitt and Angelina Jolie combination, and from now on would collectively like to be referred to as 'Swogi'.

Feeling a little left out of the team but highly amused, I dragged Swogi away from the carrots and set off up Glen Mark towards the Munro that is Mount Keen. This sudden shift in the team politics had upset the rhythm a little and the first gate negotiation was a comedy of errors. Thankfully though, no rein, saddle bag, or finger were hurt in the making; we just completed about six circles instead. The comedy continued as I found somewhere to get up on Yogi, I dropped Swift's lead rope, and she set off back to the B&B to see if there were any spare carrots left.

The carrots must have been extremely tasty indeed as this was the first time *ever* that Swift had done this. Sometimes out on the trail I take her lead rope off entirely and let her follow Yogi and I at her own pace. I had never had her 'return to base' before as she is usually content to just be wherever she is, so long as she has company. Yogi is a different story; if you let go of his lead rope out on the trail, he will often set off on a mission to somewhere. He doesn't necessarily know where that somewhere is exactly, but he just wants to get there and get there soon.

I happen to love the drive that Yogi has, to follow the trail wherever it may lead. It means I can ride him without reins or direction from my legs most of the time, allowing me to eat my lunch up top, change my jacket, take photos, or read the map. I suspect I could even lie back, pop my slippers on, put my feet up and read the paper each morning if I could only find a shop out in the hills to buy one from. He always seems content to keep going at a good pace without any encouragement from me and happily follows whichever trail we are on. He also has a turbo-boost setting for the uphill sections (he likes to attack hills with enthusiasm), and I was relying on this to drive the whole team to the top of the Munro today. Right now, however, we needed to deploy it in order to catch up with and collect our escaped member of the team.

With Swift and Yogi reunited back into Team Swogi, we continued to follow the river up to the head of the Glen at Queen's Well. The grey gravel track cut its way through the brown twiggy heather, interspersed with patches of tufty green grass. Its curvaceous twists and turns converged as it tapered in the distance at the base of the grey, craggy slopes. The river gaily glistened in the bright sunlight, the sheep mournfully munched the grass either side of the track, and I marvelled at the beautiful mountains as we approached the oval shaped corrie that contains the crown of the Queen's Well.

This marvel is as spectacular in its construction as it is in its location. The crown-shaped stone monument sits atop a natural spring and was built to commemorate Queen Victoria who once stopped there for a refreshing drink during her travels, which happened to be accomplished on horseback. The inscription reads, "Her Majesty, Queen Victoria, and his Royal Highness the Prince Consort, visited this well and drank of its refreshing waters on the 20th September 1861 the Year of Her Majesty's great sorrow".

Looking at the state of the water in the well now, I too experienced great sorrow as a drink from the well would not be refreshing for anyone, nor appreciated by the hospital staff that attended to the person brave enough to take a sip. It was covered in green slime, contained a collection of corroding copper coins and clumps of rotting sheep poo. Trying to find a bright side to yet another human violation of a natural wonder, the best I could do was conclude that the water would be somewhat flavoursome if you dared to try it.

Swogi were very impressed that they were actually following in the hoof prints of Royal Horses, although they sensibly avoided a drink from the Royal Well. I was hoping that this thought would distract them from noticing the very steep hill that I was about to ask them to climb. To distract them further, we paused at some lush green grass for them to munch on for twenty minutes. We were about to head into the hills, and it would be heather covered ground from here on forward, so I wanted them to fill their bellies. Well, Swift's belly anyway, Yogi's belly was apparently always at least half empty no matter how much grass was in front of him, as his half-Highland Pony breeding was focused on his midriff.

I kept a close eye on Swift as she kept glancing back down the glen to where she ate those tasty organic carrots for breakfast. The grass in front of her was too much of a 'bird in the hoof', however, and I managed to find a spare hand to eat a snack. The human energy levels of the team needed to be sustained, too. As we all had a munch, I tried to figure out the route from here to where we would need to join the main track heading up the hill.

On the recce I had discovered that if you followed the main walkers' track, it led you to an obstacle that would be a challenge with eight hooves in tow. It was a burn crossing that had been covered by a cattle grid construction, made suitable for four-wheel drive vehicles but totally inappropriate for horses.

To either side of this grid the fast-flowing burn contained large boulders and slippery rocks and was a potential leg breaking, skin cutting hazard that we needed to avoid. I had searched around for an alternative route but even with a trusty Jack Russell to help, I had not come up with any other option. Time had been spent filling in riverbed holes and moving a few rocks to make the side of the grid as safe as possible, but I still had serious concerns for the welfare of my companions negotiating this obstacle.

Knowing that this route across Mount Keen was occasionally used by horses from a local trekking centre, I suspected that there must be an alternative way. After contacting the estate factor, I was now armed with some instructions. These indicated that if we took a left branch after the Queen's Well and followed the main glen river a bit further, we could safely cross the burn lower down where it joined the river as a tributary. Following the path of the burn uphill would take us back to the main track.

I had tried this option from the track end during the recce and had only come across soft ground, where the horses with their weight to hoof size ratio would probably sink. Yogi, not impressed with this possibility, was reluctant to follow me now and began to get his stress head on. Yogi in stress head mode means that he just cannot keep his feet still. This action often gets him in more trouble than he would have been in if he had just listened to me in the first place, and moved slowly and carefully as directed.

Swift as usual was displaying a cool exterior with a teenager 'not bothered' attitude and thankfully followed on behind quite calmly. With a few wrong turns we weaved our way around the softer ground, did a bit of heather-bashing, and emerged in a minor Yogi panic on the track, uphill of the cattle grid. Heather-bashing is a recognised hill walking term, meaning pushing your way through knee-high heather without a path, struggling with uneven ground that you can't see down by the roots.

Yogi sheepishly acknowledged that the soft ground and heather-bashing wasn't actually that scary as he hadn't sunk that far, nor stumbled too much. Looking at the grid in the river beside him, he muttered, "It was definitely less scary than that metal horse-eating contraption over there, with hidden monsters underneath."

The sun was beating down and although it was still early in the morning, the day was heating up fast. It was going to be a hot and sweaty ascent to the top. I knew the horses were going to be working hard on this loose rocky track with steep sections ahead. We would need to take this slowly with plenty of rests if we were all going to last the day, as there was still a long way and another big hill after the one in front of us to complete.

"Slowly?" said Yogi as he popped himself into his turbo-boost setting and we started to make fast progress up the hill. When I say 'fast' progress, it was good progress for horses. What non-horsey people often don't realise is that in general, a horse will walk at a similar speed to a human - unless you have a turbo-boost, or turn up the throttle into a trot or canter.

With necessary breath-catching rests interrupting the turbo-boost walk, a hill walker soon caught up behind us. We played a stop start game for a while with the walker politely letting us go first as he stated that we would be much faster than him (Yogi of course agreed). However, it was so very hot, and the horses were getting rather steamy as the track became steeper, so I had to stop more often and eventually I invited the walker past and he disappeared into the distance. I relayed the childhood story of the 'hare and the tortoise' to Yogi but there was no let-up in the turbo speed that necessitated the frequent stops. He is an all or nothing kind of horse.

Despite the heat, the horses were doing much better than I expected and we had soon broken the back of the main climb to the shoulder of Mount Keen. The views from here were incredible and I felt very lucky to be getting such good weather at the end of May in Scotland. As we walked along the shoulder, we walked towards a decision to be made. Do we head to the top of Mount Keen for the team to conquer a Munro together, or do we skirt around the base of the final part of the hill along a flatter track?

The problem with making a bid for the summit was that the track down on the other side was not suitable for horses. We would have to descend the way we climbed up, then double back and take the path around the base anyway, to where we needed to go. It was climbing a hill for the sake of climbing it and a team discussion ensued. I was keen to climb Mount Keen because it was there, and it was possible to do (in theory). Yogi was keen to climb Mount Keen because it was there, and it had potential to enhance his celebrity status. Swift was most definitely un-Keen.

Swift is a horse that is still very 'green'. I used to think this term was utilised to describe a young and inexperienced, wet behind the ears horse, but I now know this expression defines something else entirely when used to describe my mare. Swift was 'green' in the political and environmental sense; she was passionate about energy conservation. Everything Swift does is carefully considered in terms of its energy rating and once an action is figured out, the exact appropriate amount of energy will be applied and not a joule more. With the solar energy beating down from the sunny sky above, there was no way that Swift would be persuaded to generate more of her own heat by climbing a hill that didn't need to be climbed.

I argued that Mount Keen was considered by many to be one of the easiest Munro's to climb and that if we were ever going to top out a Munro as a team, this was obviously a good place to start. With a quick glance from Swift to the big yellow star above, I knew I was fighting a losing battle. Despite team member differences in opinions and personalities at times, we do have a three musketeers "One for all and all for one!" policy, so everyone must agree to a plan or it just doesn't happen. Knowing that we were only on day three of a potential eighteen, Yogi and I conceded that on this occasion, climbing a hill for the sake of climbing it on a very hot day probably wasn't the most sensible option and round the side we would go. Swift surprisingly expended some unnecessary energy on a moment of happy tail swishing and mane shaking at the outcome of this decision.

The track around the side was peaty in nature but thankfully dry and solid enough that Yogi's feet remained calm. This meant we could all enjoy the spectacular views and I could take about a thousand photos. To our left was a patchwork pattern of brown and green, where rotational burning was creating areas of heather of differing heights. This process rejuvenates small areas with young shoots for mountain livestock and moorland game birds. Gamekeepers prefer plump grouse for their clients to shoot and the older heather and grasses are tougher and less nutritious. The revitalizing practice plumps up and benefits natural wildlife too, by the proximity of patches of blooming plant food next to older heather areas where they can hide safely from eagle-eyed predators.

The patchwork quilt reached the end of the divan in the distance as it dropped down to the floor of a deep valley. The mountain wall on the other side of this was a hazy mix of blues and greens. The wall reached up as high as it could to the bright blue ceiling, bounded by a cornice of fluffy white clouds. To the right we all glanced up at the peak beside us from time to time, only two of us wishing we were up there. As the view across to Royal Deeside unfolded, I explained to Swogi that this was where the royal horses lived.

Excited as they were to be exploring the royal valley below, there was still a difficult descent to conquer. 'Difficult' is a considerably more polite term than the description noted in my trip diary. I won't repeat that here but suffice to say it was a horrid combination of steepness, loose rocky boulders, and soft peat. Swogi mostly chose the soft peat option but every so often it would give way under a hoof or two and we all slipped and slid our way down into the valley. I hated this descent nearly as much as Yogi did (Swift as usual displayed indifference), but clinging on to a bright side, I was glad we weren't attempting to climb up it instead.

To recover from the descent, we rested on the grass by the river in the valley below (the end of Glen Tanar) for a good thirty minutes, giving all members of the team time to eat, drink, and be merry for a while. Again, we were about to head onto heather covered ground for the rest of the day - heather covered, that is, apart from the boggy parts that I still hadn't mentioned to Yogi.

The next path was one the horses and I had tackled before, but in the opposite direction. It consisted of a thin, peaty track through the heather with one soggy, steep-sided burn to cross. Finding a place to get equines over this burn the last time had been a little challenging and I had failed to find the path hidden (in heather) on the other side. We had ended up heather-bashing back down to the main Glen Tanar track, which was possible but not exactly all that pleasant.

I knew that from this direction the track would be easier to spot on the other side of the burn, so I wasn't overly concerned about losing it this time. What was concerning however, was that we would now be heading uphill along this tiny trail. Coming downwards the last time Yogi was content to follow on behind, but this time the incline would cause him to upgrade to his turbo-boost setting. I would therefore struggle to keep up with him as the ground wouldn't be safe enough for me to be sitting on his back.

True to form, the journey suddenly became sweaty and tough going, with a horse on a mission to walk faster than me and refusing to walk behind me. His best offer was to let me walk at his shoulder and for him to pull me along. With the track so narrow, this resulted in one of us heather-bashing and the other being afforded the trail. This was not a battle I always won, and we stumbled our way upwards towards the peaty, steep-sided burn.

I had the feeling that the horses would recognise this section from last year and without any hesitation they followed me down the steep slope, deviating from the walkers' track to find a suitable equine crossing. They neatly hopped the burn and had soon scrambled up the other side. This time I paid close attention to where the walkers' track was now situated; we re-joined it and Yogi and I resumed our power struggle to the top of the hill.

The top was reached without us falling out with each other - only just - but only one of us was dripping in sweat! We were now entering the boggy section and I apologetically explained the route to Yogi as Swift cheekily did bog monster impressions behind his back. It wasn't the worst bog I'd taken the horses through by a long margin. It was also only one of two short boggy sections to negotiate in our whole journey across Scotland. Considering Yogi's feelings, I had devised an itinerary that avoided the boggiest routes but that involved a three-day detour to achieve this.

"Besides," I pleaded to Yogi, "You have done this route before and survived."

My powers of persuasion won the negotiations and the whole team agreed to continue. 'All for one', we set off across the soft ground interspersed with numerous ditches. At first the horses were handling it well and in a wonderfully calm manner. Then, one of the Swogi duo decided that it would be better to change to jumping everything instead. I knew where my suspicions lay as Yogi was starting to look a little wide-eyed, and Swift had her green energy-conserving tendencies to use in her defence.

Many of the ditches could just be stepped over by normal horses, but with my 'special' Swogi duo deciding to jump them all, I was lucky not to be flattened at one of the ditches as they decided to jump in unison, right towards where I was standing. I only had time to close my eyes and breathe in to make myself as thin as possible, as they landed each side of me in a perfect horse-human-horse sandwich formation.

As the sandwich approached the next ditch which really could have been negotiated by a large step over, the bread again decided to jump. Yogi went first, and in his haste to get his front end across to the other side, he completely forgot about his rather ample rear and left both of his back legs to fall in the ditch behind him.

He scrambled out as Swift neatly leaped over in her usual efficient manner and I assessed the damage. Apart from the surprised look on his face and the damage to his pride, he seemed otherwise intact and seemed sound and happy as we moved on forward. 'Sound', not in the modern sense of cool or awesome, but sound as in the equine term meaning not lame or limping. Eventually we reached the main track on the other side of the bog and we paused for a few moments to breathe a sigh of relief with the firm ground under our hooves and feet. Yogi had already spied that this main track continued in an uphill manner and was metaphorically chomping at the bit to engage his booster switch.

I reminded him that he technically doesn't have a bit to chomp on (the metal part in the horse's mouth) as both horses wear bitless bridles. Shrugging his shoulders, he found some grass to chomp on instead, but I had to keep an eye on him in case he sneakily pressed his turbo button and set off without me on a mission to 'somewhere'.

The decision to ride my horses bitless was one that had crept up on me gradually. Yogi had arrived with a huge snaffle bit on his bridle and, as I learnt to listen to my horse more, I realised that it was far too thick for his small mouth and that he found it incredibly uncomfortable. This was why whenever I used it to ask him to slow down, he would throw his head in the air to try and relieve the pressure in his mouth. When throwing his head in the air his brain was not only shaken around a bit, but it became completely engaged with the evasion of pressure. He would then forget that

I was asking him to slow down, so I would have to apply more of a pull, and we created a rather vicious, non-slowing circle.

I switched to using a thinner French link snaffle (Western variety), and he seemed to be much more comfortable. I was more comfortable with arrangements too, as the brakes began to work better. If he was happier, then so was I, and I was content to leave it at that. Then along came Swift who was a different kettle of fish entirely as she hadn't had a bridle on at all, let alone one with any type of bit on it.

Acquiring Swift at the age of two (her not me!), it became my responsibility to start her as a ridden horse. Although I had started a few horses before, I had only done this to the stage of sitting on them for their first few rides. I had never really trained a horse to become a proper working ridden horse. We were going to have to learn how to achieve that together with periods of guidance from more experienced friends.

I didn't really know how to introduce a bit to a horse, but it hadn't become a priority yet in the starting process as Swift was happily doing all I asked of her just from signals sent through her rope halter. However, I was now at the stage of jumping up on board and needed a friend to help make this a safe jump to take. The friend who came to help happened to be in favour of the use of bitless bridles and before I knew it, Swift was trying out a 'cross-under' variety.

And that as they say, was that. Swift went perfectly in it, incredibly light to the touch in any direction, probably because she had already started to read my mind at this early stage (I just hadn't noticed yet). With the vets then pointing out a singular huge wolf tooth at Swift's next dental check-up, I decided to keep her bitless permanently. A wolf tooth is an extra tooth that horses sometimes get. They often fall out of their own accord, but if they don't, then it's an operation to remove it if you want to use a bit in their mouth as otherwise it would be in the way. If riding bitless avoided an unnecessary operation and Swift was happy, then I was happy too.

My realisation of how well the bitless solution was working for Swift coincided with a weekend away with Yogi to a Western-style riding event. When I returned and looked at the photos of us attempting some barrel racing, I was shocked to discover that in a high number of these photos my boy had his mouth wide open. He was clearly not as happy as I thought he was.

I had presumed that since I mostly ride from the seat and use the Western technique of neck-reining my turns, very little pressure would be noticeable in the horse's mouth. The photos proved otherwise, so now I had a mission to convert Yogi to a bridle without a bit. It just wasn't my style to add more pieces to the bridle to force him to keep his mouth closed, when I could clearly see he was only opening his mouth due to the discomfort he felt. I would rather take the time it would take to retrain and to find a solution that we were both comfortable with.

This conversion didn't turn out to be as trouble free and rapid as Swift's acceptance of my new way of thinking. Yogi objected to the head hugging action of the cross-under bridle, and he didn't like the nose pressure of an English hackamore, an Orbitless or a Zilco Flower (all different types of bitless bridles). With these he acted just as he had in the snaffle and threw his head up in an attempt to evade the pressure across his nose. It was costing me a fortune in new bridle attachments, but I was determined to not give up just yet and I happened upon a website where you could order custom made bitless nosebands. I decided to give it one last try and ordered one in Yogi's favourite colour, green (grass is green you see).

This noseband had an Indian bosal action where the reins tightened straps underneath the chin. It would still apply a degree of pressure around the nose, but in a different way to the options listed above. I am not sure whether it was the colour or the bosal action - but BINGO! He liked it and we had a solution. Yogi now had a floppy bottom lip out on the trail (a sign of a relaxed horse) and was no longer throwing his head up if I had to apply the emergency brakes. It took him a few months to completely forget that he no longer needed to open his mouth when I was putting the bridle on or taking it off. There was no guilt felt on my part at all, as I giggled at his confusion.

These days, out on the long-distance rides that we do, the bitless option works well as the horses can comfortably munch grass as we go, making sure their digestive system stays healthy despite the long days of activity. Swogi were demonstrating that fact perfectly right now, eating the long grass and heather in the middle of the solid track leading up the hill. It was getting late; we still had another large hill to climb and we had an appointment with a gamekeeper to meet us with a key to open two locked gates. We had better get moving.

As we set off on the harder ground, I took the opportunity to reassess the silly Yogi Bear to double check he had no ill effects due to his ungraceful negotiation of the last big ditch. I watched him walk before getting on him and he seemed to be moving fine. I lined him up at a rock from which to mount and he obligingly moved into position without me asking (a good sign). I gathered up the reins, noting that he didn't step away (another good sign), and swung my leg over the saddle. He stayed completely still. Good signs complete, he didn't start prancing about like a drunken ballet dancer, an action that usually meant that Yogi was feeling sore.

With the history of soreness due to his back injury, I had just tested all the signs that would usually tell me immediately if he was feeling any pain and the tests were thankfully negative. The rate he then set off up the hill as his turbo drive kicked in laid any worries I had to rest. Yogi appeared to be okay after his miniature ordeal. The track was good, with soft heather in the middle, so we made fast progress upwards and the stunning views over to Glen Muick gradually appeared. From the top of the hill I checked for mobile phone reception, found some, and called the gamekeeper as agreed, to let him know that we were not far away.

As we rounded the hill and climbed right to the top, the famous jagged outline of Lochnagar came into view and I could see the route of tomorrow's ride way in the distance. The dark ridgeline of Lochnagar's face was freckled with patches of white snow, but despite the matching clouds there was no merging of land into sky here. Lochnagar defined its tops firmly, with a thin but impermeable black marker pen.

We descended into the Glen of Muick to meet the friendly waiting gamekeeper, David, at the first gate. This gate I knew would be unlocked, but he had met me at it regardless in case I hadn't realised. Quite tired by this stage of the day, I handed him Swift to lead down to the house and we chatted about the hoof boots they were wearing and whether they would stand up to days on the hills if worn by deer ponies on a working estate. I concluded that I couldn't see why not, since they were withstanding what I was doing with my horses no problems at all.

Swift, I was glad to see, hadn't taken offence at my dismissal of her company, and after drawing a blank from frisking David's pockets for treats, she was busy keeping him on his toes by trying to stop and graze at every blade of grass. She knows better than to try that sort of trick with me but can at times be a complete monkey with anyone else leading her. This was one of those monkeying times apparently.

We approached the locked gates that protected the precious breeding stags from walkers who may forget to close the gates, and protected the unsuspecting walkers from the excited stags during rutting season. I thought it wise to rescue David from Swift before we walked across the lush green grass of the field. Emerging at the small holding on the other side of the field that included the keeper's cottage, David escorted me through to a large field for the horses and a small enclosure in which I could pitch my tent.

"You can close the gate of the enclosure so you are right next to your horses, but they can't bother you through the night." he said.

I wondered if he had ever met horses like Team Swogi before and knew that without the gate, Yogi would try to share my dinner whilst Swift would see if she could fit in my tent.

My kind host for the night had already supplied the field with a couple of buckets of water and set about helping me unload the saddle bags and saddles. I wondered whether his wife would mind if I stole David to help me throughout the rest of the journey. Considering the newness of my marriage and the smallness of my tent, I decided it was best not to ask this question as his wife appeared on the other side of the fence with their two daughters by her side. The eldest daughter was a typical pony obsessed young lady. I could totally sympathise with her obsession and I admired the horsey t-shirt she had worn especially for my arrival. I explained that I would love to let her ride one of my horses, but unfortunately it probably wasn't the safest idea.

Yogi copes well with small children riding him, but they need to be big enough to get up there mostly under their own steam. If you try to lift a small kid onto his back, he panics for reasons known only to him. This young lady, although determined and desperate enough to give it a go, was just too little to risk the Bear's insecurities. Swift was out of the question too. She was yet to be properly introduced to children and in fact had only carried five different people, one of those being me. Although the other four riders had been carried without incident, she had the athletic and mental ability to 'floop' if her introvert brain became overloaded and thus inverted.

Floop is a technical term that describes the action of putting your head between your knees and jumping up and down with all four feet in the air (if you have four that is). Your brain flips upside down, your eyes roll into the back of your head, and you snort a lot afterwards too. This happens frequently with rider number one on board as that rider tries to expand Swift's comfort zones and her life experiences. Eventually, after a short period of leaping and cavorting, accompanied by a reassuring hand on the neck, the floop will come to conclusion.

With a floop still being a possibility with young-brained Swift, the pony obsessed young lady was going to have to content herself with some Swogi cuddles instead. As the horses drifted off to set about shortening every single blade of grass in the rather lush field, David and his family went back to their house. They left me with a firm invite to pop up if I wanted to use the bathroom or wanted a cup of tea, or anything else at all really. They made me feel very welcome indeed.

For the first time this trip, I unpacked the tent from the saddle bags along with the wee camping stove that was yet to be ignited and began to set up my camp. Tent upright and secure, and before I fed myself, I fed the horses adding extra salts as they would need those replaced after such a sweaty day. The horses had a huge field to enjoy but as always on these long journeys, they tend to keep an eye on me in the unfamiliar surroundings and didn't stray far from the fenceline, near where my tent was pitched. I enjoyed their company and the scenery of the hills behind them as I drank a cup of tea and made myself dinner on the stove.

With all three stomach's satisfied, a comfortable feeling emerged. The hardest day was done and dusted at least for this section of the journey. The road ahead was easier, and I should probably start to relax and worry less. I popped up to the keeper's cottage for a bit of company and a most welcome, long drink of ice-cold water. I also borrowed a bit of Wi-Fi to update my blog and let my nearest and dearest know I was still doing okay.

I enjoyed the entertainment provided by the pony obsessed daughter showing off in company (well why not?) in her horse covered onesie, but I felt sleepy. It had been a long day, so I slipped away to say goodnight to the also sleepy Team Swogi before crawling into my tent. Crawling is an accurate description as, trying to keep the equipment weight down, I always use a one-man tent. It is light weight, very waterproof, and comfortable once you are in, but it's always a bit of a challenge to get in there and end up with the sleeping bag wrapped around the correct part of your anatomy.

Contortion complete, I was soon snuggled in and, as I fell asleep reading my book (one of my three luxury items), I could hear Swift not so softly snoring on the other side of the fence. Yogi of course was still in the process of cramming as much grass into his belly as he could possibly manage in the nine or so hours of field rest remaining. I could hear the grass being torn during his mission, it created a soothing rhythm mixed with Swift's snoring and soon ... had ... me ... zzzzzz.

Day 4:
Glen Muick to Gelder Shiel
(Distance 21km, Ascent 506m)

I awoke to the sounds of Swift *still* snoring! It was only fair, as I had promised Swogi a lie-in this morning. There was not as far to travel today, it was relatively flat (compared to yesterday anyway), and apart from one small section, the track was good under hoof so the horses would be able to stride out. The team therefore had no rush to get moving this morning - apart from me, that is. I was certainly in a rush to get out of my sleeping bag and out of my tent, as it was like a sauna in the little cocoon and quite stifling.

It's not really a hardship to be driven out of your tent by the heat of the morning sun, even if it is earlier than planned. Sun in Scotland is rare enough, but for it to be *hot* sun first thing in the morning is something special indeed, and I was keen to experience this unusual phenomenon. I wriggled into my clothes in a manner that Houdini would have been proud of, unzipped the tent and peered over to the horses on the other side of the fence. Swift was flat out, in the same spot where she had been when I went to bed. I wondered whether she had been there all night. She seemed to be okay though, as I could see the occasional ear twitch to ward off the flies.

She often sleeps flat out like this, and I had long ago discarded the heart-stopping fear that comes with discovering your much-loved horse lying like a completely expired and resting-in-peace horse. I no longer rush towards her shouting and waving my arms looking for the smallest sign of life. The little minx, I think, does it on purpose as she seems to hold her breath until you get within one foot of her. This distance, measured to perfection, is just short of the point where you collapse to your knees, believing your worst fears to be true. At this stage she finally takes a breath and gives the slightest flick of her ear in your direction, followed by raising the one eyebrow that remains in view. The ear would flick to point out the direction of the loony human prancing about like a gibbering wreck, and the eyebrow would raise as her eyes rolled in teenage disgust at this fool of a human being.

She wasn't fooling me this morning though; I had no trouble knowing that she was breathing as I couldn't hear myself think over the sound of her regular snores. Yogi was lying down enjoying the sunshine too. He was obviously exhausted after his mammoth midnight munching mission, but he still had enough energy left to graze any blade of grass within striking distance of his teeth while he lay there. He is half-Highland Pony after all, and they *never* miss a grass opportunity.

I made myself a leisurely cup of tea and a bowl of porridge, then slowly set about striking camp. There was a tranquil feeling to the air; life was good! We had accomplished one of the hardest days of the whole journey and only the very last day would compete for that title. The route was easier from here on, and to top it all, the sun was out. I was looking forward to the dramatic views that today's easier trail would provide without the need to slog to the top of a hill. There was also the anticipation of finishing the day at a beautifully situated bothy, where I was hoping to meet up with fellow walkers or cyclists having their own adventures.

Bothies are reasonably commonplace in Scotland but can be found (more rarely) in England and Wales too.

They are simple huts or basic shelters, usually unlocked and available for those in need of a mountain refuge. As the Mountain Bothies Association describes them, "it's like camping without a tent." Often a bothy will house a simple sleeping platform and may have a wood burning stove or fire, but if you want to stay cosy and warm then generally you need to provide your own fuel. This one, I knew, didn't have a fire, but was comfortable, had running water nearby, and even a composting toilet to save me digging a hole with my trowel - the joys of wild adventuring!

Originally they would have acted as temporary accommodation for estate workers, but these days they are frequented by hill walkers, mountain bikers, and those on cross-Scotland horse adventures. There was, therefore, a strong possibility of company this evening, and I imagined us swapping tales of our travels over a cuppa and maybe a wee sip of whisky (my hip flask being my second luxury item). With the prospect of meeting other like-minded folk tonight and less burdened by the responsibility of keeping my four-legged friends safe over tricky obstacles, as we wouldn't meet any significant ones for a few days now - I was feeling relaxed.

As I packed the bags, I realised that I hadn't washed the horses' feed bowls from the night before. I returned from doing this in the stream, and both horses immediately jumped up out of their slumbers with hope written all over their faces. I guess they weren't so deeply asleep after all and I vowed to remember that trick for next time Swift played at being deceased. They both mugged me as I came back through the gate into the field, desperate to see what was in the buckets. Each nose individually frisked me for treats, checking that buckets, hands, pockets (all six), hat, and socks (for good measure) were all empty. This was done twice to be double or rather quadruple sure and, disappointed by the un-productive search, they settled for sunny morning scratches instead.

There is always apparently great pleasure to be found by presenting the itchy bit that you can't quite reach to a human with an opposable thumb. You can tell when the thumb is in just the right spot as it results in the horse pulling an amazing parrot face impression with top lip fully extended. 'Pretty Polly' impressions explored and thoroughly demonstrated, I continued to pack at a leisurely pace. I was just adding the finishing touches to the saddles and saddle bags when David's wife was dragged around the corner and over to the fence by the pony obsessed daughter, who was wearing yet more horse-themed clothing in our honour. They accompanied us as we walked through their fields and waved goodbye as we set off down their lane to join the main Glen Muick road.

By 'main' road, I mean that it is a single-track road that links the Glen Muick visitor centre and walkers' car park with the rest of the world. Single-track it may be, but it is often busy with walkers' cars and buses carrying people to walk up or ogle at the famous Lochnagar mountain. None of us were keen to play in front of buses and since it was a Saturday, the probability of meeting a few was quite high. I also find riding on tarmac to be rather tedious. Instead, we were going to head in the wrong direction for a short distance to cross the river and ride up the other side of the glen. This would place us on the more peaceful side where the Queen is rumoured, on occasion, to walk her Corgis, away from the traffic on the main glen road.

It was really very hot and, as we reached the track on the other side of the river, we were all glad to find that we would be in the shade of the trees for most of the day. We could still enjoy the sunshine peeking through the trees and the crazy shadows it created, but without getting over heated or frazzled.

The horses were feeling good, we were totally in-tune with each other, and the travelling rhythm was well and truly established. I was completely relaxed and chilled, except for my smile muscles which were working in overdrive.

This was exactly why I wanted to do this journey in the first place. I wanted to be out there, remote, in the hills with amazing scenery, travelling under our own steam at a pace that allowed observation of every little detail around us. I pictured the team working in well-oiled unison and enjoying ourselves.

That certainly seemed to be the case this morning as Yogi was humming a little tune to himself and, unusually, Swift had appeared out from underneath her teenage hoodie. She had shed her variety of grumpy faces and was actually smiling. I was surprised and delighted to be able to collect some non-goofy photos of her for the first time in a long time. She was taking an interest in her surroundings rather than her own front feet and I even had a few words of reply from her as I chatted during our progress up the valley. It made a change from the usual teenage grunts and shoulder shrugs.

I was enjoying myself so much that I thought a wee celebration was in order. With Yogi content as always to follow the track ahead, so long as there were no bogs to deal with, and Swift content to follow Yogi (without lead rope this morning), I kicked back, put my feet up, let go of the reins and went in search of the hip flask stashed in the saddle bags. I knew the sun was still below the yardarm, but only just, and I didn't think that my nan would disapprove too much as she always had an early tipple on a special occasion. This felt like a special occasion to me, as I proceeded up the Glen in a nirvana-like trance with camera in one hand, whisky in the other, and a beautiful scene unfolding in front of me.

It was lovely to be in this complete tranquility while I could see that the main road up the glen on the other side of the river was busy with walkers, cyclists, cars, and buses. We met only one group of people the whole morning; a cheery group of heavily laden Duke of Edinburgh's Award scheme walkers who also appeared to be enjoying this unusually sunny, Scottish weather.

Never below the yardarm

A swathe of yellow gorse created a colourful foreground across the flat river valley with the dramatic rise of steep, heather covered mountains looming behind. The base of the hills was sharply pronounced at the head of the valley by the thin sliver of the shimmering Lock Muick, fighting hard to be included in the view. I was pretty content to be a part of this splendid scene, although I admit that the contentment may have been influenced a little by the current lightness of the hip flask.

Eventually I realised that we had come to a stop. The horses had paused for longer than their usual occasional munch on the move. Yogi was flicking his ears from left to right and back again while Swift was most definitely rolling her eyes at me.

"Erm … sorry guys, I was a little distracted there!"

We had reached a fork in the path and Yogi was politely enquiring in which direction I'd like him to proceed. I sheepishly asked him to head to the right into woodland.

In my hasty embarrassed decision, I'd forgotten that I was supposed to go a little further along before forking right, as that track was better for those with four hooves. Consequently, we soon reached a bridge over a boggy ditch that both horses sensibly refused to cross. To be fair I would have done the same as it hardly looked safe for those with two feet, let alone four. I jumped off and had a quick hunt around for a better crossing place. As I searched, I wondered whether I should back-track and go around, as I suspected that Yogi would refuse a ditch jump after his little incident the day before.

Yogi proved me wrong though and popped over it no bother at all; I guess this sunshine not only puts everyone (yes, even Swift) in a good mood but it is a giver of courage too. Someone should have told the Lion from the Wizard of Oz to emigrate to Australia. It would have given an extra interesting twist to the plot for the story at least, and to be honest the clue was always in the title. 'Cowardly Lion (now sun-kissed and courageous) teams up with Skippy the Bush Kangaroo to conquer the Wicked Witch of the West,' sounded catchy enough for a sequel I thought. How light *was* my hip flask?

Conveniently, on the other side of the ditch, was a perfectly situated log which appeared delighted with promotion to its new role of mounting block. I jumped back on and waved goodbye to the log in gratitude for the height boost it had generously shared. We wove our way through the shadows of the trees, and I took a few deep breaths to savour the deliciously sharp, sweet, and refreshing smell that pines exude when baked in hot sun. No offence to makers of multi-purpose cleaners that claim to make pine-fragranced disinfectant, but I've never found any product that smells quite like the real thing.

The smell is produced by the release of compounds called terpenes, and pine oil is popular in natural medicine due to its wide range of health benefits. Used in aromatherapy, the essential oil is believed to have a strengthening effect on mind and body. It helps circulation, eases stiff muscles, and reduces anxiety and stress. This essential oil seemed like a valuable addition to my equipment for the journey and I wanted to bottle the smell up to take with me as we left the trees behind to emerge on the main Lochnagar track.

The track was lovely and soft under hoof, but I knew the good conditions wouldn't last. Not far around the corner the track would steepen and become covered in large loose rocks. We enjoyed it while it lasted and with the horses striding out in turbo mode, we soon caught up and overtook a pair of hill walkers. They were a little startled to discover what was coming up behind them but recovered enough to offer some friendly banter about how easy I had it, that my horse would carry me on up the hill.

I didn't even contemplate entering this debate. If they had seen my state of exhaustion the previous day, trying to battle against Yogi's turbo as I struggled to walk beside him on the steep trail through thick heather and peat, they may have seen a different side to this *easy* mode of transport. I may have described the bog jumping spell yesterday that followed this exertion in a light-hearted manner, but it was hard and dirty work too.

It is funny how the romantic perception of travelling by horse is as an easy option. I blame Western films myself as in them it *never* rains, *never* blows a gale and is *never* cold. Horses stand still *all* night in a Western and *never* need food or care. The cowboy *never* loses his hat, *never* needs to get off and walk and *always* has food for the fire (despite tiny saddle bags). The horses are *impeccably* behaved and *never* have their own opinion.

The horses or rider *never* get tired and it is warm enough to sleep out under the stars *without* the need to put up a tent and without a *single* Scottish midge or clegg (horsefly) in sight - no wonder it looks easy! However, there is rather a lot of gun shooting and arrow firing in Westerns and I'd rather tackle the Scottish weather and midges if I'm honest.

I was just about to get out of ear-shot of the walkers when one called out to ask why the horses were wearing slippers. Slippers? They really did have this image of an easy option deeply embedded.

"They aren't slippers," I replied, "they are hoof boots, to protect their feet as they don't wear metal shoes."

I was reasonably sure that these walkers didn't know

much about horses, but they were surprised that we could do what we were doing without the use of metal nailed to hooves. Many people that profess to know much about horses are also surprised by this concept.

I explained, as I do to many I meet on the trail, that I don't really believe that it is good for the horses to wear metal on their feet day after day, hour after hour. The rigid shoe interferes with the hoof's natural shock absorption, has long-term effects on joints, and reduces the natural venous return system, whereby the soft part of the hoof (the frog) aids the return of blood to the heart as it is compressed with each step. I don't find it practical to use metal shoes on long journeys in the hills anyway. If a horse loses a shoe and I am days from a farrier, I could potentially have a sore or lame horse, or forfeit days on the trail trying to find a farrier with time to help me. If I misplace or damage a hoof boot, I can carry a spare, or repair it.

On this trip, due to plenty of training, Yogi and Swift were only wearing front hoof boots as their back feet had hardened up and generally take less impact anyway. The walkers were clearly impressed with this new way of thinking about horses and their hooves. However, I could tell that my explanation was lengthier than anticipated and their attention was starting to waver.

Team Swogi and I, waved our goodbyes and moved on up the valley with the magnificent ridge line of Lochnagar guiding us onward to our left. Shortly, as anticipated, the track became steeper and covered in loose rock. Hoof boots or no, I jumped off to give Yogi an easier time of it, even though I didn't relish a repeat of yesterday's battle with Yogi's turbo-boost setting. A rethink on the uphill-off-horse system was required!

Swift was content today to follow behind without

being led, I decided to use hers and Yogi's ropes to long-rein him ahead of me. Long-reining is basically a system of steering your horse by walking behind as if you were in a carriage. Thankfully, I prefer long lead ropes, so I was able to follow Yogi's rounded rump without danger of a tail swish in the eye, or worse (but I'll leave those details rather vague). This new system worked perfectly; Yogi was extremely happy to be in the lead, I was getting a pull along up the hill, and Swift was merrily snacking her way along the trail behind us. We were soon through the broken track and I jumped back on to enjoy a better view than that of a horse's bottom.

"My bottom is a lovely view," Yogi pointed out, smirking at Swift. "Perfectly formed without a single spotty blemish on it."

"At least Claire could have entertained herself with joining the dots if she had been following me, as my bottom has additional ASSets." replied Swift, sticking her tongue out.

For once, Swift was the one cracking the bad jokes and I was the one rolling my eyes at her. I told them to *stop arsing about* and marvelled at this change of sun-induced team dynamics.

Far in the distance I could see the little group of trees that surrounded the bothy, but it was seemingly taking an age to get there. This was primarily due to the sheep-dog nature of the track leading to it. The bothy was *right there*, but the track insisted on running way out to the right, round to the left, then back to approach the bothy from the least expected direction. Also, I love staying in a bothy and I was enthusiastic and impatient to get there; a watched bothy never gets any nearer it seems.

I was reminded of a time when, as part of a team of four girls on a sea-kayaking adventure, we were crossing the Minch - the stretch of water between the Isle of Skye and the Outer Hebrides - which was a distance of about thirty-four miles. We'd left from Skye via the Isle of Fladda-chuain to head north to the Shiant Isles for an overnight rest to break the journey. The Shiant Isles were made famous by Adam Nicolson in his book *The Sea Room,* and promised swarms of sea birds and plentiful sprawling seals. We were impatient to explore the shapes of the islands and the wildlife they held, and to stay in the bothy he described in the book.

There was a fierce head wind for the whole sixteen miles, however, and the island took an age of time to appear any closer. The constant threat of tanker traffic in this stretch of water that probably wouldn't see four small boats, let alone be able to avoid them, enhanced the feeling of the island remaining just out of reach. Only on the final approach, distracted by floating puffins bobbing-along beside us, did we appear to make any sort of steady progress towards them.

On the way to the bothy today, the view was exquisitely extensive with a green heather foreground, leading to an expanse of brown patchy heather onwards to the blue-grey tiers of hills. As with the Minch experience, distracted by the abundance of layers stretching as far as the eye could see, I stopped bothy watching and we suddenly arrived at its door. Swogi did a rapid assessment of my overnight camp choice: fresh water? Green grass? Trees for butt scratching and shelter? Enough breeze to keep midges away? With their four main criteria satisfied, they snorted their approval and let me start to untack and unpack.

There hadn't been an opportunity for the horses to take a drink since leaving the Glen Muick valley and Swift was clearly torn: should she head for the stream for water, or should she get stuck into that grass before Yogi claimed it all as his? She decided that the grass had it and I duly constructed the corral around them both.

As a gal is oft to do, Swift soon changed her mind and I found myself making trip after trip, up and down, back and forth between stream and corral with one water bucket at a time. I'd return to the corral with a full bucket only to find the first one completely sucked dry and an Olivia Twist begging for more with an empty bowl. I'd lost count of refills, but knew I was just about to give up and instead take the horses to the water, despite warnings in John Heywood's proverb collection of 1546, when finally I returned to the first full bucket and horses that were having a satisfied snooze.

I lugged all the gear into a corner of the bothy, careful not to take up too much space to allow room for others and made dinner in a midge free environment. Have I mentioned how much I love to stay in a bothy? Myself and my stomach now satisfied, I ventured back outside to amuse myself for a while with my camera in this dramatic location under the shadow of Lochnagar and the dazzling sparkles of the sunset-lit stream.

I wandered a short way up the track towards the ridge, finding an assembly of lichen-speckled, gigantic boulders. You could almost believe they'd been placed by humans, balanced in the style of a Neolithic monument. The wind rustled through the thick reed-grass at the base of the stones, making their caps of deadened flowers look like thousands of spirited people. They swayed in unison, ringing the purple heather bells beside them in worship of the solstice gods.

Venturing back down to the horses to capture them on camera in the golden sunlight, I noticed that Yogi wasn't looking very happy at all. For one thing, he was surrounded by lush green grass and he wasn't eating any of it, not one single blade. Trying not to panic, for I'd never seen a non-eating Yogi before, I stood and assessed the whole situation.

He had stress lines etched deep into his face and since nobody was asking him to do something he'd rather not do, I took this as an indication of pain. He was standing all tucked up too. His front feet were in a normal position in relation to his shoulders, but his back feet were pushed forward under his belly, when really they should be firmly situated under his hips.

Now I was starting to panic. He looked like a horse that had colic. Horses have extremely sensitive bellies and it doesn't take much to upset them. An upset can result in abdominal pain caused by gas accumulation, obstruction, or inflammation of the gastrointestinal tract. It can be fatal if left untreated and the condition causes a high number of deaths among domesticated horses. If he had colic out here, this was very bad news indeed as we were a very long way from a vet.

I observed him a while longer. He wasn't getting any better and I was getting very anxious. Where were the walkers or cyclists who I had so looked forward to sharing adventurous tales with at the bothy? If someone else was here, I could maybe send them for help or at least discuss logistics with them of how I was going to get my sick horse out of here, but no; I was alone, and very scared for my horse.

I wandered around the corral and offered Yogi some grass out of my hand. Would he eat it? If he would still eat a little, then maybe his belly wasn't so sore. He ate from my hand and my heart rose a little, but he showed no interest at all in moving to feed himself. I felt all around his belly and he didn't glare at me once. Surely if his belly was sore, he would be annoyed at me touching it? I listened for bowel sounds - with no stethoscope to hand, my ear against his side was going to have to suffice, and yes, he had normal bowel sounds (unlikely to be a gas build up or blockage then). Maybe this wasn't colic after all?

Is he just exhausted? Did I do too much too soon in the trip? Is this my fault? What else could it be? The thoughts rushed through my head. I looked again at how he was standing. Had he hurt himself after all, doing that silly bog jump yesterday and now that he had stopped moving, he was feeling sore? He hadn't shown any sign of stiffness or lameness during the day, but I know myself that a pulled muscle sometimes doesn't really present until a day or two afterwards. He is a bit of a wimp when it comes to pain too, so maybe Yogi was just being a drama queen. This wasn't going to stop me worrying about him though. I hated seeing him suddenly so unhappy.

I gave him a big neck hug and didn't get the usual nose bump, snuffle or snort in return. He remained tight-lipped and distant and wasn't going to tell me what was wrong apart from that he was in pain, somewhere. I sat down on a rock outside the bothy, found the one spot that my mobile phone could send a message, and shared my concerns with another rock - my husband.

As a paramedic I know that gut feeling - or to give it the posh term, intuition - is a recognised phase of diagnosis, and my gut feeling was telling me that there wasn't a problem with Yogi's gut. Dave convinced me not to panic and if signs weren't indicating belly problems, then it probably wasn't belly problems and I should wait and see what happens.

I shuffled around on my Yogi watching rock to try and get more comfortable, as I could be here a while. Solitary rock sitting, in danger of inducing piles, midge swatting, and shivering in the cool wind had no good effect but it made me feel more useful. The fretting on the rock wasn't quite the social, warm, and comfortable bothy experience I had so keenly anticipated either. An hour went by and nothing had changed; no belly kicking, belly biting or rolling - signs so very characteristic of colic. All he did occasionally, was lift a back leg straight up underneath him like he was trying to stretch something out. At half-past-nine exactly (yes, I was clock watching as well as Yogi watching), he suddenly put his head down and started to casually graze.

The relief was immense. I suddenly felt quite exhausted and my legs had decided that I'd overshot my bedtime and had already gone to sleep at least twenty minutes ago. I staggered up, wobbled my way over to the bothy, and got ready for bed. One last check on Yogi half an hour later and I crawled into my sleeping bag. I knew it wouldn't be long before I'd be awake again and out to do yet another check. Even though it no longer looked like colic, I wasn't taking any chances and I'd be doing hourly observations through the night.

Day 5:
Gelder Shiel to Mar Lodge
(Distance 23km, Ascent 266m)

I stumbled out of the bothy at eight o'clock. I'd last been outside to check Yogi at half past five, and since he had been perfectly fine then I'd allowed myself a bit of a sleep and a lie in. Regardless of my visit only two and a half hours ago, Yogi greeted me with his usual 'good morning' soft whinny and Swift shrugged her shoulders and swung her spotty butt in my direction in a 'saw-you-earlier' kind of way.

All appeared to be pretty normal then with Team Swogi. To make sure though, I braved the midges despite having the luxury of the four walls and roof of the bothy and cooked my breakfast porridge outside. From here, I could better observe Yogi's behaviour while I battled to eat my porridge with added midge protein and fished out those determined to do backstroke in my morning cuppa.

Yogi seemed absolutely fine. There were no longer any stress lines on his face, he was pushing Swift around to make sure he had the tastiest grass, and there was no sign of him doing that funny stretch thing with his back legs. Whatever was wrong last night, there was no sign of it now. Relieved but not completely fret free, I cleared out of the bothy and packed up to go.

Swift, being quite young-brained (Appy's can be slow to develop), wasn't really ready to be the lead ridden horse yet, so I was reluctant to switch Yogi to packhorse at this stage. This idea would have given Yogi an easier time with less weight to carry in case he was still sore, but Swift would be reluctant (the polite way to say she'd refuse) to go up front.

I loaded the bags up on Swift to her usual teenage complaint of rolling eyes and, "Why me?" and set out walking with Yogi by my side. At least, that was the initial idea, but Yogi was full of beans and Swift and I couldn't keep up. He set off at quite some pace with no sign of stiffness or pain and even jogged a little. He seemed to find the landscape as eerie as I did.

The stream to our left looked beautiful as it babbled along happily with a sparkle in its eye, but in contrast, the rock formations all around it were menacing with their fierce, troll-like snarls. The terrain reminded me of a trip to Norway many years ago (for oil industry work) where the ground seemed completely devoid of soil, as bedrock reared its head everywhere you looked.

After another twenty minutes of trying to keep up with Yogi, I bravely stood on a troll's head and tried to get on him. I paid close attention to what Yogi was saying and knew that if he was sore, he wouldn't let me get on his back. Yogi wasn't saying anything about being sore and was completely enthralled by the fact that I was standing on a troll's head.

"You aren't brave, you're stupid!" he said. "Everyone knows that if you make a troll angry first thing in the morning, then they wake up with a craving for the taste of horse."

Swift sniggered. "I've heard that an angry troll develops particular cravings for the taste of spicy *ginger*!"

I'm not sure if Yogi really believed what Swift was saying, but he certainly didn't hang about to find out if it was true. As soon as my butt hit the saddle, we were off. Off in the direction of Mar Lodge where I had booked a patch of grass and a camp spot for a rest day.

"Rest day, did you say?" asked Swift, reading my mind

again, and suddenly lived up to her name with a spurt of speed and a turbo-boost of her own that I didn't know she had.

The rocky trolls stayed in the hills as we dropped down to more kind-hearted, forestry surroundings. The ambience was softer, but the track was rough with pale, loose, fist-sized stones for a short while and Swogi favoured the lumpy grass at the track sides instead. The lumps didn't appear to impede their haste however, as both turbo-boosts stayed very much in place. A lone pine on the left, standing proud like a flag, signified the boundary of harsh hillside with more lenient lowlands.

After about an hour, all turbo-boosts came to a crashing halt at the sight of the bridge in front of us. I'd forgotten to check my map against the information given to me by the rangers at Mar Lodge. They had mentioned that there was one bridge I might like to avoid with the horses and that I should instead take the high road rather than the low road. It was too late now (to get there before anyone) and I searched around by the bonnie, bonnie, banks of the river for a sneaky route round this bridge. There wasn't any sneaking to be found.

Back at the bridge I thought the problem through. It was solid enough, and wide enough; the snag lay in its unusual construction. Built like a wooden cattle grid of sorts, the horses weren't going to like it and may stumble or fall to their knees if they tried to cross it, although the bars were close enough together that a hoof wouldn't fall through. As I stood thinking about the long diversion I was now going to have to take, Yogi took matters into his own hands and nimbly crossed it without incident. He was so quick with his decision and execution that I didn't have time to stop him and neither did Swift.

Swift and I now had a new problem, of having one horse on one side of the obstacle and one horse on the other. Yogi was happily munching grass on the far side of a bridge that I was happy to cross, but it's often difficult to work out if Swift was happy or not. I tentatively approached her, chatting about the lovely grass waiting at the *rest* stop on the *other side* of this inoffensive, harmless, teeny-weeny bridge. She tentatively approached the bridge and I held my breath. I also held her head up for most of the crossing as it wasn't at all graceful. She stumbled her way across with eyes open wide, but thankfully without falling to her knees. She also mumbled her way across, mostly swear words directed at both Yogi and me.

I gave Swift a gentle stroke on her neck to say thank you for her bravery. Unlike Yogi, she is not a horse that likes a hug. Her bottom lip quivered briefly in appreciation before she abruptly remembered she wasn't supposed to need a human. Enjoying some attention is a sure sign of weakness, and she is a tough nut stroppy teenager.

"Hmph!"

With a shake of her head and one of her *looks,* the moment was well and truly over. One of these days I will permanently unleash the lovely soft soul that is hidden inside this spotty heart. For now, though, I have to be content with only the occasional glimpse of softness when she forgets to close the door.

The bridge not suitable for horses truly reclassified, we jigged our way along on a soft track and soon approached an area the horses had been to before, near the Old Invercauld Bridge. They both seemed to know where we were from a previous long-distance trek and both had a spring in their step. Reaching the picnic place we'd used last time, I reminisced about being here before with additional equine and human friends and decided to stop for some lunch. The chosen lunch stop was next to a carpark, and I knew it had excellent facilities - it's amazing how a simple picnic table and a basic toilet can become luxuries after only a few days on the trail. The other advantage here was a fence to tie the horses to - within reach of tasty trees and grass to keep them occupied while I was otherwise engaged.

As I ate my lunch, I listened to the sounds of the river, magnified by an increase in speed and gradient underneath the bridge. My pre-Swogi era involved happy hours playing under this bridge in a kayak, and as earlier memories of this location surfaced, my thoughts turned to my husband back home.

Reasonably early in my river kayaking learning curve, he had brought me here to practice rolling in moving water. Rolling is a technique to bring the boat the right way up again if you are unlucky enough to flip upside down. At the time Dave owned a kayak shop and often left a sign that stated "Gone product testing" on the shop door. This was one of those times and he was testing out a new, small playboat (a kayak designed for trick manoeuvres) and a new dry suit in order to honestly advise his customers through personal experience. That was the excuse he used anyway. This specific experience didn't go quite the way he was expecting however, and he was the one who appeared to need the rolling practice.

The playboat was a little more playful than anticipated and 'skinny hips' Dave, being a loose fit, had fallen out when he had flipped upside down. The boat wasn't the only thing that had flipped, and suddenly the novice found themself trying to rescue the experienced instead of the other way around. Proudly managing to push him and his boat to shore without even so much of a snigger (as I really needed to concentrate), I was abruptly confronted by a tirade of foul language. I'll provide a cleaner transcript here, but it went something along the lines of, "This dry suit is completely *flipping* useless, I am *utterly* soaked through!" and "I'll not be recommending this pile of *rubbish* to any customer of mine!"

I was surprised by this development, as the make of suit he was wearing was, in my limited opinion, one of the best out there and the manufacturer had a very solid reputation. I banked my boat and went over to console him. As I approached, I noticed that the suit was well thought out and the makers had even included a zip for a gentleman to relieve himself through.

"A pee zip, that's a good addition to any dry suit," I said to Dave, "but is it supposed to be left open whilst swimming?"

I can happily report that once this product had been correctly tested with all zips closed, it was completely watertight and was recommended to many a customer. As an aside I still have some of their equipment over fifteen years later that is still going strong - such a shame the company no longer exists. My ability to hold back the laughter also no longer existed, and Swogi exchanged glances of confusion as I appeared to laugh out loud at nothing that they could see. I apologised for disturbing their lunch munch and went back to my daydreams...

The bridge we were near now - the Old Invercauld Bridge - was built in around 1752 to provide a military crossing of the River Dee. Although the last of the significant Jacobite risings had taken place by then, the threat of another still remained and military presence was still commonplace, as were improvements to infrastructure to ensure efficient mobilisation of government troops at time of any crisis. The Jacobite risings were a turbulent time in Scottish history, spanning from 1689 until 1746. It was a complicated mix of allegiances, uprisings, and tactics that were driven by lineage, power, wealth and dominance of religious groups.

To summarise this complicated period, James Stuart VII (as he was known in Scotland) or James II (as he was called in England) held Catholic beliefs and held the crown in England, Scotland and Ireland. The English parliament favoured Protestant rule and supported Mary II (James VII's eldest daughter) and her husband (the Dutch William of Orange) to overthrow the throne. James VII fled to France where he lived in exile supported by this Catholic nation.

The Jacobite motivations for revolt lay in establishing both a Scottish throne, a claim to which James VII still legitimately held, and restoring Catholicism as the ruling religion. James's claim to the throne aided a move toward much sought Scottish independence, and added to the motivational mix were various money and power aspirations held by certain influential individuals.

Six attempts were made to reinstate the exiled Stuarts to the throne with varying amounts of French and Spanish support. The clan chiefs and lairds were able to mobilise large numbers of loyal fighters to battle at a moment's notice. Usually this moment was one they thought would be to their advantage, such as when English troops were distracted and engaged in battles overseas. Loyal the fighters might have been, but they were often unskilled peasant crofters who had a 'call to arms' itemised as a clause in their tenancy agreements.

As often witnessed in all eras of history, the 'commoners' became the cannon fodder of political agendas intended to make the wealthy prosper.

The Jacobite rebellions finally culminated in the Battle of Culloden in 1746, with which the romanticised story of Bonnie Prince Charlie is so famously linked (watch Braveheart the movie). The Bonnie Prince was the grandson of James VII and he also fled to France following his defeat at Culloden. There was a high price on his head, but he still had plenty of support from various clans in the Scottish Highlands and, although Culloden marked the end of this era, there remained in this area a sympathetic and sentimental view towards their 'King over the water'.

A century later, as use of the Invercauld bridge increased, Prince Albert funded a new road bridge in 1859 to improve privacy around the nearby Balmoral Castle. The Old Invercauld Bridge is now a footbridge and has a rather humped-back shape. I could so easily imagine the stomach flip if your carriage driver approached it at some speed in times gone by.

The happy memories and historical links decided to stay a while, lingering around the picnic table in the car park as we continued onward to follow the course of the River Dee in its upper most reaches. The springy steps also continued, and I mused that there couldn't be much wrong with Yogi as he asked time and time again to upgrade the jigs to a canter. His rhythmic chant of, "Can-I-canter, can-I-canter, can-I-canter" almost lulled me into it but, thinking of Swift and her bags, I declined his offer (repeatedly).

It was another sunny day, although not as hot as yesterday as the sun was accompanied by a rather stiff, cooling breeze. As we emerged from the forest, a view across the Upper Dee Valley opened up. The river snaked its way back and forth across the wide, flat floodplain that it had constructed over the years. We were all entertained for a time by some small calves in the field to our left, as they played in a muddy puddle then bolted back to their mums, startled by our appearance.

At times, the track under hoof was grassy and uphill. Perhaps inspired by the nearing rest day or lulled by Yogi's seductive canter chanter, Swift suddenly cantered up alongside, ears pricked and without complaint about the bags she was carrying. Yogi immediately took this as consent by me to move up a gear and we enjoyed the faster pace on the uphill sections. New mountains in the distance introduced themselves as they appeared around each twist in the trail.

As a result of this faster pace, we arrived at our evening stop and rest location earlier than expected. I'd stayed at Mar Lodge before with the horses and have always been made to feel very welcome indeed. Given our early arrival, however, I was surprised to find everything already set out for us.

Mar Lodge is a member of the British Horse Society's *Horses Welcome Scheme,* which offers a quality-assured list of equine bed and breakfast accommodation. To qualify for this scheme, the horse accommodation must meet certain standards, although horses rarely expect or require more than a bucket of water and a safe patch of grass for both bed *and* breakfast. The human accommodation, quite rightly, is not considered important enough to receive a rating and I'd be staying in my tiny tent for the next two nights.

A ranger from the Lodge had set up a corral for me, thinking how difficult and tiring it must be to travel on my own with two horses, and had filled a bucket of water for the horses to take a long drink. She had obviously not watched very many Western movies and seemed to understand the reality of the situation, rather than the romantic/easy option falsely portrayed on-screen. This corral, though kindly constructed, was a little on the small side for two hungry, trail-beaten, celebrity horses (according to them), but was a welcome holding area whilst I started the process of de-booting, untacking and unpacking. It was nice to be able to do this at a leisurely pace without having to rush to construct my own corral around the horses, who always think that the grass is greener just a bit further away.

I even took a moment to enjoy a luxury cup of tea before proceeding into full camp assembly mode. Unhurried, I set about building a bigger corral using my own equipment. My corral kit consists of a couple of rolls of electric tape, some tent poles (collapsible to fit in the saddle bags), tent pegs, guy ropes, duct tape, and baler twine. No homemade equipment kit would be complete without duct tape and baler twine. Whatever it is you were constructing would simply fall apart without these essential items.

I found a spot nearby for my tent, making myself comfortable and organised to cook tonight's dinner. As I walked across to move the horses into their new bigger corral, I noticed for the second night in a row that Yogi was standing still, stress lines on his face and *not* eating. This just wasn't making any sense. How can he be so full of beans, fluid and loose in his movements, no sign of pain or lameness, happy for me to get on his back during the day, but when he stops at night seems so obviously in pain?

I checked his back and legs using many of the stretches and exercises I'd learnt from when he had an injured back, and again I couldn't find anything obviously wrong. I moved him into the new corral and he dropped his head down to start grazing. He obviously wasn't as bad as last night, but he still wasn't right. With an experienced horsey friend arriving tomorrow, I'd ask her opinion and maybe a rest for the day and night in a warm rug (she was bringing some with her) might help ease whatever it was that was wrong.

I watched him carefully as I cooked and ate my dinner. He was at least eating with more enthusiasm this evening, but was still doing that strange stretchy thing with his back legs every so often. Not worried about colic now (the symptoms just didn't fit), and with me being a bit more relaxed in a place where there were other people and better access to help should Yogi need it, I crawled into my tiny tent for an early night and a deep sleep.

Day 6:
Rest Day at Mar Lodge
(Distance 10km, Ascent 130m waterfall walk)

Emerging lazily from my tent at whatever time it was (no need to check today), I found the horses also having a lie in. Both were still lying down with legs neatly tucked up underneath them and they seemed relaxed and happy, although a little on the damp side. It had rained slightly overnight and there was a chill in the air. Yogi, half asleep, gave a half-hearted attempt at his usual good morning whinny and Swift opened half an eyelid in my general direction.

It wasn't overly cold, but since Swift was lying tucked up and not in her usual flat out display, I figured that this was because it wasn't quite warm enough for full horizontal. I was glad that my friend Fiona was arriving shortly with horse rugs so that Team Swogi could get nice and cosy for the next twenty-four hours. This would set them up well for the next days ahead and I hoped would help Yogi recover from whatever it was that was ailing him.

As I cooked and then greedily ate my porridge, I admired the impressive lodge building in front of me. The Lodge itself was originally built in 1895 by the Duke of Fife, but had to be rebuilt after an extensive fire in 1991. Although a relatively modern building as a result, it was reconstructed with impressive and tasteful architecture that befitted its equally impressive setting, nestled between the River Royal Dee and the foot of the Cairngorm Mountains. No longer a grand family estate house, it is now split into luxury holiday apartments.

As I set off towards the back door of the lodge where I

had been promised 'sneaky access' to a much-needed shower, I noticed that the door to the ballroom was ajar. The ballroom is in a separate building to the lodge, and has a spectacular display of red deer stags' heads lining the walls and ceiling (2,435 in number, I am led to believe). I popped my head around the door but didn't stop to count them all, as I found the sight a little eerie truth be told. That is a huge number of magnificent animals to no longer be running free on the hills.

Deer management has been an issue since the mid 1900's, when deer populations escalated to extremely high levels to the detriment of the local environment and to the deer themselves. I have a divided opinion on deer management, which is based on the love of all types of nature, a soft heart, and very limited knowledge on the subject. It is probably not a dispute I am qualified to debate. Suffice to say, there must be a balance struck between providing an economy for sporting estates (and the local people in rural areas that they employ) and nature conservation.

The Mar Lodge Estate covers around eight percent of the Cairngorms National Park and is owned and managed by the National Trust for Scotland. It is, I understand, one of the biggest and most important nature conservation landscapes in the British Isles, thus has a need to maintain the deer population at a manageable level. This maintenance is what causes controversy for some. Another Cairngorm estate faced huge criticism when they carried out a one-off, large-scale cull of deer on their estate as numbers had risen out of control. However, they now have thriving glens abundant with diverse traditional flora and fauna and are praised by many for the restoration of a native landscape and woodland regeneration. The battle between what Man thinks is nature, and what true nature delivers when left alone, will continue for as long as mankind does. A situation that is not unique to the Highlands of Scotland.

Returning fully refreshed, but only smelling slightly less of horse from what felt like the most amazing 'sneaky' shower in history, I couldn't help but notice a rather bright orange blot on the landscape. This blot looked entirely out of place in some respects, but perfectly suited in others. The blot was an all-terrain, rugged, fully capable for all adventures Land Rover (called Bernard) and signified the arrival of my friend Fiona.

Greetings, hugs, and rugs were distributed in the right proportions and directions (along with a few Land Rover matching carrots, much to Swogi's delight) and we came up with a plan for the day. Firstly, I had kit to repair; then there was a trip required into Braemar, the nearest village, for a restock of trail food and hip flask content (the essentials, essentially). Following that were a few interesting waterfalls that I wanted to show to my friend. Fiona's fascination with every little bit of nature from tiny wee bugs, shapes of shells, colours of stones, to bubbles in a stream, would make her squeal with delight at how close I could get her to the waterfalls. I was looking forward to rewarding her support crew efforts with a fun-filled walk later in the day.

First though, I had Yogi's reins to repair (from day two which now seemed a long time ago) as I'd rather not have the temporary karabiner fix turn into a permanent one. Also needing some attention were the D-rings that

I attach the saddle bags to on Swift's saddle. I'm not sure whether they are badly designed in the first place (if so then my only criticism of an otherwise fantastic product), or whether Swift - when I'm not looking - loosens them off, in the hope that her load might get lighter without me noticing. She was looking over rather sheepishly in my direction as I contemplated this, so I had my reservations.

As I sat by Bernard's back door with my task in front of me, Fiona offered some sound but apparently strange advice. Looking over my shoulder, in proper Harry Enfield style, she said, "You don't wanna do it like that." Luckily her alternative suggestion was much more helpful than the father-in-law from the sketch show would offer, and is something I still use today. Who knew that dental floss is a fantastic substance to make super strong repairs with?

Fiona knew apparently, and not only does it come in a self-contained box handy to store in a Land Rover (or saddle bag), but it's easy to thread through the eye of a needle and is incredibly strong. So strong in fact that I've never had to repair Yogi's reins again and they have seen plenty of miles since then. The D-rings are another matter however, and I remain Swiftly suspicious about how they happen to unravel, especially since dental floss deliciously tastes of mint.

Repairs realized, we moved on to the replenishment of reserves and set off in Bernard to Braemar. The road to Braemar is about six kilometres long, single-track, and provides magnificent views of the Dee Valley. As Fiona drove, I enjoyed looking across the river at the mirror image of the view that Team Swogi had admired as we arrived yesterday. The lumpy brown heather at the side of the road looked somewhat coarse compared to the flat and fertile floodplain below. The lush green grass there was grazed by cattle in amongst the complex jigsaw of river twists, interlocking spurs, and oxbow lakes. The red roof of Mar Lodge in the distance was a small splash of colour in this vast landscape, prominent against the dark green forestry on the lower slopes of the foothills but dwarfed by the mountains towering behind.

I was grateful for the lift into town this time. On a different long-distance trek and on a different rest day, I had walked the twelve-kilometre round route to collect supplies. Despite the readiness of my thumb for hitching, I'd not had the opportunity to deploy it as not one single car had passed me. I'd had to walk the complete distance there and back. The extremely tasty hotpot with a side of chips and a pint that I stumbled across whilst in town, however, had made the arduous amble deliciously worth it.

Shopping successful, and supplies stashed back at basecamp, it was time to show Fiona the local delights that the Lui had to offer. The River Lui is a tributary of the River Dee, close to a famous constriction called the Linn of Dee where the mighty river squeezes through a natural rock gorge. This is most dramatically viewed from the ornate Gothic bridge that spans it. Whereas most tourists may travel to see the Linn and perhaps some might follow the path up the western bank of the Lui, few explore the eastern bank of this little river. On the eastern side there isn't a proper path, but if you know where to look, a tiny trail leads through the heather for gorge-walking enthusiasts to follow.

As it happens I did know where to look, as during my pre-Swogi era I was enthusiastic about all things wet and waterfall. Working as an outdoor sports instructor, one of my favourite activities was gorge walking and this was one of my favourite gorges to play in. The Lui provided an exciting array of sizeable waterfalls to clamber up or slide down plus tight, steep-walled canyons to swim through or jump into if you were so inclined and safely equipped.

Today though, Fiona seemed content to be led to within touching distance of the waterfalls without any swimming or wading required. We paused in marvel at the rainbows formed through the waterfall's spray as the sun poked through the clouds from time to time. We watched dippers bobbing in and out of the river edges, peered into the canyon depths where the water disappeared into the abyss, and admired the twists and turns of the gnarly trees that were dotted along the bank.

As we emerged content and revitalised back onto the road, a horse and rider appeared. Or rather, a rider and two horses appeared in a somewhat similar set up as Team Swogi. Up until then, I'd rarely met - in person or in horse - anyone else who travelled like I do, other than frequent trail partner Yvonne. There are many long-distance riders (more than you may realise), but it's the minority who go out solo with a packhorse and enough equipment to be self-sufficient for numerous days in remote hills. It was lovely to chat with a like-minded individual - who was considerably more experienced than me - during a happenstance meeting before heading away on our individual exploits.

Back at camp I began the discussion that I had been avoiding all day. What did Fiona think about the Yogi situation? Should I continue, or were his signs and symptoms indicating something that should have me abandon the mission? We extracted a reluctant Yogi from underneath the warmth and comfort of his rug, poked, prodded, and stretched him in all manner of places, then trotted him up for each other in turn to see what we could find. We found very little out of place apart from the swing of his ample half-Highland belly. He was showing no signs now of anything ailing him and was completely sound in walk and trot. No sign of reluctance to move his feet or legs in the correct places on tight turns, either. The only thing he appeared to be worried about was how soon he could return to the corral.

"Where," pointed out Yogi, "Swift is busy eating all of *my* grass!"

We put his rug back on, popped him back in with Swift (both actions to his liking), and discussed options. Fiona was going to bike and walk with us tomorrow, so maybe we could see how Yogi proceeded rather than head for home right now.

"Home?" Yogi said. "I love being at home where it's so comfortable in the shelter and where all that delicious food is."

I wondered if I should take rugs going forward? I'd have to try and fit them somewhere on Swift, increasing her load.

Swift sniffed the air and said, "Looks like it's going to warm up, why would we need to carry *heavy* rugs?"

We took our discussions away from the horses and over to the stove to have a cup of tea. The 'all for one' pact had its limits with comfort-loving, food-obsessed, and work-shy members of the team and I felt discussions might be more productive out of ear shot with someone who had no such bias.

The end of the next day would take us much closer to home and the day after even more so. Once through Glen Tilt, the next glen on our route, we would be travelling roughly parallel to the A9 - the main trunk road running through the North of Scotland. This would provide a more accessible and easier rescue by the fifth emergency service, consisting of Dave with the horse trailer. Sounding options out with Fiona, and considering Yogi appeared fine, we agreed that the best option was to head onwards tomorrow and see how things were at the end of that day.

The trail tomorrow would start well on a wide, off-road vehicle track, but would eventually reduce in size to a narrow, sheep-width path. This tiny path would have a steep heather covered slope uphill to the right and a steep downhill slope to the left. At its worst sections, the track consisted of a mixture of loose soil, heather, and slippery rocks. The steep downward slope to the left terminated in a fast-flowing river which is exactly where anything else would terminate should it fall down there too.

Mark Twain once said, "Good judgement is the result of experience and experience the result of bad judgement." and this is exactly why Fiona was joining me on the trail tomorrow. I'd made that bad judgement once before and was determined not to do so twice. In my opinion, and at the current stage of team development, this narrow path would be too dangerous to ride and lead on my own and I needed a second pair of hands to keep the second horse safe.

In my early days, on one of my first solo treks, whilst collecting the bad judgement and experience, I'd been faced with a similar kind of trail. The only difference was that the sheer slope upwards had been on my left and the loose, gravelly downwards slope to the river was on my right. To be fair to my decision making and risk assessment skills, the track started out wide and appeared safe, but it became gradually narrower and narrower until I reached a point of no return. Horses don't have the tightest turning circle unless you can teach them to rear up and pirouette on their back legs, and neither Swift nor Yogi knew this circus trick.

I had been leading Yogi behind me and, thankfully, had gone to the effort of tucking his reins away and attaching a lead rope to his headcollar. Not knowing Swift or her capabilities too well at this early stage, I'd tied her lead rope to the pommel (sticky-up part at the front) on Yogi's saddle. I thought this would prevent her from heading home and would help guide her with the right way to go. Since I'd tied it with a quick release knot in a place I could reach rapidly, I believed it was safe practice should anything go wrong.

How wrong could I be? I'd thought we were all proceeding in a careful and conscientious manner; yes it was tricky, but everything was fine - until it suddenly wasn't fine anymore. In the blink of an eye, Yogi - probably daydreaming - had missed his footing and had just stepped off the edge. It all happened so incredibly fast, but I remember watching the lead rope start to go tight between myself and the rapidly descending Bear and I also observed the same thing happening with the lead rope between Yogi's pommel and Swift's headcollar. No time to detach her, the quick release system was useless.

Yogi is heavier than Swift, so the physics and momentum had not been in her favour. In that split second the main thought in my head was *"She's going to go over the edge too!"* The advantage of my outdoor sports background emerged and the ingrained reaction to taking an impact on the end of a rope kicked in. I widened my stance, dropped down on my heels, and quickly adjusted my hand grip to brace myself for the force of the shock as the rope went tight. As the situation unfolded, seemingly in slow motion, I saw the shock on Swift's face as she also seemed to realise what was about to happen.

I was completely gobsmacked to see her reaction. Wide-eyed, she firmly planted both front feet, balanced her weight back on her haunches, and - like me - appeared to be ready for the impact she was about to take on her lead rope. Braced and prepared as we both were in the split second we had been afforded, the physics still didn't add up. It just didn't seem possible that we'd be able to break Yogi's fall.

Sometimes a little bit of luck is all that it takes for you to survive your bad judgement and convert it into a worthy learning experience. Luckily for all of us, both lead ropes reached the end of their capacity at exactly the same time. Mine, being strongly attached to Yogi's headcollar, and Swift's attached to the front of his saddle, had a rotating action that spun him round more than stopped his fall. This action meant that his front knees and back feet found purchase and he rapidly stopped sliding. Swift and I had also stopped sliding towards Yogi and the edge that he had just disappeared over.

Holding my breath, I watched as he tried in vain to get his front two feet on the ground; but it was too steep and too loose. He scrambled and scrambled, mostly using front knees and back feet, whilst I hauled and hauled on his head. I used strength I didn't know I had but I have no idea what Swift applied (witch-like powers of levitation?), as my eyes were firmly on Yogi and his struggle. Bit by bit he managed to scramble back up to the tiny track. It felt like hours of labour, but it was over in minutes and I collapsed to my knees exhausted on the trail. Yogi had been panting hard and shaking from nose to tail with a large amount of adrenalin pumping through his system. I staggered to my feet and had a brief check for any sign of injury, but with a more pressing action to take, I didn't look too closely. I threw my arms around his neck and promptly burst into tears.

As poor Yogi was smothered in hugs, kisses, snotters and tears, I became fully aware of how lucky we'd all just been. There had been so many *'what ifs'* running through my head and none of them created particularly pleasant outcomes. *What if* I'd only had hold of the reins? Not only would they have been shorter and more slippery to grip, but they would probably have snapped quickly under the pressure. *What if* Swift had been pulled over the edge too? *What if* Yogi had fallen right to the bottom, badly hurt himself, and I'd needed to try and find help? The cliff fall happened miles from anywhere or anyone and I knew this glen had zero mobile signal. I would have been forced to leave the horses there and walk an hour or two for help.

I clearly remember the shudder that had descended my spine. The *'what ifs'* were not what I'd needed to be concentrating on at that time. What I'd needed to be thinking about was getting out of there safely as we had still been in a dangerous place. I'd reluctantly extracted myself from under Yogi's mane and given him a more thorough check all over. Astonishingly, I only found a couple of bruises and scrapes, but nothing that needed any first aid attention. I squeezed beside him as far as I dared on the narrow trail to reach Swift, to check her head and neck and say a massive thank you for her essential help in preventing Yogi's demise. For once she was completely speechless with no negative or positive response to my gratitude and attention.

Everyone had been stunned but unscathed and I'd stepped back to take stock of the situation. I still had no choice but to proceed forward and at that point I suddenly realised again how lucky we had been. If Yogi had scrambled back up and had ended up facing Swift instead, then I really would have been in a pickle - with no room to turn either horse. With a brief flashback to the moment I'd thought Swift was going to be pulled over the edge too and I unclipped her lead rope entirely.

Lesson well and truly learnt. My sure-footed, deep-thinking, spotty gal was safer unattached. This left her vulnerable if she made a mistake, with no one there for her at the end of her lead rope to break a fall, but at least she wouldn't be caught out by a mistake that someone else had made. I'd left this statement rather generalised at the time, as Yogi had been looking sheepish enough without me piling on the guilt.

With no option then but to proceed in a forward manner, the next hour or so had been a time of intense mental concentration and worry. The trail ahead of this little incident had grown more challenging before it improved, with two major rockslides across the tiny track to negotiate. Now fully alert and awake, both horses had been much more attentive and careful with their feet. However, I did have my heart in my mouth watching Swift carefully negotiate the narrow trail through the final rockslide on her own, before emerging back onto the safety of a wider, flatter track where Yogi and I had been waiting.

The flatter track was good for another hour but again petered out - or rather, it 'peated out'. Worn out from the cliff hanging incident, the last thing any of us needed was the couple of hours of peat bog jumping, river crossing, and heather-bashing that then followed. It would probably have been fine in dry weather, but it had been very wet in the run up to this excursion and so conditions were somewhat challenging. Yogi hates bogs and I did wonder if he would ever trust me to choose a route ever again.

This bad judgement turned learning experience means that I now recce any intended route for solo treks to assess for dangers and challenges such as these. I do this myself, rather than relying on someone else's opinion as to whether a trail is horse safe or not. Although I could unclip Swift and leave her to follow along tomorrow's similar trail, (in the alternative glen) the risk of her missing a step and having a similar experience to Yogi but without help to stop her fall, was a risk I was not prepared to take. Despite her moody teenager attitude, I do happen to love her dearly.

Thus, Fiona had been assigned to join us by bike at first, along the initial wide trail, before carefully leading Swift in-hand along the narrower part. Fiona would turn back once the trail widened again and recover her bike from a hidden spot in the heather to increase the speed of her homeward journey. This was not a trail I would now attempt alone with two horses and I was grateful to have another friend willing to support my eccentric exploits. I might be a bit of an oddity, but it's nice to know that I don't have to be odd on my own.

With the night turning cooler, I was glad that the horses were cosy in their rugs. Fiona retired to her bunk bed in Bernard and I said good night to Swogi before crawling into my tiny tent. I suspected a fitful sleep was ahead, as the next three days would be more challenging than the last few and I just can't help worrying about keeping my horses safe. Thinking about the Yogi incident, then camping in the same place as we had done at the end of that day all those years ago, wasn't going to help me avoid nightmares about cliffs.

When Yogi fell off the cliff

Day 7:
Mar Lodge to Forrest Lodge
(Distance 26km, Ascent 333m)

After a fitful sleep, I emerged from my tiny tent to a day that embodied the famous Scottish word *'dreich'!* The world was monotone in appearance, it was cold, and it was drizzling. The weather had certainly changed since yesterday, and it felt like the change was set to stay. I suspected that I wasn't going to see much of the yellow thing in the sky for a few days to come.

Trying to raise our spirits, I said a cheery good morning to Swogi who were up and about grazing. Yogi replied with an enthusiastic good morning whinny and Swift afforded me a huffy "It's wet" grunt. I also woke up Bernard, by gently knocking on one of his windows to see if he would tell Fiona about the cup of tea I was tentatively offering.

Luckily, Fiona is a morning person. She had slept well, was grateful for the early tea, and was soon up and about assisting me to pack the saddle bags. Not for the first time this trip, I was welcoming the extra helping hands and wondered if I could sneak a person into one of Swift's saddle bags without her noticing. I thought my chances were slim at best, despite Fiona's petite form, so I'd have to settle for temporary companionship and help instead.

The next three days would be a substantial diversion from the aim of completing a cross-Scotland adventure in a straight line, for several good reasons. Top of the list was that the direct line would take us down the glen described yesterday, featuring endless miles of bog jumps and a potential cliff hanging incident. Obviously,

I planned to avoid hazards such as these, but there were also other reasons for diverting down a different glen (Glen Tilt this time): I'd never tried this glen by horseback before, it was extremely pretty, and it boasted interesting history in terms of geology and access rights - two subjects close to my heart.

In my pre-pre-Swogi era (pre-outdoor sports instructor) I'd studied geology. In attempting to make a living out of my love for rocks, the oil industry was the original reason for my move north to settle in Scotland. Geological mapping and engineering geology was my thing, but unfortunately short in employment opportunities when I left University. Petrophysics is where I ended up and I wasn't particularly good at it, nor did I especially enjoy it.

Petrophysics involves staring at squiggly lines on a computer screen, trying to interpret in 3D terms what they signify about rock type, porosity and permeability, all for a client's financial benefit and this just didn't float my boat. Despite departing the oil industry to spend most of my time floating in a boat as an outdoor instructor, I never lost my fascination with 'proper' geology, the sort you can see and touch in the field or glen.

We should perhaps quickly skip over the fact that in my third career, I now stare at squiggly lines on a defibrillator and interpret what they signify in 3D terms for a client's health benefit. This interpretation sometimes involves lifesaving decisions, thus making those squiggly lines suddenly feel more real-time and consequential than those in the petrophysics world ever felt. Those who may need to call for an ambulance in my patch, may be relieved to note that health and survival benefits distinctly surpass financial benefits in engaging my squiggly line interest levels and motivating the standard of my interpretation skills.

Back to the geology: Glen Tilt runs in a north-easterly to south-westerly direction along the Loch Tay fault line. Nothing unusual about this, as Scotland has many fault lines that transect the country in this direction due to oblique compression between north and south during the land movements of the Caledonian Orogeny. During the orogeny, as mountains were built, glens were also formed (the peaks and troughs of the time) as the movements of tectonic plates crushed land masses together 490 - 390 million years ago. As the plates collided, faulting occurred, the most significant of which in Scotland being the Great Glen fault; one hundred kilometres in length, it links the east and west coasts of the country.

Many of the fault-line glens are considered essential transport routes today and played strategic parts in Scotland's human history. You don't have to be a history guru to recognise that the Great Glen would have been a busy thoroughfare during the Jacobite risings in the 18th century, especially as it starts at a place called Fort William, has Fort Augustus at its halfway point, and finishes near Fort George.

Human history is the main reason for Glen Tilt's geological notoriety too, although nothing to do with Jacobite clans. Historically, Glen Tilt was probably the venue for one of the first ever geological field trips. Such trips typically consist of hunters armed with soggy sandwiches, a notebook, pencil crayons, a hammer, and a magnifying-glass apiece, intrepidly searching for clues of rocky dimensions.

Rivers eroding adjacent to fault-lines provide opportunities for geeky rock hunters to find a wide array of different ages and types of rocks on display, laid bare by the river's hard labour. The River Tilt must be very proud of its achievement in exposing the answer to the origin of igneous rocks, albeit a shared achievement with the man wielding the pencil crayons who worked it all out.

In 1785, a Mr James Hutton found evidence in Glen Tilt to answer the 18th century's huge controversy of how basalt and granite rocks came to be. It was an exciting time in geology, with Neptunists quarrelling with Vulcanists over whether the Plutonists were correct that granite rose from a subterranean underworld, obliterating bedrock as it forced its way into life as we know it. The Plutonists, lead by Hutton, won this raging academic battle due to the differing rocks types he found on either side of the Tilt. It must have been a huge relief to mankind when Hutton, the father of modern geology, published his *Theory of Earth* in 1788 with all rocks positioned in their correct category of sedimentary, metamorphic, or igneous, concluding a period of sleepless nights for all.

Hutton, however, wasn't the only one to take a stash of soggy sandwiches to Glen Tilt in the midst of a battle. A party of Botanists in 1847 led by a Mr John Balfour found themselves (with their sandwiches) in the rain and at gunpoint in the middle of a dispute, this time about access rights. The Duke of Atholl claimed that they were trespassing and, despite the rain and darkness, they must return the twenty or so miles on foot to Braemar.

Less science-fiction sounding than the geological one, this battle was taken up by the then recently formed Association of Public Rights of Roadways, against the 6th Duke of Atholl. The battle culminated in a victorious Victorian conclusion in court, that found in favour of the people. It was decided quite rightly by the courts that the route between Braemar and Blair Atholl via Glen Tilt was a long-standing Drovers Road, and therefore was a public right of way.

This was the start of the public pushback against landowners in Scotland who were preventing a right of access to the countryside. It was also the start of a named association helping the public to defend their rights. The association doing this now is called the Scottish Rights of Way and Access Society (ScotWays), and they help to safeguard The Land Reform (Scotland) Act 2003 which gives the public the right to responsibly roam.

Without this roaming right, I wouldn't have been able to contemplate my cross-Scotland adventure at all. That said, access with horses can still be an issue on certain estate lands, with cattle grids, fences, style access only, and padlocked gates. The Land Reform Act and ScotWays (amongst others) help negotiations with landowners and support the public to solve these problems, allowing the public to exercise their bodies and their rights on foot, cycle, or horse.

I remain very grateful to Mr John Balfour for starting this process and hope that his sandwiches weren't too soggy in Glen Tilt. I am pleased to report that he seemingly deceived the Duke that day and snuck through the glen to the warmth and comfort of a local inn on the Blair Atholl side, without having to walk the twenty miles back in the dark. I think I would have liked Mr John Balfour with a shared love of nature, enjoyment of fine ale, the draw of a warm fire, an unwillingness to be intimidated by status, and a common-sense approach to human rights.

Given the twofold historical context described, how could I cross Scotland without exploring this important glen? How could I consider taking the more direct route, taking the horses back to the place I'd vowed 'never again'? The three-day diversion was a bit of a no-brainer in decision making terms and, despite the extra miles it would entail, I was rather looking forward to it.

All packed up and ready to go, I had a quiet word with Yogi and again asked him if he was feeling okay.

"I'm fine, let's go! I don't care where, somewhere, anywhere, but let's go now so we can get there. Is that the trail we're following over there? Let me at it!"

This was a normal response from him, so I concluded that the rest day under a warm rug had helped whatever had been wrong. I set off on foot beside him regardless, allowing him time to warm up his muscles and allowing Swogi to accept the new two-wheeled member of the team.

I watched in amusement as Fiona, in trying to be sociable, was attempting the longest slow-bicycle race of her life. Sociable as it was, this arrangement didn't last long and we were soon heading up the glen in a more purposeful manner. I'd jumped up on top, Yogi had turned on his turbo-boost setting, and Swift was following on behind, stopping to munch grass here and there before trotting to catch us up. Meanwhile, Fiona was whizzing about back and forth exploring and taking photos. It wasn't the best weather for photography, the light was grey and flat, and heavy drizzle was still falling from the sky. However, it's a rarity indeed for me to be in front of the camera rather than behind it and Fiona managed to get a few dramatic photos of Team Swogi in action, negotiating streams, bridges, or tricky terrain together.

All was wet but well until just before lunchtime. We crossed the third cold, rocky stream in a calm and controlled manner and decided to stop for a rest. Within five minutes of stopping, both Fiona and I could tell that Yogi was not a happy Yogi once again. The facial stress-lines were back in place, I could see pain in his eyes, and he was doing that strange stretchy thing with his back legs again. This just wasn't making any sense at all and I knew then and there that I needed expert advice. I couldn't work out what was happening to my boy on my own, so we paused further for discussion on how to access the nearest vet. Not only was I so incredibly grateful for Fiona's help in negotiating the thin and dicey track today, but I was glad of her being there to sound out my options.

The resulting decision was that my best way to veterinary help was to continue forward to a lodge nearer to the end of the glen. There, I knew, was someone who kept horses, was knowledgeable about them and would, I'm sure, help me find a vet to see to Yogi. I'd also be much better positioned closer to home for a rapid retrieval from hubby should the vet's advice suggest this. We were at the start of the tricky track now anyway, where I had already planned to dismount. We decided to proceed slowly and carefully and even when I reached the wider track again, I'd continue to walk rather than ride.

With the decision made and determination restored, it was time for Fiona to stash her bike in the heather, pick up Swift's lead rope, and start to get closely acquainted with the moody teenager mare. I whispered a quiet, "Good Luck with that!" in Fiona's direction as Swift pulled a goofy scowl as if to say "Who are you, who put you in charge, are you qualified for this and why are you presuming it's okay to be in MY personal space right now?" Fair questions I suppose, but sometimes it's about how you ask them.

Thankfully Fiona has a cheery disposition. Ignoring Swift's scowls entirely she followed on behind me, remarking how exciting and atmospheric the glen now appeared, as it narrowed and steepened with the river squeezed in beside us. Like most teenage behaviour, displayed for maximum attention seeking, it is often a successful strategy to ignore it until it goes away. Swift soon gave up her efforts and grumpiness as she accepted Fiona's guidance along the thin trail.

We were in a dictionary definition of a V-shaped valley, the river afforded only the smallest amount of room in the crux, with the path etched into and clinging onto one of the steeply sloped sides. The thin trail was slippery and wet in the drizzle, but perfectly negotiable with one horse each and a little bit of care - except for two areas, where there were smooth slabs of rock across the trail. These rocky slabs sloped down to the river over the trail and would involve a bit of a clamber.

Now, clambering over smooth, slippery slabs might be perfectly acceptable for those of us with two feet and hiking boots, but that kind of activity is most unacceptable for those of us with four hooves to supervise. I only need to provide three words to form the image of what that might look like: Bambi on ice!

To avoid these sections and equine acrobatics, I had mentally marked the approach to the slabs during my recce and had explored the alternatives. The best alternative in both cases involved heading straight up the heather covered slope to our right, and bashing our way through for a while before descending back down through the heather to the trail again. The key was making sure I knew where to head uphill, as if I left it until we were right next to the slab there wouldn't be room to turn the horses very easily on the thin trail.

Marking important navigational points during a recce can be achieved in a variety of ways. Here I had relied on memory to recognise a distinctively shaped stone on the approach to the first slab, and geology (a breccia on the stream side) to indicate the point of no return at the second slab. During other expeditions I'd used deer antlers, specific plants/trees, fence posts, a placed pile of stones, and had drawn arrows in sand, hoping that they'd still be visible and in place when I returned with the horses weeks later.

Generally, I only need a little hint to indicate a diversion, left as a reminder of obstacles that hooves may struggle with on paths designed primarily for feet. In the main, my lifetime pastime of exploring and wandering around in wilderness had set me in good stead for map reading skills at a higher level. The higher level, that is, of sitting upon a steed. I won't claim to be an amazing navigational guru, but I am confident with a map and compass and only occasionally become misplaced.

You may think that map reading skills would be the same wherever you sit, but they become somewhat transformed from the back of a horse. You can't open the map out as fully as you might like. Not unless you would like to rapidly depose of that (horse-eating) map at a flat out, wide-eyed gallop (Yogi), or whilst bouncing around in floopy circles (Swift). Although to be fair, both my horses have become tolerant to this over the years and don't bat an eyelid these days when I open the noisy flap-in-the-wind sail thing.

Taking a bearing becomes a challenge of speed and cunning. Trying to get an accurate reading with no flat surface to work on and a horse that won't stand still adds a new dimension. Opportunistic as they are, a horse will often take the chance to search around (and around, and around) for the tastiest bit of grass to munch, while you are temporarily distracted by degrees.

The "How far have we come?" question is more complex to answer too, as the speed of travel very much depends on the mood of your companion that day, hour, or minute. It also seems to be more dependent on terrain under hoof than I've ever experienced with terrain under hiking boot. Average speed can be a very flexible estimate on horseback indeed, whereas it remains a reasonably predictable rate when using your own two feet.

Added into this approximation of timing is of course the recording and allowance of faff factor. You may think you have the average speed nailed, but have you allowed for the time spent watering a thirsty horse, untangling a rope, negotiating a sticky gate, or picking up items you've dropped? Much slower to rectify with two feet and eight hooves all involved.

On that note, every navigational tool must always remain attached to you or the saddle, as any unexpected movement may cause you to drop them. Retrieval involves a tiresome and time-consuming dismount, hunt for missing item, and remount before any directional continuation occurs. Navigation on horse is different but I always seem to find my way somehow and right now we'd arrived safely at the Bedford Bridge, a suspension bridge spanning the River Tarf.

Described as a foot bridge on the map, it traverses the Tarf just before it combines with the Allt Garbh

Buidhe, the river we had been following most of the day. The Tarf struts its stuff one last time with a series of spectacular waterfalls immediately above the bridge. It has a swaying suspension design, so a foot bridge it most definitely was, and the hooves were going to have to wade through the confluence below. With an eye on the bridge's inscription 'This bridge was erected in 1886 ... to commemorate the death of Francis John Bedford aged 18 who was drowned near here on 25th August 1879', I encouraged the horses with the fact that even Queen Victoria had managed to ford the river here in 1861.

We were preparing to cross the river but also to part ways with Fiona. The track on the other side of the river would return to an acceptable width for us to continue on our own. Fiona stated her surprise at how easy Swift had been to handle and how well she had behaved all day. I began to wonder if I'd made a mistake and had collected the wrong horse from the field when we'd set off that morning. Initially a little intimidated by Swift's lanky size and grumpy faces, Fiona had worked it through and they were now completely bonded.

I was surprised to discover a flash of jealousy that Swift was being friendly and looked sorry to see Fiona leave. I was sorry to see Fiona leave too, but I'm not sure I'd ever seen Swift look sorry to see ME leave. I've always had the distinct suspicion that as soon as my back was turned, Swift does a little dance behind it, blowing raspberries for good measure! Swift gave Fiona a nuzzle and I gave Fiona a thank you hug as we turned to find the best place to enter the river.

I had another three kilometres to go before reaching the location of probable help. I should have been travelling a further seven kilometres this day to reach the planned overnight stop, but getting a vet to Yogi was now top priority. Well, fording the river was the immediate priority, which was part of the top priority, and - not being able to ride Yogi - we were all going to have to get our feet wet. It was deeper than it looked in the middle and it was more than just my feet that got wet. Trying to stay cheerful and trying not to think about what the vet might say later, I concluded that walking the last hour of the day would keep me warm and I was sure that my boots would dry out in a few days' time.

I thus arrived unannounced at the lodge rather soggy and dishevelled, but upon hearing my plight I was made very welcome indeed. The horses were offered a field, I was invited to stay the night, and the owner was straight on the phone to her vet to see if they could come out this evening (which they could at 7pm). I had dumped the saddles and bags in the horses' field, and I was kindly offered a lift up there in a four-wheel drive pickup to bring it all back down to where I was to stay for the night.

I was feeling a little tired, mostly mentally tired from watching every footstep Yogi had made that day. The vet was on their way and I was worried about what they might say. As I jumped into the pickup, feeling distracted, I caught my thumb on the seat and bent it in a direction it really shouldn't be bent. Well kick me while I'm down why don't you. I swallowed a yelp of pain, fought back the tears, and observed with interest that my thumb - swelling rapidly - no longer did exactly as instructed.

I appeared to have hidden this incident well as my rescuer was none the wiser. I already felt foolish enough as it was, turning up on their doorstep in need of assistance. If there was a stronger word than independence to define my self-reliant nature, then I'd use it to describe (stubborn-as-a-mule) me. I wasn't going to admit to myself or anyone else that my right thumb being out of action might pose a problem going forward. It's not like travelling with horses required much knot tying, buckle fastening, or hand grip, right?

In thumb-throbbing pain, I packed up my gear, cooked some food, and settled in for the night whilst waiting for the vet to arrive. They arrived right on time, having travelled approximately thirteen kilometres up a rocky trail in a trusty (and completely non-rusty) Land Rover. I didn't even consider how much this evening call out was going to cost but if the newness of the Land Rover was anything to go by, let's just say the vet practice was not undercharging.

A lovely man appeared from behind the wheel but as he introduced himself, I grimaced. Not only had I forgotten to mention my hurty thumb prior to the strong handshake, but he was a MAN. Yogi really doesn't like vets, most likely due to his back-injury history and having spent a lot of time in their company whilst they poked, prodded, and stabbed him with things. Usually only female vets have a chance of getting near him as he descends into stress-head mode at the slightest sniff of disinfectant or glimpse of latex gloves hiding in a pocket. In an uncommon direction of sexism, my thoughts were that this might not go so well.

I explained this likely scenario as we approached the field and the vet wasn't phased in the slightest. He immediately took Yogi's lead rope from my hand, oozed confidence and leadership through to Yogi's brain, and the Bear was instantly putty in his hands. Those hands were all over Yogi's back and legs and weren't finding anything particularly wrong. Stunned by the vets composed authority, Yogi was doing everything asked of him and was behaving impeccably well.

As a result it was a thorough assessment, yet the only thing discovered was that Yogi had an incredibly strong back. The vet was particularly impressed with how well defined and sturdy his back muscles were, and to hear this was heart-warming and pleasing. This was a testament to the years of hard work focussed on that area by myself and various physios, but it didn't solve the present predicament. Not even his comment that, "This is a lovely little horse and perfect for what you are doing" could cheer me up, as it didn't explain the mysterious symptoms.

Yogi, on the other hand, was looking rather smug about all this flattery and attention. He wasn't overly perplexed about the mystery, had changed his view slightly about vets in general, and appeared content to return to the grass in the field. I felt foolish yet again; like occasions over the previous days, Yogi was no longer showing any signs of pain or discomfort. Did the vet even believe me that I'd observed the worrying behaviour and thus had called him out all this way into the wilderness?

"Fiona saw it too," I spluttered, "I know there is something wrong."

The vet replied that there might be, but whatever it was couldn't be very serious. Yogi just wasn't lame, and he was moving everything in the way it should be moved. The vet agreed with my assessment thus far, that as strange as the symptoms were in presentation, they weren't raising any red flags of danger or concern. The conclusion reached was that Yogi should be good to continue and it's likely to just be sore or stiff muscles.

The vet advised, "Some anti-inflammatories would help for the next few days; also consider switching Yogi to packhorse for a while, to give him an easier time."

Three thoughts sprung to mind immediately following this guidance. Would Swift be prepared to go up front this early in her Appy brain development? Would we be back to square one in terms of teamwork and travelling rhythm? Would horse-strength anti-inflammatories help a throbbing, sprained thumb?

As I watched the vet drive away and prepared the horses' dinner with medicine hidden in Yogi's bucket, both horses cantered over in pre-feed enthusiasm. I reflected yet again that despite all the signs and symptoms, there really couldn't be much wrong with Yogi. I wished I could say the same about my throbbing thumb that was, by now, twice the size it used to be.

I said goodnight to the horses and ambled back down the track. Despite feeling completely exhausted, I needed to strap up my thumb and set about adjusting the saddles, to swap ridden for pack and vice-versa in preparation for tomorrow's change of order. I would also contact my husband as best I could, in a place with no mobile signal, by using my satellite device. Tomorrow he was to meet me to facilitate safe crossing of the main A9 road at a duel carriageway section, and I'd ask him to bring the horse trailer down "just in case."

Day 8:
Forrest Lodge to
Dalnacardoch Lodge
(Distance 29km, Ascent 514m)

You have no idea how difficult it is to unzip a sleeping bag in the morning 'I'm too hot' panic, with only one thumb working. Especially if the only thumb that remains working is the one on your non-dominant hand. The difficulty faced then, however, was nothing in comparison to stuffing that same sleeping bag tightly into its stuff sack in order to squeeze it into the saddle bag. Not many things became easier after that as I prepared breakfast, fetched the horses from the field, and attempted to get saddles and bags secured with one very hurty and inoperable thumb involved.

I was feeling completely devoid of oomph and was beginning to wonder if I was coming down with something. Maybe it was just because I couldn't stop worrying about Yogi, but I certainly couldn't allow myself to be ill right now as I had a trek to complete and horses to look after. Yogi in particular, obviously, but today I needed to find some energy to deal with the challenge that would present of Swift being up front. I gritted my teeth and pretended I'd found my get-up-and-go.

Swift had been up front before, but mainly in familiar territory. She'd managed small sections in new places too, but only for short periods of time. Usually she'd last a while and almost seemed to enjoy it, but then the responsibility would become all too much and her brain would have a fart. At least (thankfully, I thought) at the point of brain overload now, she mostly just stopped dead in her tracks rather than digress into full floop mode like she used to. That was a positive wasn't it? She'd manage okay today, wouldn't she?

Well it wasn't looking likely! I'd tied the horses on breakaway strings next to a large stone wall as I was getting ready. Suddenly two low flying jets appeared out of nowhere and all hell and both horses broke loose. The breakaway strings had done what they said they would do on the tin, and Swogi were now munching long tasty grass in the driveway with Swift being reluctant to be caught.

Low flying jets don't usually spook Team Swogi and we've dealt with a variety of overhead aircraft many a time before without fuss; low overhead helicopters in glens carrying huge bags of stones for path repair, through to large noisy Hercules flying by during rides on the beach. Yogi previously lived near the Lossiemouth RAF base and had taught Swift that they weren't anything to worry about. Today the lodge and the stone wall had acted as a sound barrier to their arrival and I totally understood the horse's reaction when the jets appeared with a sudden BOOM, as I'd jumped along with them at the noise. We'd startled as a well-versed team then, but right now, there was only one of the team playing a cheeky game of cat and mouse as I was refusing to join in with her.

Luckily Swift was tacked up and ready to go, so I packed the last few things up onto Yogi and set off beside him, without her. Two can play at this game, and in thirty seconds flat Swift was hot on Yogi's tail, afraid of being left behind.

"Not today my gal!" I announced in triumph. "You're it and you're up front."

To try and get her into the mindset of leading the

team, I swapped Yogi for Swift and walked beside her for a while to let her warm up. Mentally, Swift was perfectly happy with this arrangement, but I suspected this would change once I jumped up on top.

My suspicions proved to be well-founded. I'd managed to find a large fallen tree to scramble up on top of my lanky girl after the initial spell of walking. This is not an easy task for the vertically challenged (with a damaged thumb), but it appeared that walking forward without a Yogi bottom in front of you was not an easy task either. Swift was in total disbelief. "But, but, but ... I'm PACKHORSE ... not lead horse" was the statement going round and round her immature Appy brain. This change of status was taking a while to sink in, and it hadn't reached as far as her feet yet.

We had the choice to follow a wide vehicle track or cut across a grassy area. I thought the grass would give her less to worry about in terms of route choice as she could go anywhere she liked, but I hadn't allowed for the apparent problem of sheep fluff. There were little bundles of wool everywhere and Swift's Appy brain was knitting it all together into a complicated yarn. We were making extremely slow progress - knit one, purl one, two steps forward, one step back.

I was having to use all the tricks in the book to get a horse with 'sticky feet' unstuck. If she wouldn't go forward, I'd move her front feet sideways before asking her to go forward again. She would oblige for a few steps but would then drop a stitch and start to unravel. I was weaving as much reassurance into the conversation as I could, but what should have taken twenty minutes was now pushing on for an hour, and there was still a long way to go today.

I wasn't used to pushing a horse with my legs. It's

something I tend to avoid doing when riding Yogi, as generally the main task at hand is to continually ask him to slow down with my seat. On Yogi, it's best not to have your legs anywhere near his sides, as go-faster encouragement is the last thing he needs. A short way into our day's journey and my legs were already complaining that they were working far too hard.

Knit one, purl one

I was, however, working on the "stitch in time, saves nine" principle by persevering to get her to go forward now, hoping to reap the benefits later on, but in the end I admitted defeat and had to jump off. I wondered if another half hour walking beside me, but in front of Yogi, would improve her confidence. I had to start making progress on the day's mileage anyway for my own sanity. Yogi was blissfully unaware of all the drama up front. He was delighted with the slower pace on top of all that delicious grass. Munch, munch!

I'd been walking about another half hour when I came across a young couple out for a walk themselves. They stopped to speak to me, asking why I hadn't camped near them last night. It turned out they were renting a cottage on the estate and had been told by the owners that I'd be stopping nearby overnight. When I hadn't arrived as planned due to stopping short to see the vet, they had been a little worried. They were relieved to see me fit and well but surprised to see me walking.

"Do you walk the whole way with your horses?" they asked.

I held back the expletives in my explanation, but not my frustration aimed at the situation in general. It isn't Swift's fault, but it's incredibly exasperating that despite the hours of work and training I've put into her over the years, she still can't find her inner confidence. My frustration was rapidly turning into a general bad mood, as my throbbing thumb was even more painful than our lack of progress. When the young couple asked if there was anything they could do to help, I thrust Yogi's lead rope at them and said, "Hold this while I get on Swift, I'm going to try again." They looked exceptionally un-horsey, and particularly surprised at this request, but, they had offered. Yogi didn't give them any bother, but the chap looked incredibly nervous approaching Swift to hand me the end of the lead rope once I was back on top. I didn't blame him at all, as Swift was full of fidget and had her best effort at a terrifying mare-glare firmly displayed on her face.

In all honesty I wanted to ask them to walk ahead of me for the next few miles to allow Swift to follow, but I thought that was a step too far since they were currently heading in the opposite direction. The assisted mounting was going to have to do in terms of a support boost. This was my mountain to climb; I'd set the challenge so I'd better just get on with it. I was determined to continue climbing but I hadn't necessarily intended to climb it up the north face and without any ropes.

Unfortunately, the boost didn't last long and it took a whole ten minutes to get past a sheep-scratching station, where many a woolly hide had taken advantage of the comb-like properties of a barbed wire fence. Regularly spaced snags of fleece flapped happily in the wind reminding me of travels in India, Nepal, and Bhutan where prayer flags are hung in all manner of places to bless the surrounding countryside.

The prayer flag colours represent five elements: blue for sky and space, white for air and wind, red for fire, green for water, and yellow for the earth. They promote peace, compassion, strength, and wisdom. The more commonly found horizontal flags are called Lung ta (meaning Wind Horse) and often depict a powerful or strong horse in the centre. The woolly substitutes today didn't seem to be promoting much wisdom nor inspiring much strength, despite their equine connections.

Off we set again (knit one, purl one, drop a stitch, unravel, repeat) and, making awfully slow progress, we continued down the valley. The valley was beautiful, but very much underappreciated and neglected due to my attentions being focused elsewhere. Back on the track, Swift finally grasped what it was that I wanted her to do. She seemed more content to be up front and her feet were less sticky, but her brain was still in overdrive. She was moving forward, but I'd call it a shuffle rather than a walk, as her feet needed to move as slowly as her brain could process everything she was looking at. "Is that dangerous ... can I go that way ... what's behind that tree

... am I going the right way ... should Yogi really be behind me ... does he know what he is doing back there ... it's an important job you know ... is that wool a baby sheep ... can I really step over that stick ... are you sure I should be up front?"

We descended the valley in a cloud of doubt, alongside the River Tilt and into the trees on the approach to Blair Atholl. We were still proceeding at a snail's pace but were finally making progress. The river near Gilbert's Bridge was desperately trying to attract my attention by noisily and delightfully increasing its gradient in a cascade of drops, but all my attention was still focussed on knitting a comfort blanket for Swift. It was an energy draining, leg aching process that was about to meet what I thought would be an enormous test.

We were heading onto the track that runs right alongside the shooting range and the flag was raised to indicate that it was very much in use today. Now I became the indecisive member of the team. Should I jump off Swift again just in case, or do I proceed as is and hope that her brain copes with the addition of a further challenge? If I jump off, we might be back to square one again when I get back on later. I absolutely did not want to take those numerous steps backwards and sideways.

Before I had fully made up my mind, the first shot rang out with a loud CRACK! Both horses threw their heads up into the air and paused in mid stride, then as fast as that had happened they both dropped their heads and merrily continued down the track. Well, when I say merrily ... Yogi was as happy as could be, but Swift was still protesting slightly about having the burden of all the decision making to do. However, I was glad to discover that the shooting didn't seem to make her protest any more than she had been doing thus far today.

I nearly fell off her with elated shock - sometimes this girl can be full of surprises. I offered up an apology to my previous field neighbour who had frequently been subject to under-the-breath mutterings in his general direction. The farmer next door had regularly used ferrets to chase out the rabbits in his field, shooting the rabbits at most inconvenient times for me and undoubtedly for the rabbits. For example, when I was changing the horse's rugs, or tacking up or cleaning out the horse's feet. The sudden noise of the gunshot often caused the horses to startle with fright, sometimes resulting in me getting a little bit squished.

Fortunately, the regular exposure to this had trained my horses well, and they were no longer so concerned about gunfire. Right now, I reckoned I owed that farmer a pint of beer or two and I forgave him several crushed toes and a handful of bruises. For the first time today, I was feeling so very proud of Swift and a little more positive despite our slow progress. My thumb suddenly didn't hurt as much (okay that bit is a lie), and it felt somewhat spectacular to be riding so close to an active firing range with two calm horses. Maybe we could swap the midges and pouring rain of reality for the gunfire and arrows in a Western movie after all.

We were staying this side of the river as, instead of descending down into Blair Atholl, we'd be heading west to travel along an almost forgotten stretch of General Wade's Military Road. The route was part of the Dunkeld to Inverness stretch of road, built around 1728, but only a small part of it remains unobliterated by construction of the modern A9 trunk road. This network of military roads was constructed to help the British government 'bring order' and attempt to control the local populations during the Jacobite rebellions.

There wasn't much of the original road surface evident on this section, although hidden in the trees was one of the initial bridges. I loved that this inconsequential structure made you ponder on the numerous footsteps and hoof falls that would have passed this way in times gone by. I doubted the bridge had changed much since the 18th Century, despite restoration in 1985, and I contemplated that the rebels and soldiers would have travelled with horses as their aid, in a similar manner to myself, as they journeyed into battle.

My current battle was somewhat different in nature. On one side, we were incredibly behind schedule, and it was going to be a late arrival at the camp spot. On the other, we were passing close to the retail legend that is The House of Bruar, and they sell mouth-watering ice-cream of every favourite flavour. The fight was on between the pull of caramel delights versus the very real need to push on.

Despite the obvious complications of trying to eat ice-cream in a busy car park with two food-inquisitive horses and only one working thumb, the force was strong, and I was ready for combat. The internal battle, however, was won by a left-field external opponent, as I'd totally forgotten about the tiny tunnel between myself and the double cone victory. Even without saddles and bags, it was going to be a tight vertical squeeze for Yogi, so Miss Lanky Swift wasn't going to stand a chance.

"Do they do carrot flavour?" enquired Yogi. "'Cause if so, we could leave Swift here and I'll fetch her some."

"Thought you two didn't like to be separated!" I answered, amazed.

"Yeah ... but carrot flavoured ice-cream is my

favourite!" Yogi stated, licking his lips.

"Hmph! Some loyalty … he who eats alone chokes alone, you know," snorted Swift. "You won't leave me alone though, will you?" she added, nervously.

I settled the argument before it escalated. "One for all and all for one, if we can't all fit through the tunnel, then nobody is going through."

Our ice-cream crusade was thwarted before it had begun - we turned away to the path that many defeated armies had walked on before, and looked forward to meeting up with faithful hubby towards the end of the day instead. Again, I would be crossing the A9 and doing so at a dual carriageway section. Two sets of eyes and ears to assess for traffic were better than one, and since I was now travelling close to home, it wasn't too far out of Dave's way to help me accomplish a safe passage.

The incredibly slow progress had put us way behind schedule for the intended meet. Dave would soon be at the designated spot and I was at least two hours away. I gave him a call to apologise on Swift's behalf and he decided to meet me further south at the first A9 crossing of the day. This was a single carriageway crossing and although traffic would be moving fast, I had felt safe enough tackling this one by myself and thus hadn't pre-arranged any help.

As we mooched our way along General Wade's Road, Swift suddenly picked up her head and accelerated. She was striding out well and Yogi was having to jog to keep up. I looked around in every direction to try and discover the reason for this sudden turn of events.

"Look over there … it's a mini Yogi … it's ginger and it's fast … it's in front of me and I'm going to follow it!" Swift had spied a shiny young roe deer which, startled by our arrival, was leaping along the track in front of us.

I was grateful to General Wade for building such straight roads, in Roman style, as although the deer was outrunning us it was visible for quite some distance. It seemed that having any ginger bottom to follow, is enough to give an Appy brain courage. We managed a whole kilometre in a beautifully smooth, faster pace before the hesitant gait returned. It is flashes of potential like this, that keep me committed to this mare. One day I will eventually find the key to her true capabilities and she is going to be incredibly awesome.

The key was stuck in the lock for now though, as the deer disappeared into the depths of the valley to the right. We continued our dreary drudge of doubt down to the A9 but soon had our spirits and confidence lifted by Dave's arrival as he walked up the trail to meet us. Although Dave's bottom isn't ginger, it still gave Swift a bottom to follow and again she walked out at a good pace and we were soon on the other side of the A9 in deep discussion.

It was already six o'clock and I still had about seven or eight kilometres to go. I was mentally drained and physically not in great shape. My thumb was throbbing and my legs and back ached too from pushing Swift along. These were all muscular grumblings of a nature I'd dealt with many times before, but there was something bigger than these. I felt fatigued to the core and I'd rarely felt like this before. I sincerely hoped I wasn't coming down with flu-like symptoms that I'd experienced a lot of recently, as I was only approaching halfway through my planned journey.

As requested, Dave had arrived with the trailer in tow (for Yogi, just in case), and the temptation to load up the horses to travel to the night's stop was just as strong as the lure of the caramel ice-cream had been. The cherry on top of the cake of temptation was that it was also starting to rain hard. One of the many reasons that Dave is perfect for me, is that he always finds a way to instil common sense when I'm about to make a rash decision. So, with the words, "You can hardly claim to have crossed all the way across Scotland by horseback, if you miss out eight kilometres in the middle," we came up with a more sensible solution.

We unloaded the saddle bags from Yogi. I would continue riding and Dave would meet me at the end of the day, having set up the corral for the horses and pitched my tent. This would save me time and energy which I hoped I could carry forward and make use of the following morning, as tomorrow's ride was due to be yet another long one. Especially with Swift adamant in her refusal to live up to her name.

The last section of the day would be on tarmac, on the old road running parallel to the A9, and we would be visible to anyone commuting north and south. As we continued in our damp, doubtful, and drained debacle, I felt solace knowing that we would give the motorists a fleeting glimpse of times gone by, when the pace of life was slower and free of modern-day stresses. Not free of stresses by any means, just different ones to contend with and, despite the testing times the day had presented, I still preferred a slow-paced horse to a fast pace of life.

In times gone by (around 1861), the Queen and Prince Consort had stayed at Dalnacardoch Lodge, near where we were camping tonight. It wasn't unusual for the Queen to be touring Scotland, as she was very much in love with the place by then and had already purchased Balmoral Castle. However, I'm not sure what sneaky shenanigans they were staging at Dalnacardoch that night, as they apparently arrived under the cover of darkness and in undercover disguise.

Described as arriving in a shabby carriage, with a shabby driver and a shabby pair of horses, I surmised that we weren't too dissimilar, especially with Swift's princess-like dictation of demands today. As Swift suddenly picked up her pace, I thought this royal story had inspired the princess into action, but no - it was just the sight of our shabby trailer sitting at the end of the road.

Horses aren't stupid and, on seeing the trailer, both anticipated the food inside it, the hay to munch, and the warm journey home at the end of their ride. I decided not to mention how far off the mark they both were and concentrated on emitting hay and warmth vibes to Swift. THAT they could have, but I blocked Swift's mind reading skills from thoughts of tomorrow's adventure continuation and the lack of a lift home for possibly many days to come.

Amused at their reaction to seeing the trailer, I remembered another long-distance ride where I'd met gates that were impassable for the horses and had accepted a lift from a friend for a short distance, to avoid a busy main road. My friend appeared on a side road to meet us with my van and trailer, just as we emerged from a forest trail. Having explored many options to get round the gates in a time and energy consuming failure, I was now too tired to be disappointed that I'd have to use motorised transport to complete the day. There was nowhere for my friend to stop, so I had to follow her down the single-track side road for a little while to find a lay-by in which to load up the horses.

Yogi became distraught that the saviour of the trailer was moving so quickly away from him and broke into a rather bouncy trot. How they recognise my vehicle and trailer over any other passing combination remains a mystery to me. We clattered down the road at a fair rate of knots, finishing our day's ride in an unintended, sweaty heap. Slowing the Bear down when the top of a hill or the end of day is in sight isn't always easy.

Reaching the trailer this evening, Dave helped me untack and pop the horses in the corral. He'd also thoughtfully managed to retrieve the rugs from the other side of the Cairngorms by meeting up with Fiona the day before. By now the rain was stair-rods, a term I hadn't fully defined in my head until this moment in time. I was glad the horses would be cosy for the night despite the weather conditions. There had been no sign of discomfort from Yogi today, but a warm night would only be beneficial as would the anti-inflammatory I again hid in his evening feed.

My tent was looking particularly uninviting I had to admit, and being only a short drive from home, the force of temptation was strong again. The horses weren't the only one seeking out home comforts. Dave was coming back in the morning anyway to see Swift safely along another narrow steep trail, and I was contemplating joining him at home overnight. I felt fatigued and unwell and sorely in need of a boost.

In times of trouble over the years, a cuddle with my big dog Danny (a Large Munsterlander) always lifted my spirits. Tully had an uncanny knack of cheering me up too, but big old Danny was a fluffier, calmer influence. He was also nearing the end of his time on this planet. I missed him and every moment in his company was now more precious than ever. Could I leave the horses here and head home for the night? The horses were safely corralled in a bigger field and wouldn't come to any harm if they escaped the enclosure. Nobody would know ... then "What happened to one for all and all for one, by the way?" drifted over from Swogi in a gust of horizontal sleet and a draught of disapproval.

In resignation, I said a particularly un-cheery goodbye to Dave and took my stove to the relative shelter of some trees to cook my evening cuisine. It was still damp and cold under the trees, but I took a moment to appreciate the tasty beer Dave had kindly brought. There is more than one way in the world to raise one's spirits. I didn't linger long, as I was starting to shiver, and upon returning to my tent discovered that I'd left the door slightly ajar and the rain had taken full advantage of my mistake. Crawling into my wet sleeping bag, I hoped that this would finally be the low point of my adventure. Thinking back to the high point so far - the tranquillity of Glen Muick in the sunshine - the contrast seemed vast.

Better days on the trail

Day 9:
Dalnacardoch Lodge to Bhran Cottage

(Distance 25km, Ascent 438m)

I 'd slept an exhausted but fitful sleep. My tiny wee tent had withheld the overnight downpours well, but the sound of the rain lashing the fly sheet had interrupted my rest several times through the night. It was still raining this morning but had settled back to a more clement dreich rather than a torrent.

As I hovered over my porridge while it cooked, I mulled over the previous tough day. Despite my frustrations at the slow pace, we had got here in the end. I was actually quite proud of Swift for stepping up to the mark when thrown in at the deep end. With the amount of rain overnight, I was also wondering how deep that end might turn out to be today, when we reached the river crossing that we had to complete towards the head of the next glen.

At this point, I was in two minds whether to continue or not. Wasn't this the proper time to pull out, considering I wasn't able to ride my boy? As we were such a short distance from home by road, it would make for an easy extraction. On the other hand, Yogi seemed fine yesterday with the easier job to do - although it had made my job a whole lot more difficult. In the scheme of things, looking at how far we had already travelled with uncertainties surrounding his health, we didn't have far to go now, to at least achieve this journey to home - the place I viewed as the half-way point of the cross-Scotland adventure.

At home we were due to have another rest day

anyway, and maybe after another packhorse day followed by rest, his sore muscles would be recovered and he would be ready to soldier on. If not, then I would have to complete this journey in two separate sections once he was well. Separating this cross-Scotland journey into two parts - finishing this part at home and starting the next from the same - would be a much easier process as far as logistics and psychological motivation were concerned.

As Dave arrived, I'd made up my mind. I'd walk the whole way today. Doing this would mean that Swift could carry pack, Yogi would have zero load, and we'd make better speed than we'd managed yesterday. It would be a day on foot for me, but since Dave was joining me also on foot until lunchtime, it would give us time to chat and catch up. Dave was to help us past another tricky thin section, steep up to the left and steep down to the right this time, alongside Loch an Duin. With us both walking, we'd be at a similar sort of head height and it would make for a more companionable time together.

Today we'd be following an ancient drover route through the Dalnacardoch hills, emerging out at the head of Glen Tromie and the route - the Gaick Pass - was unquestionably magnificent. Looking at Ordnance Survey maps of the area, you'd read 'Forest of Atholl' followed by 'Dalnacradoch Forest' followed by 'Forest of Gaick', but you'd struggle to find a single tree in sight. According to Scottish National Heritage, around 5,000 years ago I'd have been riding (or walking) through a boreal delight of Scots pine, birch, rowan, aspen, juniper, hazel and oak. The land is now reduced to peatland and moorland, mostly due to human exploitation but also the development of a cooler, wetter climate. As much as this is a shame, it allows some dramatic long-distance scenery that otherwise would have been hidden by an array of bark and leaves to display its full potential.

The scenery would start to get more interesting at Loch an Duin, and similarly the trail we'd be following would get more interesting too. In order to avoid some hoof-swallowing peat bog, we would have to deviate from the walkers' trail. The deviation would lead us to attempt to cross the wall of a small dam in a somewhat gymnastic balance beam fashion. The emphasis was undeniably on the attempt, as I wasn't sure if the, 'one for all and all for one' ethos would survive this certain obstacle.

Walking along chatting to Dave had certainly passed the time, and we'd arrived at the test of team ethics all rather abruptly. In front of us stood a narrow concrete wall, with a deep pool of water on one side and a gentle stream of outflow emerging through the sluice gate on the other. Would the horses step up and onto the concrete wall? If not, I really wasn't sure what solid alternative we could find, so I just kept all fingers and toes well and truly crossed.

There was a low, metal handrail on either side to dissuade the horses from stepping off the concrete in either direction. It was a stylish construction considering few would ever visit to admire it, as the posts for the rails curved away from the dam leaving large open gaps at your feet. The rails, therefore, wouldn't stop the horses from stepping off entirely - I was just hoping Swogi would apply a little common sense and stay firmly in the centre of the concrete strip. This concrete strip was solid, but not particularly wide.

In pure Yogi style, the way ahead may be narrow, but so long as it was solid and clear in front of him, there was no hesitation and we were off and over the dam in a blink of an eye. "I'm heading somewhere this way, please try to keep up!" In true Swift style, too, if Yogi's bottom was in front and he thought it was safe, then that was good enough for her and she followed calmly along behind his behind. I was yet again filled with pride, wonder, and appreciation at the way my horses could tackle the challenges I so often threw their way.

All we needed to do now was track around the hill in a peat-avoiding, heather-bashing manner, to eventually drop back down to the thin trail we'd now follow along the shimmering loch. Not as steep down to the right, nor as steep up to the left as previous experiences described, but I was still glad of the extra pair of hands to ensure the second horse remained safe.

It was such a majestic setting, with the swathe of green and purple heather sloping down to the steel grey flat of the loch before reaching the steep, concave rise that formed the hills on the other side. I paused many a time to take photos of this stunning scene. Yogi, always obliging, stood proud in pose to try and outdo the dramatics of the backdrop behind him. Swift would do the same, but upon hearing the click of the lens would suddenly pull the goofiest face you'd ever imagine.

"A clown like you should be in the circus!" I told her.

Swift sniggered. "Catch me if you can!" she said, then promptly stuck her tongue out.

Oblivious to Swift's impish antics, Yogi was trying his best to teach her a posing lesson. He thought, like most things he teaches her, that it was just taking a while to register with her complex Appy brain.

I kept my eye on Swift in her impish mood. If she was feeling like this, then Dave could be in for a hard time leading her. They'd had a give and take kind of relationship so far over the years. Dave did all the giving and Swift constantly took the mickey out of him. At first, I found it amusing that Swift would behave perfectly for me, but as soon as Dave the beginner horseman tried to take charge, she'd take full advantage of every single gap in his equine knowledge.

Poor Dave was often dragged about, nipped, threatened, and left struggling with half a rug on (or off) an uncooperative horse. He was very much taken for a ride in all but the correct sense where a horse was concerned. Amusement soon turned into unease though, as someone was going to get hurt (most probably Dave) if I didn't intervene. With a little tuition from me and a surprisingly natural aptitude for equine communication techniques, Dave started to gain the upper hand.

I hoped Dave hadn't played his best cards yet though, as Swift was most definitely behaving like the joker in the pack today. Thankfully, however, the thin trail was becoming more of a challenge and Swift became fully focussed on placing her feet in the right order and the right places. She didn't get a chance to turn her impish attentions to any remaining chinks in Dave's armour. The two kilometres of thin trail were negotiated safely in no time at all, and it was time for Dave to head back and leave me to my onward excursion. I'd see him again soon as the route passed by our hometown of Kingussie the next day, so it would have been rude to ride on by without stopping there.

Team Swogi were now back as a threesome, and as we continued on our way the track soon widened out to a good quality, off-road vehicle track again. A few kilometres later we reached the second of the day's lochs. Sandwiched between two steep sides, Loch Brodhainn was even more picturesque than the last. Yogi really had his work cut out now, to strike a pose able to surpass the beauty unfolding behind him. Now I might be a little bit biased about how handsome my boy truly is, but I really do think he managed to pull it off (but only just).

The mountain sides curved up in perfect symmetry and so spectacularly from the loch that the vast waters, belittled, looked like the last sip of wine in the bottom of the glass. This analogy of course would also work with the last sip of tea in an old-fashioned china cup, but it seemed an awfully long time since that glass of wine I'd savoured at the House of Mark.

At the end of the sip of wine, we'd be approaching Gaick Lodge. It isn't an overly impressive building on the outside at least, but it makes up for that in status and situation. The present lodge in its glorious setting was built around 1820 by the Duke of Gordon and replaced the much smaller structure of the original building, claiming rights to be called one of the oldest shooting lodges in Scotland.

The original building's fame is the consequence of a well-known catastrophe, when an immense, rumbling avalanche completely and utterly flattened it. The story is a little contested, but the tale in the glen roughly follows: around New Year's Eve at the end of 1799, a huge storm was raging. A shooting party were staying in the depth of the glen at the lodge on a mission to stalk venison for the festivities. They were also staying in a considerable depth of snow, with more falling and strong winds blowing.

The lodge is positioned close to the base of a

mountain, but it's difficult to believe in these warmer climes that sufficient snow could have gathered to cause the size of avalanche that struck. But gather and strike it did, completely obliterating the lodge and all its contents. Unfortunately, the contents included Captain John Macpherson, four of his men, and their hunting dogs.

The lodge in those days was more akin to a bothy type building, a strong stone structure with a thatched roof and heather beds. It was in these heather beds that the bodies were eventually found, after a lengthy, back-breaking dig by local men. The Captain, apparently a cruel man, wasn't the most popular of fellas and became referred to posthumously as the Black Officer with the White Death. Black of course referring to the colour of his heart and soul!

Before we could set our eyes on this famous spot however, we had a river crossing to do. The Allt Gharbh Ghaig (pronounced Garry Gig) is also a renowned feature of the Gaick Pass, its reputation gained by having a rather reactive personality. Heavy rainfall or snow melt can create an angry, intense flow that isn't shy in carrying rocks and scree to bruise or swipe you off your feet. Attempting to cross during one of Garry's spontaneous rages could be a wet, painful, but exciting experience.

With the amount of sleep-disturbing rain that fell last night, I was worried about what kind of mood Garry was going to be in today. The mountains can sometimes do strange things to the weather and create pockets of microclimates, some long-term and some temporary.

Last night it seems the rain was pretty much concentrated over the soggy pocket that was my tent, as Garry, well-rested, was merrily and gently bubbling along this afternoon with no rain-fuelled anger in sight.

He was still over twenty metres wide though, and reasonably deep in the middle for those with diminished vertical stature. As I glanced around the Swogi team, I could clearly see that I was the only one with this specific shortfall. On my own, I could probably have rock hopped across and managed to stay reasonably dry, but with, Mr 'Keen-to-get-to-the-other-side' and Miss 'I-want-to-stop-and-play-sploosh-splash' there was no hope of hopping dryly. Would it set back Yogi's recovery if he carried me across? I knew it was only twenty metres or so, but it might be slippery, involving extra muscles for balance, and I was remembering back to the river crossing in Glen Tilt that seemed to set off his pain that day. However, he'd had a full day and a half not looking sore at all. Surely, I thought, the twenty metres wouldn't hurt him.

The opposing thought of being wet to a mid-thigh height (if I was lucky) again and of walking another ten kilometres in soaking soggy boots was having a strong influence on this decision. I led Yogi over to a rock and asked him if I could possibly hitch a lift. All the positive signs were there again that Yogi was feeling fine, and he politely waited for me to jump up on top. He attacked the river challenge with his usual enthusiastic mindset and strode confidently into the water with a splash to get to the other side.

"Splash did you say?" responded Swift, and Yogi and I waited patiently whilst she played her usual game of 'How high can we sploosh?'

When I say we waited patiently, I paused with amused

patience, but Yogi - who always wants to complete the job he's started - wanted to get to the other side *now*. On narrow river crossings, we rarely have a problem as Swift is through it and out the other side before her brain is truly into splash mode. On longer crossings, we only ever get halfway before the game commences. Her relationship with water is always a sight to behold. She initially presents with the view that she shouldn't have to get her feet wet at all and always looks around for a bridge. When that can't be found, she reluctantly concedes and proceeds to fully immerse herself in the experience by submerging her feet and everything else she can possibly plunge in the water too.

The game consists of lowering her head, dunking her nose in the water, then splooshing it back and fore, then side to side, to see how wet she can get herself and everything around her. When that doesn't create enough satisfaction, she'll switch to pawing the water frantically with a front hoof, just in case she's missed the odd dry bit somewhere. I began to wonder if I would have stayed dryer attempting the rock hopping option.

I also began to wonder if I'd actually manage to stay on top of Yogi, as I was currently at full stretch holding him back with my right hand (still with poorly thumb I might add) and trying to get Swift to move forward with her lead rope tugging my left hand. At the point of no return, with my left arm stretched straight, and my body laid back over Yogi's bottom, she finally finished her game and stepped forward with no cares in her world at all. Game complete, and a happy Swift grinning from large ear to large ear, we reached the other side. I jumped off Yogi and let the horses graze for a moment to see if Yogi showed any signs of pain. The negative answer was a huge positive for me, but I would still walk for the rest of the day.

This was the day of three lochs and we would soon be at the largest one, again sandwiched between two steep-sided mountains. The track alongside this one was nice and wide, and level with the water's edge. This larger loch was less of a sip of wine from this angle and more like a puddle of spilt real ale. Still a lovely nectar, but spread out across the table. Each loch had seemed more beautiful than the last, and this was the grand finale of the day. Even Swift had become inspired by its splendour and was busy outshining both the scenery and Yogi in her diva-like poses. Finally, I could capture her magnificent looks on camera, if only for a moment. Yogi rather humbly accepted defeat and dropped his head down to get on with the job of the day, which was getting to the end of the trail.

Swift had also started to drop her head down more and more, but mostly to munch the grass at the side of the loch. She was falling further and further behind and I resorted to putting her lead rope back on. With Yogi content to follow me (and/or the trail) at a reasonable rate, and so many photo opportunities to keep my hands busy, I came up with yet another hands-free option.

I popped Yogi's lead rope on him, tied it to Swift's, and ran the combination up over Yogi's saddle to make sure it stayed tangle free. Thus, Yogi could tug Swift along, providing enough encouragement for her to keep up with him and I could walk along with camera in hand. Now able to observe Swogi from a distance, I could see the stress lines beginning to appear on Yogi's face again. I was thankful we didn't have much further to go today and a very short distance to home the next.

Tonight, we were to reach Bhran cottage at the head of Glen Tromie and, keeping the pace down for Yogi's sake, it was going to be yet another late arrival. Here, I was meeting trail partner Yvonne who was having her own cross-Scotland adventure. She was riding from Spey Bay to Fort Augustus, an alternative direction to cross Scotland and a somewhat flatter and shorter option.

Shorter it may be, but not without considerable challenge for Yvonne and her team. This was her first lengthy solo trip and one of the first with her present arrangement of equines. It takes time to iron out the wrinkles in a towing combination and Yvonne hadn't really had a chance to get the ironing board out of the cupboard yet. We were both looking forward to enjoying each other's company from here to Fort Augustus, as we planned to meet in the middle and continue our journeys together in mutual support for a few days.

Yvonne often comments about how easy I make the riding and towing system look, and this is where the appreciation of the glue that holds Swift and Yogi together comes in. I know how lucky I am to have two horses that gel so well and complement each other's strengths and weaknesses so completely. Yes, there are drawbacks to fast versus slow (physically and mentally), but there are many positives too.

Swift can slow or calm a fast or excited Yogi, and Yogi can encourage and ignite the laid-back attitude of Swift. Where one horse is nervous of an obstacle or challenge, the other is often nonchalant about it and will proceed ahead, explaining to the other that there really isn't anything to worry about at all. It's a combination that has complimented each other right from their very first meeting which happened more abruptly than planned. Yogi was in a long, sloping field and was happily munching grass at the bottom of the hill. Swift was being introduced to the field through the gate at the top of the hill. She was only a two year old at that time, but had been keen on energy conservation from birth and hadn't looked particularly lively so far. I thought it would be fine to let her into the field to meet Yogi in her own lazy time and on her own mañana terms.

She surprised us all with a switch to terms which were decidedly 'manic rather than mañana' and hurtled down the hill at excited top speed to meet him. Now, I don't think Swift had ever seen the need to turn to page two in the Highway Code for stopping distance calculations higher than twenty miles per hour, and completely miscalculated her 'crazy rather than lazy' timings. It didn't look like she was going to be able to stop prior to making any sort of pleasantries or introductions, that was for sure, and for a moment I thought she would just fly on past him. For the first time I fully appreciated why she had been christened Swift and wondered if there was any racehorse in her ancestry that I hadn't been made aware of.

Swift had grown suddenly in her second year and her legs were much longer than she thought they were. She wasn't totally in control of these gangly things yet, and that lack of control was very much in evidence as her brakes failed and she slammed hard into the side of a rather startled Yogi. Out from the tangle of fur, manes, tails and feet, emerged a few bruises but a bond that was as solid as the impact that started it all and that as they say was that.

As for the bond that Yvonne was working with, it was there from the start too. Yvonne was travelling with two Highland ponies who happened to be mother and daughter. Katy, the mum, had been a broodmare for most of her life, and despite being a little long in the tooth she had not been sat on (as far as we were aware) before Yvonne bought her. Katy's daughter Skye was still a young, inexperienced, and green pony (green as in equine terms, not Swift's energy conserving terms), but had done plenty more under saddle than her mum.

Like Team Swogi, Katy and Skye had somewhat opposite personalities notwithstanding their close kinship. Katy was a complete introvert in character and Yvonne needed mind reading skills better than Swift's to work out what was going on in her head. Skye was a head tossing, rule bending snort of a horse, full of fun, merriment and mischief.

Combining these two into a wrinkle-free, smooth team was never going to be easy, especially when you consider that both were classic Highland ponies. They equally displayed the recognised characteristics of the Highland Pony breed, those of stubbornness and strength; qualities of character that helped them survive the worst weather, masses of midges, and gruelling ground conditions found in Scotland. However, if you were asking your Highland Pony to do something they didn't want to do, then these qualities united to give you a considerable force to reckon with.

I was proud of Yvonne for getting as far as she had already come with her new companions, and admired her ambition and determination for undertaking the journey she was doing. I was looking forward to hearing about how her first few days had transpired and hoped that she had had a successful time.

When looking for a good match as a trail partner, it is important to find someone with a similar sense of adventure, a shared sense of humour, and the same level of grit and determination. To prevent you falling out under sometimes challenging situations, you also needed to be able to forgive each other's outbursts, cope with each other's grumpiness from time to time, recognise each other's strengths and weaknesses, and muck in with all the jobs that need done no matter how exhausting or unpleasant they may be.

No matter how much Yogi's fast pace had worn out Yvonne and her ponies in the past, she always worked hard at the end of the day to assist me in setting up corrals, pitching tents, and collecting firewood. We might be mismatched on speed on the trails but everything else worked well, so long as I had the occasional beer and Yvonne had a regular supply of Diet Coke (ref grumpiness comment!). Yvonne was adept at keeping spirits up during adversity and seeking out solutions to problems, whereas I was good at map reading, tying knots, and opening gates.

The slower pace of horse travel allows the land to sound its voice. If you rush through distracted by dialogue, then you might miss its whispers. Although delightfully chatty, Yvonne is often content to travel in mutual silent absorption of surroundings. At other times the land, when angry and loud, needs drowning out by a merry tune, or occasionally a harmonious verse will celebrate and enhance the cheery mood of a place.

Yvonne has a wide-ranging repertoire of songs at her disposal; an amusing ditty to enrich the moment, through to a rousing ballad to feed a weary soul. Once attempting a high pass in high winds and driving rain, we were soaked through and cold to the core. I was up front with Swogi, with Swift's head tucked under my arm and Yogi swearing and spinning behind me, trying to turn his bottom into the driving rain.

It was tough going, navigation was challenging, and enjoyment was at an all-time low. Through the rain and wind a rendition of 'The Flower of Scotland' floated strongly through. I couldn't see Yvonne through the mist, but I could certainly hear her stirring spirit. Doubt wandered away lost in the swirling clouds, taking with it all despair and a little of the discomfort too.

I would struggle to ever find a horse to match Yogi's turbo-boost walk, so I had accepted that I was always going to have to deal with riding with slower equines. I may as well therefore ride with someone I completely enjoy the company of, and I appreciate that I would be hard pushed to find a better matched, mad-as-me, eccentric trail partner than Yvonne.

Having the ideal match in travelling companion has instigated and/or been the make or break of many adventures over time (Hilary & Norgay, Mallory & Irvine, Armstrong & Aldrin, Butch Cassidy & the Sundance Kid, Lone Ranger & Tonto, Dastardly & Muttley, Dumb & Dumber), but I like the illustration of importance given by Dr Samual Johnson in his accounts of *A Journey to the Western Isles of Scotland* which he also completed mostly on horseback: "...and [it] was in the Autumn of the year 1773 [I was] induced to undertake the journey, by finding in Mr. Boswell a companion, whose acuteness would help my inquiry, and whose gaiety of conversation and civility of manners are sufficient to counteract the inconveniences of travel, in countries less hospitable than we have passed."

As I arrived late and tired at Bhran Cottage, the evening was suddenly full of neighs, whinnies, and squeals of delight as Swogi realised their pals were hiding around the back of the cottage. The squeals of delight erupted from me too, as Yvonne - in true trail partner style - had already constructed a corral for me next to hers. The delight continued when Yvonne's sister Wendy, who appeared in her car with a few provisions for Yvonne, uncovered a bottle of wine in the boot.

Sheltering from the dreich weather in a tiny section of the ruined cottage, we swapped our tales of success (as well as woe) over a quick bite to eat, a glass of wine, and a can of Diet Coke. Oh, the other good thing about having Yvonne as a trail partner, is that should you be lucky enough to fit in a pub visit on your trek, she will probably drive you home from it at the end of the night as her preferred tipple is often non-alcoholic.

After saying goodbye to Wendy who had to get on her way, we discussed route options for tomorrow. Possibly due to the wine's Dutch courage, I decided to try riding Swift again for the last stretch home. Even though there was much to catch up on, we were both exhausted and soon retired to our tents. I whispered goodnight to Swogi and, as I crawled into bed, they were both lying flat out and looked extremely relaxed and content in the company of their great trail friends too.

Day 10:
Bhran Cottage to Newtonmore
(Distance 21km, Ascent 195m)

I woke up with the realisation that today's end of trail would be the end of the trip for Yogi. I had seen the stress lines on his face begin to appear again yesterday afternoon, and observed him doing those funny stretches with his back legs a few times in the corral that evening. These were clear indications that this was something he wasn't just going to be able to walk off, despite having several days of me doing the walking and him not carrying me.

It had been an incredibly long, drawn out decision as I played the wait and see game on my own, then did so again after the reassuring advice from the vet in Glen Tilt. It would have been a much easier conclusion to come to if he'd just been hopping lame. Not that I was wishing that on him by any means, but this slight niggle that something wasn't quite right, contradicted by seeing him striding so well up the hills, was confusing to say the least.

Yogi had done such an amazing job of carrying on regardless when clearly in discomfort, but enough was enough. Now that we would be home this evening, I knew I would not ask him to do any more for me. I would get his own vet out to see him during our rest day, but whatever their advice, Yogi would not be completing the trip.

I now wasn't sure whether I'd be able to complete the trip either. Even if I travelled super light, Swift was just not experienced nor confident enough yet to manage the challenges ahead on her own. Swift was also far too much of a teenage grump to cope with a sudden new pairing with a different horse. On top of that, Yogi (the softy) would go to pieces if his partner in crime left him, and the last thing he needed was days and days of pacing and stress.

Previously, I'd tried to work on the separation anxiety that Swogi displayed when apart. I'd tried building it up gradually by taking one or other of them out of the field, even just down the road for five minutes before returning. I'd tried taking one away in the trailer for a quick drive; I'd tried separating them for longer periods too, when getting help with Swift's training. No amount of gradual build-up or sudden separation worked. They just couldn't tolerate being apart.

Once when Swift was away for a week's training, I'd put Yogi in with two other horses, companions he knew from chatting over the fence. He had spent four days completely ignoring his friends and instead dug out a trench along the fenceline with his persistent pacing up and down. He didn't eat, sleep, nor drink for those four days and turned into a hoarse horse by constantly calling out for Swift. He also became extremely tucked up in his belly, and I rushed to get Swift back early before he made himself ill with colic.

Frustratingly, I note that if the horses separate themselves from each other, one at one end of the field and one at the other, then that is utterly fine. They are even content to be out of line of sight, if one is in the shelter and the other is right round the house in the trees. If I should dare to try and separate them, however, even just either side of the trailer, then all hell breaks loose. This probably explains how I ended up doing this whole riding and towing thing in the first place, which fortuitously had led to bigger and better things than I'd ever imagined possible.

I didn't know what to do. I could bow out gracefully and plan to complete the rest of the adventure later in the year or next summer, but I felt an incredible burden on my shoulders to complete it now. You see I'm not one to miss a trick of supporting a charitable cause in any way I can. I'd publicised this adventure well in advance and as well as I could on social media, to attract as much sponsorship as possible. The charitable cause I was supporting was Prince Fluffy Kareem (PFK).

I had first discovered this charity via a friend online and with my soft heart turning to jelly at the sight of suffering horses, I was moved to offer support. I sat open-mouthed at my computer looking at horrific wounds being treated by natural remedies such as manuka honey, combined with antibiotics sourced through charitable donations. *Horrific* is probably an understatement. I just couldn't believe that such undernourished animals with gapping, pus-filled infected wounds could possibly recover. In the UK, the vet would immediately assume a solemn tone and explain that euthanasia was for the best, but PFK was demonstrating time after time, that treatment in many cases was possible and successful. I connected with their determination, their 'never surrender' attitude and their tender loving care.

PFK help working horses, donkeys, camels and their owners in the pyramid region of Cairo, Egypt. Not only do they help to heal the horrific wounds, injuries and illnesses the working animals endure, but they take time to educate the owners on better animal care. Many of the local methods used with animals and to treat their ailments are very much out of date compared to Western medicine, or are based on superstition. Facing extreme poverty themselves and with families to feed, the owners either don't have a lot of choice to rest/treat their animals (their only mean to earn a living) or they don't know any other way.

PFK works immensely hard, in a setting full of deprivation, mistrust, tradition, and strong beliefs to help make it a better place for equines, camelids, and their human families. If you ever find yourself at the pyramids, look out for their trademark fluffy nosebands and saddle cloths, handed out to prevent the sores caused by the traditional use of harder materials such as metal chains across soft noses.

The international admiration that PFK has had brought attention to my campaign, albeit on a reasonably small scale. So far, I had raised a thousand pounds for the charity and pledges were still coming in. How could I let PFK, the animals and all my supporters down? Somehow, I had to find a way to continue, even if it meant doing so with hired or borrowed horses. I felt sick at the thought of attempting what I knew lay ahead with characters and capabilities of companions unknown, but I also felt sick at the thought of letting everybody down. Giving myself a shake, I reminded myself to sort this mess out one step at a time, and the first step on the ladder was to get Swogi back to their field at home today.

Now you might think that having an extra human to hand would reduce the morning faff, but the faff had doubled in size with four equines to prepare. I also had the job of swapping the saddles over again into the riding Swift and towing Yogi combination, as I'd been too tired to do this on arrival the night before.

We sorted and packed, and set out in a grey and blustery day that was thankfully dry. Chatting to Yvonne the night before, we'd relayed our individual struggles; mine of the Yogi worries and the battle to get Swift to walk out up front, and hers to get Katy to walk forward at all. Skye it appeared was happy to stroll along, but Katy was often reluctant to be towed and would frequently stop with sticky feet that, in a Highland Pony fashion, couldn't be persuaded to move.

Usually we all relied on strong leadership from Yogi, but with him transferred to packhorse, the design of a different running order was required. The resulting plan would make the most of their strengths and also exploit their imperfections (we hoped) to maximum effect. Yvonne would lead the way riding Skye up front, followed by Katy, with Team Swogi following along behind. It was hoped that Swift would gain reassurance from her pals in front, and the menacing faces she'd pull at Katy's bottom would gently threaten Katy to keep her feet firmly flowing.

The method was a success and we were making respectable progress down the single-track road, following the twists and turns of the charming River Tromie. We entertained each other with more tales of trail tribulations from our previous days, and Yvonne even sang an amusing song or two.

We were soon at Tromie Bridge where we would join a trail on the opposite side of the river that was medieval in origin. Comyn's Road was centuries old and had been constructed due to a love of real ale. Yet again I found myself identifying closely with ghost figures from the past. The love of real ale and passage through the hills is probably where the similarity ends though, as the Comyn family were much higher in status than I'll ever achieve.

The Earls and Lords of the family held titles on both sides of the hill, both in Blair Atholl and Kingussie. They had built this route, substantial enough for wheeled carts, in order to improve links between the two. The link created at the end of the thirteenth century was considered of extreme importance to transport fine ale up to Badenoch (the Kingussie area), from where it was brewed at an Inn in the Perthshire village of Blair Atholl. It's a long ol' way between the two settlements by horse-assisted transport, as I could now testify first-hand, so the ale must have been of exceptional quality indeed.

Although this route was used for centuries, a later pass in a more direct line across the hills - the Minigaig pass - became more popular. This became the main trade route for drovers and travellers and Comyn's Road was reclaimed by the land. Once across the Tromie bridge, the Minigaig Pass follows the older Comyn route and here you can tread where many a merry (possibly ale-filled) cart driver passed on by, a long time ago.

The Comyn family were of considerable historical importance in many a Scottish skirmish. In an impressive flourish of name-dropping, Lord John Comyn III, who had fought alongside William Wallace, came to his end at the hands of Robert the Bruce (allegedly) over a feud regarding the claim to the Scottish Throne. As my thoughts were drawn to the unfortunate demise of another of the Comyn clan, I was trying my hardest to block out Swift's mind reading talent, as I didn't want her to get any ideas on how to lighten her load.

Poor Walter Comyn had fallen from his horse up high on the road's plateau. His horse galloped away, with

Walter's foot trapped in the stirrup, and what was left of him was left by the side of the road to die. Now I wouldn't want to speculate which family member it was that was most partial to a drop of the exceptionally fine ale, but...

Since Swift was looking curiously around at my right stirrup, I quickly returned my mind to the present and realised I'd temporarily misplaced Yvonne. I'd wandered on ahead to open a large deer gate and had thought that Yvonne was not far behind. Had Katy decided to dig her Highland heels in again, with Yvonne stuck in a no-tow zone?

The situation was very much different to my fears, as I could see Yvonne cheerfully chatting to the inhabitant of the house next to the bridge, whilst Katy and Skye helped pull weeds and flowers from his garden. The gentleman from the cottage was gesticulating widely with his arms pointing up to the top of the hill. Yvonne was listening intently, nodding and smiling in all the right places.

Katy and Skye were politely nodding and smiling too, although not, I suspect, in the right places. Busy stuffing their faces, I had the distinct impression that neither of them were particularly following the conversation unfolding. They were too busy exploring the taste sensations that a cottage garden had to offer and were trying to open the gate to sample the full range of available treats.

Although Yvonne and I have many similarities on the trail, we have some marked differences too. I was more of a Yogi mind-set and was always focussed to crack on with the day's adventure. Yvonne, although always determined to finish what she started, was more Swift-like in approach and could lose herself in time and place when conversing with people we met.

I knew I had about thirty seconds before Yogi and I would start to fidget, and Swift would tuck into the grass. I estimated that there was at least ten minutes of Yvonne's conversation yet to take place. I already had the gate wide open and Yogi, spying the trail ahead, said, "It's this way isn't it? Haven't we been here before? That's the trail home - what are you waiting for? Let's go!"

"Snack break then," Swift spluttered, in between mouthfuls of grass. Sigh ... this was going to be a long, arm-stretching ten minutes.

As I was now well accustomed to travelling with Yvonne, I knew better than to be annoyed. I had often been utterly impressed by the treasures unleashed by her simple exchange of words with a stranger; accommodation for the night, a field for the horses, a short-cut explained or a refreshing drink, are a few of many examples. Being Miss Self-Reliant myself, I was in awe of her ability to easily chat with someone and simply ask for help.

Conversation complete (which, by the way, was all about a different route that the landowner was adamant we should take, but which I had deemed less suitable for those with four hooves) and fidgeting finished, we were on to familiar territory for Swogi. We'd done the Comyn's Road before and Swift was suddenly snappish about the slow pace being set.

The ear-back scowls, teeth-bared frowns, and Highland Pony-directed expletives were all too much for the sensitive Katy. Yvonne was now experiencing a different kind of towing problem, with Katy moving her feet faster than ideal, as she flustered to get ahead of Skye to get out of Swift's tooth snapping reach. It was very much time to change tactics.

As Swift strode out, leading the whole herd towards home, I again experienced the fantastic potential that I knew lay within her. The familiar ground, and the confidence given by the bigger herd of horses she knew well, was having a turbo-boost effect that even Yogi was proud of. We proceeded at a fast pace, across the open ground towards Kingussie with magnificent views of the Monalaidth Mountains looming ever closer.

The wide track was soft and grassy, forming an obvious route through the heather-coated land through which, every so often, a young silver birch raised its head in a splash of pale bright green, all leaves a dancing, delighted to have grown tall enough to push the heather aside and be able to soak up the sun. On the horizon a thick layer of dark green trees concealed the River Spey, yet they clearly indicated its channel by their presence. Behind this green line, the patchy lower slopes of the Monalaidths reached up to their dark grey tops. The dark colour was in sharp contrast today to the numerous high white clouds.

Within no time at all, and a lot of jigging from the Highland Duo to keep up, we were on the minor road leading toward the famous Ruthven Barracks and on into Kingussie town. The barracks, set on a mound in the marshes, are an obvious prominent feature when travelling along the A9 and attract many a tourist to pause in their journey and explore the history they contain.

Before exploring that ancient history though, history in the making was taking place behind me. Yvonne, tired of the jigging along in pursuit of a swift Swift, had jumped off Skye to walk and, now that we'd reached the road, she was searching around for a suitable spot to jump back on. Although Skye is small in stature, Yvonne - also small in stature - would struggle to mount from the ground and she'd spied a peaceful truck driver enjoying his lunchtime piece (local dialect for sandwich).

Waltzing confidently up to his cab with Katy and Skye in tow, she was deep in discussion to ask him to hold Skye's opposite stirrup whilst she clambered up on board. The truck driver appeared to be reluctantly agreeing in a somewhat terrified manner. The powers of Yvonne's persuasion had struck home yet again, and he emerged wide-eyed from the comfort of his truck to oblige her polite request. Laughing at her gall and her succinct success, I realised yet again how much I had to learn about asking for help to make for an easier life. All back on board, we rode towards the barracks and its grand position high above the marshland, with the Monalaidths gloriously grey in backdrop behind.

It should come as no surprise that the first to build a castle on the strategic mound were the Comyn family in around 1229. After all, they would need a large cellar to store all that delicious real ale brought over their road. They were strategic thinkers indeed, as they built the castle before the road and were therefore ready to receive and store their orders once the beer bringing began.

Many other orders came into play, for battlefields rather than beer, over the following years. The castle and later the barracks changed hands (and sides) numerous times during the Catholic versus Protestants and Scottish versus English scuffles. Its initial strategic position was as the only ford and ferry crossing to traverse the middle stretches of the lengthy and mighty River Spey. Its later strategic advantages were just as important, in being a central point between east and west and north and south on the network of General Wade's roads.

The Ruthven Barracks, commissioned by the government, were built in 1719 as one of the four infantry facilities located to control key routes through the Cairngorms. There wasn't much left of the castle at this time as it had been burned during battle in the late 1600's at the ignition of the Jacobite revolt. Stable blocks were added in 1734 as General Wade recognised the worth of mounted troops.

"Quite right too!" exclaimed Yogi, who considered himself to be somewhat battle scarred and deserving of appreciation and medals.

The battle of the barracks

As a result of its tactical position, the Ruthven mound was never going to have an easy time and the structures it supported were flattened, stormed, and burned numerous times over the centuries. Finally burned and abandoned by the Jacobite rebels around the time of their defeat at Culloden, it remains relatively unchanged from that day. As the rebels disbanded, they gathered at the Ruthven remains to hear the orders: "Let every man seek his own safety in the best way he can."

I'd ridden a horse through a castle or two in my time and enjoyed the different sensation and connection with history it imparted. I looked longingly at the track to the right that lead up the mound to the historical site.

"NO WAY JOSÉ!" shouted Swift, to pull me back into line. "That right is UP and left is HOME, are you seriously thinking I'll oblige?"

Oh, well, I thought, maybe some other time then and I'll get Yogi to take me up there.

"Up where? I like ups," said Yogi, popping his nose out from under Swift's tail.

We continued down the road, reached the railway crossing at the edge of town, and despite no gates being lowered and no red lights lit up, we came to a very solid STOP.

"Wooooahhhh!" said Swift, with her front legs splayed and her nose sniffing the tracks, "I'm not sure I'm up to the responsibility of assessing the risk on this one ... make Yogi do it."

It appeared it was time for yet another running order change.

"We'll let the younger and more sensible Skye take charge then shall we Swift?" I said.

In response there was a shrug of shoulders in a 'I'm not-bothered' kind of way.

After the railway crossing, assessed as well and truly safe for all by Skye, we were to turn left to Newtonmore rather than right for home. The original Plan A (for All

Is Well) at this junction was to proceed straight on, up into the hills around the back of the lovely Loch Gynack and descend to Newtonmore via the start of Glen Banchor.

Plan B, with Yogi-Bear to consider, was to head straight for home, and there would be no requirement now for Dave to run the van and trailer through to the neighbouring town. It would have been a good Plan B (for Bear), if I'd remembered to tell Dave that we'd moved forward in the alphabet.

Executing Plan C (for Cycle way) would involve an easy three-mile ride along a cycle track to rescue the superfluous trailer. Considering the miles and rough ground covered so far, this wasn't going to make a lot of difference to Yogi's scheme of things. Swift, however, had moved on to her own personal Plan D (for Defiance) and was trying to convince the rest of the herd that she had it all worked out.

Her plan was exceedingly simple. "Right is home, left isn't, I'm not going left, we are all going right, don't forget the one for all and all for one principle!"

I don't know whether hanging out with the stubborn Highland ponies had influenced Swift, but I could tell that her heels were well and truly dug in right now. I could also tell that I wasn't going to have any success in getting her to move from my position up high in the saddle. Sitting at a road junction on the High Street wasn't the best place to tactically win a game of ABC (or D) anyway, so I jumped off.

From the ground I had more tricks up my sleeve to unstick those dug in heels, and I could glare at her eye-to-eye - well almost, if she lowered her head and I stood on tiptoes. The stop-start, spinning around and pointing the other way with her nose or a flick of her tail, eventually subsided after ten minutes or so. Resigned to the direction we were taking away from home, she sulkily let me remount and resumed the sport of Katy baiting.

The cycle way was easy riding and we were soon looping around the back of Newtonmore to where the trailer was parked at the Newtonmore Riding Centre, locally known as NRC. The lure of a refreshing beverage in town was strong, as we'd previously had a warm welcome at one of the pubs when visiting with the horses.

Katy had charmed the crowd with a demonstration of one of her many party tricks involving food, by eating a packet of crisps (Onion Rings are her favourite). I'm sure the landlady, who had provided refreshing water for the horses then, would enjoy a repeat performance now (as would Katy) but after ten long days on the trail, the lure of home was also strong. There was a lot to sort out, most importantly a vet to see Yogi and a lot to discuss, like how I might manage to continue without Swogi. There were dogs to cuddle, a fire to warm ourselves at, fresh food and wine to enjoy too. The trail is good, but home's good too.

The horses quickly loaded and were soon ensconced back home in their field with their Highland Pony guests. We made sure they had everything they needed and left them settling in. I gave Swift a quick pat to thank her for trying her hardest at the leading lark. I'd have given her more of a cuddle, but her interest was decidedly indifferent. Yogi, however, snuggled into the big hug I gave him as thank you for his hard work and extra efforts over the last few days. I left him happily cramming hay into his mouth, in between contented sighs of "Home sweet home."

We too were quickly loaded into the car and off to the pub after a brief but much needed shower. Mountain food isn't always the most satisfying and we were both desperate for a mound of filling pub grub instead. The other reason for heading out to the pub was to find a beer mat or two, upon which to form a new plan. It's widely recognised that the best laid plans are laid out on the back of a fag packet or, for those who don't partake, then the back of a beer mat will do. I figured that this particular plan was going to take several beer mats to work out, and I apologise to the Suie Hotel in Kincraig for the amount we ended up using.

The plan we managed to devise was going to take several stages of logistical aid. Yvonne, the great pal she is, had suggested we might manage to travel together for a while before we parted ways, as she finished her journey and I continued alone. I would be able to complete my adventure by riding one of her sturdy Highland ponies during the days together, before continuing with both of them from Fort Augustus onwards.

We wouldn't, therefore, have the carrying capacity of pack ponies for the next three days and we'd need to find a willing volunteer to drop our camping gear at the overnight stops. Or, as I pointed out, an unwilling volunteer would do, and with two sets of pleading eyes pointed in Dave's direction over the top of his pint of beer, my poor husband didn't stand a chance. He agreed to drop our kit at the next two of our overnight camps.

From there we'd have to work our charms on Yvonne's husband Adrian, who was soon similarly recruited to support the logistics on the western side of the next set of hills. All arranged in theory, we would unpick the details tomorrow as we'd need more than beer mats for that. It suddenly looked possible that I would, after all, be able to finish the cross-Scotland adventure I'd started, and the sponsor pledges would be honoured.

I was extremely sad that I would be continuing my journey without my best equine friends, but if I took time to dwell on that too much, I doubt I'd be able to carry on. "The show must go on" (and all that jazz), and I just had to count my lucky stars that I had a solution. Relieved, replenished, and rapidly falling asleep, we headed back home for a good night's sleep in an incredibly comfy bed.

Day 11:
Rest Day at Kingussie (home)

After a tiny bit of a lie in, and a luxurious moment taken to cuddle Danny-boy and caress his comforting silky ears, we were soon in a frenzy of unpacking, cleaning, repacking, and restocking. The washing machine wasn't quite sure what had hit it and as much as I love my horses, it was nice not to smell like one for a while.

I met the vet at the field for yet another inconclusive event. At short notice, this wasn't Yogi's usual animal doctor and she appeared young and inexperienced. The assessment carried out was nowhere near as extensive as the one by the vet in the middle of Glen Tilt. She seemed more concerned with recommending every expensive experiment under the Sun Alliance than listening to the person who knew her horse best.

Seeing Yogi in familiar territory, and having more space to think rather than just travel, I'd become more and more convinced that his pain was well and truly in his back feet. The pattern of behaviour just didn't fit a muscular injury at all. On top of this were additional dots from before the trip that I had only just joined together. A few weeks before we embarked on our adventure, Yogi seemed to be peeing much more often than usual (an embarrassing infliction) and each time only producing a small dribble. Fearing infection, I'd subjected poor Yogi to a urine catheter test and in the process, the vet had removed a bean.

I find myself describing another scenario here, that no cowboy in the movies ever seems to face. Geldings can accumulate a waxy substance, made up of dirt and dead skin cells, inside their sheath or urethra that can interfere with urinary flow. It's an owner's job to clear this out from time to time, but Yogi and his fear of latex gloves had never let me near him. I love my Yogi-Bear dearly, but there was no way on earth I was going to do this disgusting job with only my bare hands.

With Yogi under sedation, I'd handed this pleasure over to the gloved hands of the vet. The bean removed and the urine test clear of infection, I thought the problem was solved. His frequent flow had still been a regular feature throughout the cross-Scotland excursion, but it had at least seemed to be a more comfortable process, with less grunting by Yogi required to initiate it.

As a paramedic we're taught not to get blinkered by a distracting injury, but I realised now that's exactly what had happened. Eye-wateringly broad as it was, the bean wasn't the root of the problem; it was a side-tracking discovery that was leading us up the garden path. My suspicions now were that Yogi had a wider systemic issue going on and his frequent peeing issue was one of the symptoms.

'No hoof no horse' is a well-known phrase and my barefoot journey had taught me a lesson. If your horse is unwell, they will often display signs in the quality of their hoof. Another plus for keeping your companions barefoot and fancy free, as a metal shoe nailed to a hoof will hide any subtle signs that not all is well and good. This footsore theory would fit much better with the behaviour Yogi had displayed, and I couldn't believe it had taken me so long to work it all out.

Standing with his back feet tucked forward to relieve the pressure and stretching his back legs straight up would have eased pain in the feet too. The worsening pain after cold, rocky river crossings and the way he would only display discomfort after stopping and not whilst moving (we've all been there with blisters in our hiking boots), and the fact that he was better in the mornings after a full night resting his toes, also reinforced the sore feet theory.

The trouble had started, after a night's constant grass mowing in the gamekeeper's knee-high paddock at Glen Muick. Could Yogi be slightly laminitic as a result? Laminitis is an inflammatory condition of the laminae - structures holding the hoof wall in place around the bone in a horse's hoof - and is primarily caused by too much grass (or, more accurately, too much sugar in too much grass). With his front feet protected by the hoof boots, the possible mild laminitis was only evident behind and had disguised the classic stance a horse would use to ease the worst pain felt more commonly in the front feet. I wasn't sure if it was all as serious as this, as I know my imagination can often run away with itself (with both hands in the air), but a systemic sickness certainly deserved consideration.

The vet disagreed and was still promoting x-rays, nerve blocks, lameness work ups etc, advised for those with more structural than systemic issues. On my return from the west, it looked like a trip to the equine specialists down in Edinburgh would be on the table, as I'd rather spend my money on expensive experiments that followed my line of thinking, based soundly on knowing my horse so well. Animal doctoring will never be an exact science and the tests my vet was suggesting were valid for one train of thought. Bloodwork to test my theory, however, was busy flashing warning lights in my signal-box, as I was convinced that I was on the right track. That gut feeling was there, and any vet was going to have a hard job persuading me otherwise.

For now, though, Yogi would rest up with his best friend in a safe and cosy place, in a field reasonably devoid of grass, and would come to no harm until my return. Yogi seemed comfortable enough when not tasked with the hard work of the trail and I would be home in a week. I still felt guilty leaving him in limbo, not knowing the exact cause of his ailments, but I was reassured knowing that Dave would be keeping a close eye on him and would provide regular updates as I continued on the trail.

Whilst we were down at the horses, Yvonne and I played around with some tack options. Yvonne would now be riding Katy and she needed to convert her pack saddle back to one that would fit a human more comfortably. Hunting for a fragment of familiarity going forward, I also wanted to see whether Yogi's saddle and bridle would fit well on Skye.

Luckily for me, Yvonne uses the same type of treeless saddles and, with a quick swap of saddle pad and a change of cinch (the strap that holds the saddle on under the horse's belly), Yogi's saddle was sitting well. Skye's bitless bridle was also of the same style as Yogi's, so all it took were a few nips and tucks on Skye's smaller head for me to be able to use my familiar bridle and reins. At least when heading out into uncertainty, my bottom and my hands might not notice that anything had particularly changed. I was delighted, too, about finishing my journey exactly how I had started: bitless, treeless, and barefoot. I'm not saying that this is the only way, but it's my way and I was glad I could stick to my principles and preferences.

After an hour or so of directions to the husband support crew, they had the grid references and instructions required to hopefully ensure that the riders and their kit would end up in the same place at roughly the same time. Planning complete, the rest of the day was spent resting; fire on, feet up, and fussing fluffy dogs.

As bouncy as Tully the Jackie Rascal could be when out and about, she sure knew how to quietly snuggle and cuddle too. One of her favourite places of warmth and comfort was under Danny-boy's head. She was only just a little bigger than the size of his head, so she made the perfect pillow. With his floppy soft ears hanging over each side of her body, Dan made the perfect heated blanket to keep her cosy. It was a win-win situation, and as a result this was a common daily occurrence.

They didn't seem to object about sharing as I gently inserted myself into their pile of fur, warmth, and contented sighs on the sofa. I always said that I'd never allow dogs on the furniture but as Danny-boy aged into Dan-the-Man and became that little bit stiff and sore, I'd decided on his tenth birthday that the lad needed more comfort in his life. Throws were found for an already ageing sofa and Dan took delight and full advantage of the change in house rules. I do confess that I did exactly the same as him.

As I massaged his soft silky ears and descended into a snugly, snoozy slumber, I thought upon the eleven years that had flown by with him in our lives. It hadn't been an easy start by any means. He was head-strong, stubborn, and had the strongest prey drive I've ever experienced in a dog. Alongside that, he was big, sturdy, fast, and so completely full of energy that even a long day in the hills would not curb it.

The blood, sweat, and tears that had gone into attempted training only made him at maximum, ninety percent reliable. I'd lost count of the many hours wasted, waiting for him to finish his chasing of pheasants down at the 'Dell', calling out to ears that had suddenly developed a selective deafness to whistles. We'd read all the books and tried all the techniques suggested to improve his recall, even spent a fortune on training in a borstal for badly behaved dogs, but nothing made a significant impact.

Whether it was having Tully as a recent addition to the family or Dan deciding he had finally matured at the age of twelve, he was now more reliable off the lead and had been pivotal in helping me with Yogi's training. Yogi being the 'is everything going to eat me?' kind of horse wasn't initially that confident up front on the trail. Having Swift along as company, to watch his back had certainly helped, but having Danny-boy out in front assessing the trail for danger (in Yogi's mind) had made the biggest difference.

If Dan could go through a stream, cross a bridge, or negotiate some boggy ground, then obviously a half tonne horse would be safe to do so too. Yogi's logic was a little flawed, but the teamwork worked for him and he was always very patient to stop and wait if Dan stopped in front for a sniff or a call of nature. Swift, on the other hand, would impatiently 'bop' his behind with her nose; and on a few occasions I'd had to prevent her from progressing to the use of teeth to give him 'encouraging' nips. Dan, in his happy go lucky style, would continue his business in his own set time frame regardless.

On the flip side of his unreliability out and about, he was the most relaxed and chilled dog to have around you when inside a building. Any building would do, but pubs with 'biscuit corners' were his favourite places to be. He was a regular at both the Suie Hotel in Kincraig and The Craig in Grantown-on-Spey where he'd find his fan clubs waiting for him, hopefully with treats in hand.

He was such a soft and gentle giant who would lean against your legs, charming you with those hypnotising eyes as he looked up at you over his shoulder with a big grin across his face. The look of love and pure devotion in his eyes was an art that he had thoroughly perfected. Is it any wonder the "no dogs on the sofa" rule had been broken in our house? I'd held out a long time, but eventually I hadn't stood a chance.

Sometimes a special, once in a lifetime dog comes along and that was Dan. He didn't just charm his way into pubs and onto sofas, he charmed those who were nervous of dogs and he charmed his way fully into the depths of my heart. He had the most amazing presence that meant you couldn't keep your eyes off him (probably a good thing anyway, with the mischief he'd get up to), and had the most amusing habits for daily entertainment to get you through the toughest of days, always carried out at full volume and with greatest galumphing for maximum effect.

He might have been the most stubborn, head-strong dog I'd ever lived with, but he was also the most utterly loyal dog too. His eyes, overflowing with unwavering love, watched your every move; everywhere you went, he just wanted to be right by your side. Although he loved all his friends and fans within his 'extended family', he hated to be separated from Dave and I even for a second, so toileting and bath-time was never the same again.

I knew how much me being away on this trek would be stressing the old fella out and did feel guilty about heading back to the trail tomorrow. We'd just have to get some quality time in together now to see us through another week. With one hand lost in the silk of Dan's fur and the other softly scratching Tully's belly, I drifted off

171

to sleep for a while, taking full advantage of the rest that the rest day had to offer.

The daily routine of a long-distance trek, although totally addictive, can physically wear you down. Rest days are therefore always appreciated by both horse and human. The chores at the start of the day - breakfast, breaking camp, getting everything to fit compactly and balanced in saddle bags, brushing the horses, cleaning their feet and putting on their hoof boots, tacking them up, deconstructing the corral, putting the last few items in the bags before taking the time to securely and with balance attach them to the saddles - can take between one and a half to two hours. The routine at the tail end of the day to set up camp, clean hoof boots, and create a corral etc. takes a similar amount of time.

In between these four hours, there are six to eight hours of continual movement; never stopping for longer than twenty minutes at a time. You can't ride for all this time as your horse's back will suffer, as would your own legs and behind. You alternate between riding and walking with the focus on the continued progress of eating up the day's planned miles.

The ground can be rough, the hills steep, the weather challenging, all adding to the physicality of the journey. Generally, on a two-week or longer dobbineering adventure, I'll lose a stone in weight but gain the muscles and balance of a mountain goat! There are of course easier options for horse travel such as staying in pre-organised fields and B&Bs. Not travelling so self-sufficiently negates clumpy saddle bags that weigh and slow you down. A faster pace, increased miles, and an easier progress can be made each day.

I've travelled this way and it's a great experience too. The most fun and relaxing was probably the East

Highland Way with three other friends and four horses. We were met each night by our support crew (Dave) in the horse lorry, who set up corrals, cooked our meals, and generally pampered us all (horses included) in exchange for beer, whisky, great appreciation, and a few rounds of golf thrown in.

Although thoroughly enjoyable in a different way, I wouldn't call it classic dobbineering. Dropping down to accommodation each night usually curtails that true wilderness experience and that's what I crave the most. The use of horsepower and my own steam to reach and stay in remote and beautiful places is something I wouldn't necessarily get to enjoy, if I had the constraints of returning to civilisation by night fall. In my mind and soul, the hard reality of remote is still won over by the romantic notion of a night under the stars - even if that romance is of a different ilk with equine rather than human companions!

Although I don't meet many people on the trails I choose, I do enjoy the surprised exclamations of "I didn't expect to see a horse up here" and "I didn't know people still travelled with horses." At the point of this conversation, we could be standing on an old drover's route through the hills but the walker or biker we have met might be completely oblivious to the origin of the trail. We are a novelty, a reminder of days gone by, and there is something spiritual about that historical connection way out there in remote reaches.

It's tiring, there is no doubt about that, but I find the movement and exploration addictive. For reasons I don't understand, for me to properly soak up the scenery I'm in, I must feel it whilst on the move. I'm not one for sitting still to absorb a view as curiosity drives me to get up and go see what's just around that corner, what's behind that wall, can the bottom of the lake be seen, and what's by the stream.

In the evenings, once camp is set up, I'll often explore the place I'm in by going for a two to three-hour walk. Mad you might say after travelling the whole day, and I would totally agree. It doesn't help my energy conservation that's for sure, but it settles the curiosity in my soul. I might not pass this way again and I want to ensure I've seen every nook and cranny and left no stone unturned. This probably adds hugely to my daily mileage count, but I don't allow it to qualify as it's done without horses and with a different purpose in mind.

In many ways, I'm a Yogi kind of person, with an all or nothing attitude to life. Trail days should be full of exploration and movement from sunrise to sunset. I can be restless on rest days too (like the last one at Mar Lodge), where there are still places left unexplored or restocking of supplies to achieve. Today's rest day, unusual with its home comforts and familiarity, was managing to achieve its purpose with more success than usual and in the best possible way.

Swift - 'Spotty Bum' *Yogi - 'The Bear'*

Tweeted at the Burn House

At Queen's Well

A hare and tortoise rest

A royal view from Mount Keen

Snack break below Mount Keen

The hip flask view Glen Muick

The teenager out from under her hoody

Beside Lochnagar

The Upper Dee Valley and Mar Lodge

Rare to be in front of the camera - photo Fiona Duniam

The thin trail of Glen Tilt

The joker of the pack with the small dam behind

Dave helping out - the Gaick Pass

Yogi posing lessons

The resulting diva

The handsome Bear

Yvonne and the Highland Duo

Grass obsessed Katy

Mischief maker Skye

Katy baiting

The singing shepherdess

The imprint of man

A safer Wade's bridge

Looking down to Loch Ness

The compact Highland Duo

The plank walking technique

An example camp layout

Day 12:
Newtonmore to Laggan
(Distance 18km, Ascent 300m)

We used the trailer to take the ponies the five kilometres back to Newtonmore Riding Centre and declared ourselves ready to set out on the trail in record time. With one horse each and fewer bags to pack, it created less of a faff. The day was windy and cool, but patches of blue sky were interspersed with white fluffy clouds, so it looked like a fine day to be in the hills and appeared like it would stay dry.

We were into the weekend and the riding centre was busy. The audience we had as we departed had a mixture of bemused, wistful and I-think-you're-mad faces. I didn't help the latter opinion, as I jumped up on Skye and nearly fell off the other side. I realised that despite my own saddle, the change of horse was still going to feel somewhat strange. For one, she was a whole lot smaller than Yogi or Swift and getting up on top clearly didn't warrant the amount of energy I'd applied to the process.

I thought Skye rolled her eyes and sighed, but I couldn't be sure as I didn't yet know her so well. The alteration to my mounting effort truly noted, I wriggled back into the middle to where my butt should be, and we were ready to continue our adventures. Katy, with Yvonne on top, seemed happy and was moving forward well in the riding centre's arena (where we had tacked up), so it looked like the new combination was on to a winning streak.

The first part of the day was a ride I knew well. Indeed, it was one of my favourite day rides when riding closer to home. As we climbed up into the start of Glen Banchor, I tested that all the controls were switched on and working on my new steed. Stop and turn were fine, but sideways and go forward were a little more sluggish than I was used to. Despite this I was fairly satisfied with the results, but I wasn't the only one involved in the test drive.

Skye had surmised that she might have a beginner on top, who didn't know any of the rules of engagement. I'm not surprised she came to this conclusion considering I'd nearly fallen off the moment I'd half sat on her. For Skye, as far as rules were concerned, they were there for breaking or bending. As we meandered up the single-track road, she was busy trying out the flexibility of the ruler.

Highland ponies tend to be rather grass-obsessed individuals if left to their own devices. You can't really blame them for that, as in order to survive the harsh Scottish winters out there on the hills, they have to be cunning enough to seek out - then rush to consume before any other pony - the rare patches of grass to be found in amongst the predominantly heather filled land. In a case of survival of the fattest, the grass infatuation had become dominantly inherited in their genes.

When Yvonne had started working with Katy and Skye, one of her main problems was preventing them from stopping to eat. It is perfectly acceptable to let your horse munch its way along a trail, as Swogi often do, but when more progress is reached in the munching rather than the along part of the system, then something needs to change.

Highland Pony necks are probably the thickest, shortest, and strongest necks you're ever likely to meet on an equine, and once their head is down munching there isn't very much you can do about it. To help them get the message, Yvonne had resorted to grass reins which are straps that connect the horses head to the saddle. These straps allow the horse to move its head in all directions, but not to put it right down to the ground.

Usually deployed for small kids and strong pony partnerships, it was also perfectly applicable when adults and strong, stubborn Highland ponies were combined. Over time, the grass reins had done their trick and Yvonne no longer used them. Skye was very aware of this fact and although she wouldn't dare to step out of the grass line with Yvonne, she was very much trying to jump right over it with me. On top of that she had thought it best to check out my resolve and everything I asked of her was answered with, "No ... make me if you can." Her reply was usually accompanied by a stroppy shake of her head and a whip of her mane across my face, to make sure I completely understood, then underlined with the swish of her tail for good measure.

Wondering what on earth I was letting myself in for, Yvonne explained - between her giggles - that this would all settle down in an hour or so and that Skye tested every new rider she carried. I was finding it all quite amusing too, really, as Skye's stroppy responses were delivered with mischief in mind and a light-hearted humour. There was much more character to this little lass than I'd ever given her credit for, and I was really starting to enjoy the cheeky glint in her eye.

By now we'd reached the first of the many ruined townships in Glen Banchor. The glen takes its name from the word Beannachar which is a horn-shaped riverbank, formed by a long bend in the River Calder as it descends down to join the River Spey. Along the Glen's length are numerous historic townships, remnants of the communities that lived here in past times.

The townships were small gatherings of houses built of stone, turf, and timber and were the homes of clans or kinsfolk who leased small crofts (which often functioned like collectives) from the local estate. Potato was a main staple food, and the blight that spoilt the crops (1845-1852) caused disease, starvation, and mass migrations. Although more historically linked with Ireland, the Highlanders and west coast crofters suffered greatly due to the potato famine too.

If this wasn't enough to contend with, landlords who were struggling to cope with the means to fund poverty relief for their tenants (a government requirement of the Poor Law Amendment Act 1845) could see the benefits of the emerging intensive modern methods of farming. Landlords desired to eliminate the costly burden of responsibility to their tenants and at the same time wanted to clear the land to make way for the larger scale - and more profitable - pastoral agriculture, based on huge sheep farms.

As a result, the kinsfolk were cleared out, thousands of families evicted, and their cottages burned to the ground. The bulk of the Highland Clearances occurred in the second half of the 1800s and the evicted tenants were moved to the coast, often to poor and infertile land. There they were expected to become sudden experts in herring fishing, a rapidly emerging industry. The other option was to emigrate to lands and conditions unknown, often ultimately forced upon them by their landlords under the guise of assisted emigration. The crofting areas lost about a third of their population within twenty years.

In historical records, the Highland Potato Famine

appears almost swept under the woollen blanket of the more attention-grabbing and politically emotive clearances. Described by author John Prebbles in his book, *The Highland Clearances,* "[clearances] concerns itself with people, how sheep were preferred to them and how bayonet, truncheon and fire were used to drive them from their land." Perhaps I'd finally discovered why adult sheep are so depressed. The guilt of the misery that their popularity had caused was a heavy burden to bear.

It is ironic that just past this sad reminder of the triumph of greed and power over compassion, the glen's beauty really begins to unfold. As we followed the twists and turns of the trail, the bowl of the Glen opened up. We'd reached the abandoned farmstead at Glenballoch, where the Allt Fiondugh tributary combines with the River Calder, and there was a gate to be opened up too.

As the official gate opener of the team, I jumped off to complete this task and contemplated that there were some advantages to having a much smaller horse. No longer would I have to search around to find a suitable (and sizable for Swift) mounting block. With Skye being so small I could easily get back on from the ground.

I looked longingly at the lengthy canter track that stretched off to the north-west, but one look from Yvonne and a shake of the head from Skye and I knew this would be one to wait for another day. Instead I thought back to the bumpy ride I'd once enjoyed with a kayak as my steed. The tributary was a good place to start, to ride the waves down the short but sweet waters of the Calder. This, I can report, is a journey best undertaken by those who have experience of white water and particularly after heavy rainfall, when river levels will cover the numerous rocky obstructions.

On the other side of the bridge, we wouldn't have far to go before we'd be required to weave a merry dance around areas of horse-swallowing bog. Skye, remembering her previous swallowing-wallowing experience here, was glancing at me nervously. Yvonne also appeared a bit anxious as she asked for about the third time today, "You have found a better way through this time, haven't you?"

Yet another example of why I now recce routes on foot first. On our first ride here, early in the learning curve process, I'd followed advice on the best way to proceed with hooves where the main off-road vehicle track runs out. I was leading a small group of horses and riders and was sure I'd followed instructions to the letter but had ended up in softer and softer ground. Common sense collective within the group, thought that the ground would be harder further up the hill and away from the riverside.

We'd soon realised how wrong we were. When Scottish peat is involved, the usual rules of common sense, totally don't apply. Yogi was aghast to see his pal Skye disappear up to her belly and, if that wasn't bad enough, the long-legged Swift was in the same position too. Yogi, with his fear of bogs (a rational fear, I then deduced), was wide-eyed and stressed but I was astounded to see that the rest of the herd remained reasonably calm as if it was just another muddy day out. The humans, however, weren't taking it quite so lightly.

This should have been a simple walk of about three kilometres, instead it turned into an experience of epic proportions. There were four of us floundering with five horses that day and, pulling as a team, we unstuck the ones that were stuck, and all finally returned down to the river. It took some time to find a safe route but once there, wet feet with solid, rocky riverbed underneath were preferable to no feet in sight at all. We were all exhausted and in shock at the mistake that we had made. We appreciated how close we had come to a major disaster and there was relieved laughter, horse hugs, and tears before we were ready to continue. We were extremely thankful that all we'd lost were several hours of our day.

The boggy bad judgement now logged as experience (per Mark Twain's advice) had changed today's approach to this section considerably. I'd been back in my running shoes on a recce, and today's route was a tribute to how dry and mud free I'd managed to keep them. The route would involve crossing the shallow river several times to walk along its banks and stay away from the bogs higher up.

I reassured Yvonne that I had clear markers firmly implanted in my brain and that the route was easy when you knew how. With a little twisting and turning we were soon at the first marker to cross the river; the unusual signpost was firmly implanted in the heather and consisted of an old white fridge. Thankful as I was of something as reliable as Beko to guide our way, it is incredibly sad that humans have such a low respect for the land. How on earth this fridge became dumped in such a remote place I have no idea, but it must have taken considerable effort and determination to spoil such a beautiful place.

Walking beside Skye in a companionable fashion, I

felt we were beginning to bond a little. She seemed to have finally realised that I wasn't going to relent when it came to her grass-eating demands. Yvonne appeared to be having a good time with Katy too, and the issues of Katy digging her heels in seemed like a dark and distant memory.

Walking down by the river, the immediate view was of sandy banks and bright yellow, gorse-filled slopes. The river had cut a new, smaller floodplain within the overall wider one. The main valley base was about a kilometre wide, but the river was now content to carve its path through only a tenth of that. Far away at the edge of the valley, angular hills running in parallel alignment reminded the river that, should it choose to reach out once more, it still had some absolute boundaries.

The clouds were happily playing high overhead, racing around the hill tops and temporarily relinquishing the odd patch of bright blue sky. All the exciting weather seemed to be circling around us, and the patches of blue were often directly overhead. These enhanced the river's sparkle, added a depth of colour to the yellow petals of gorse-flower, and made the grass appear a succulent shade of green.

"No ... Skye ... no ... I don't care how green it looks, you are NOT allowed!"

Perhaps my test wasn't all quite over yet...

However, our twisting, turning, and splashing route was over, and in only an hour we had reach the Dallnashallag Bothy. I caught Yvonne tapping and checking her watch.

"Did that really only take one hour?"

Compared to our previous trek along this glen, she couldn't quite believe we'd reached the bothy so soon in the day.

"I mean ... it's not even lunch time yet," she reflected.

The bothy has a small, fenced garden and on our previous visit we'd used it to confine some of the horses. Grass mowing and fertilisation is all part of the service, but before I get slated for leaving horse poo where it's not wanted, we always remove it from areas around buildings where humans are likely to tread or camp. A trusty set of Marigold gloves and a clothes-peg are essential pack items for this task. Today, however, the bothy appeared to be occupied by a large group.

Large groups aren't generally welcome in a bothy, as it means the lone walker might have nowhere to stay, or - if wanting an early night - is disturbed by the volume of noise that large groups can often create. This group looked more like official estate business, as there were vehicles on the land and even a small marquee. I suggested we stayed away, not wanting to disturb a high-paying shooting party, but as we approached, Yvonne made a beeline for the building. In true Yvonne style, by the time I caught up, she was deep in conversation with a man over the fence. It all looked amicable enough, so I too headed in that direction, reassured by Yvonne waving for me to join her.

This was no shooting party, but a party had been held. The lads were there to commemorate an old gillie from the estate who had sadly passed away. The yearly excursion to toast his memory had become something of a tradition, and included the ritual of bringing his old rocking chair up to join in with the revelries. Yvonne and I were welcomed in and soon found ourselves sitting (not on the sacred chair, but admiring it) with one hand wrapped around a burger and one hand wrapped around a drink. There was only a full fat Coke for Yvonne and a mediocre lager for me, but beggars can't be choosers, and we chose to gratefully have rather than have not.

With the ponies merrily mowing in the confines of the garden, the fences negating any requirement for supervision, it was the most relaxing lunch. Hot food midday was an exceptional treat, as was a proper seat, particularly inside and sheltered from the midges. Yet again Yvonne's sociable style had acquired us a luxurious extravagance. The downside was the difficulty of extraction from such comforts, and it would be with great reluctance that we returned to our onward mission.

We'd been in a similar position at this bothy once before, and weren't going to get lulled into another false sense of sunny security. That time, we'd sunbathed on the seats outside and left - t-shirt clad - in heat and warmth, only for that to change dramatically and suddenly to torrential rain, booming thunder, and formidable lightning a little further down the valley.

The amount of rainfall that day in only a few hours was incredible; the burns overflowed, and the trails and roads became rivers. The thunder was deafeningly loud, and we were scared that we might get hit by lightning as it crashed to the ground all around us. Soaked through we arrived at a small courtyard next to a house, on the edge of a village, and sheltered against the walls of the buildings.

We weren't sure if anyone was home, but I don't think they ever discovered that two of our party took the liberty of even more shelter than the use of the walls. Yogi and Katy, being clever comfort-seekers, burst through the small doors of the sheds, not caring in the least whether there'd be room to turn around once inside. Happily steaming in the rain-free shelter alongside a chicken or two, and having managed to turn in their individual tight spaces, they looked out smugly at the rest of us standing in the wet.

Praying they wouldn't leave any tell-tale deposits, we huddled together to keep as warm and dry as we could and as far away from the lightning as possible. The rain didn't let up however, and we still had a way to travel. After considerable time, group debate gathered momentum to the Clash of, "Should we stay, or should we go now?" If we stayed, we would get cold, we'd stay wet, and we wouldn't make any progress on our day's mileage. If we went, we probably wouldn't get any wetter than we already were and we might warm up a bit, but we would run the risk of being hit by lightning.

Deciding to move on, much to Yogi's and Katy's disgust, the lightning strike is exactly what happened a little further down the road. Thankfully not directly hitting any of our party, but it landed rocket style with an incredibly loud "ZIP ... CRACK!" only about ten metres away. I'd never seen lightning strike the ground before and hadn't realised that a bolt zips upwards to meet the strike coming down (all to do with positive and negative charges apparently). It took me a moment to realise what had happened and the same could be said for the owners of the garden it hit.

The husband, clearly confused, poked his head out of the garage in which he was sheltering to see what had happened, as his wife appeared at the back door of the house asking him, "What the hell have you done? You have just tripped the electricity in the WHOLE house!" Defusing the argument that was about to commence, I explained about what I'd just witnessed and the probable cause of their power cut and lack of lights.

"You'd be safer indoors!" the chap stated obviously, pointing at our slightly stunned group. Although the couple, now a united force, declined to allow the four horses and four riders to enter either house or garage. With no choice but to continue, we carried on through the rain, negotiating flash floods of biblical proportions. Thankfully, the thunder and lightning had also moved on, deciding they'd had enough sport with us that day. About an hour later, the sun came out to steam dry us as we rode along, perfectly verifying the reality of Scotland and its four seasons in one day.

Bolstered by the exceptional lunch and the continued sunshine, (but wary of a rainy repeat performance), we hit the trail once more. Skye was oblivious to this dramatic memory as she hadn't been in the soaking team that day, and was keenly working her way along the track that leads out of the valley down towards Cluny Castle. The scenery in this section is spectacular as the trail weaves its merry way along, facing the view across to the southern array of the Grampian Mountains. With every twist and turn you'd glimpse different snow scattered tops which appeared to wink and wave at us from their distant abodes.

"That grass is also waving at me from over there," said Skye, as she looked to the side of the trail.

"It's all in your head you know Skye, you've just had a good half hour grassy break," I replied.

"But I'm worried about starving to death in these treacherous mountains!" she snorted.

"Honestly there is no chance you will starve to death!" I said, given how widely my legs were wrapped around her large belly.

"My genetic make-up reminds me that it's sensible to keep an eye on all grass opportunities you can," she replied in defence.

"An EYE though not TEETH!" I shouted, as she attempted to snatch a clump to rip it from its roots.

The trail eventually emerged from the glen, seemingly in the back garden of the castle. It didn't feel quite right to be riding so close to the residence, on meticulously maintained gravel driveways splitting lovingly lopped lawns. I'd always sincerely pleaded with Swogi not to leave a messy, smelly deposit right in the heart of this immaculate neatness. This time, however, the pleading request was concentrated on imploring Skye not to leave hoof marks on the grass or destroy the garden's flowers on either side of the drive as she was tempted by a nibble or two.

Cluny Castle was the strong hold of the MacPherson clan, who originally sided with the King of England. The Camerons (allegedly) showed them the errors of their ways and they swapped to the cause of the Jacobites. The MacPhersons then became part of a unique confederation of twelve separate clans, grouped together under the identity of Clan Chattan.

Clan Chattan supported the cause of Charles Edward Stuart (Charles III aka Bonnie Prince Charlie). Following the Jacobite defeat at the Battle of Culloden, Cluny Castle was burnt to the ground by government soldiers - no doubt as Bonnie Prince Charlie made his famous romantic escape into the hills and stopped in every cave, sheiling, and hollow along the way (or so every tourist attraction claims) before running off to the safety of France.

Queen Victoria is reputed to have considered buying the rebuilt castle but must have viewed the property on a day like I described earlier, as she decided the weather was too inclement in this area. Instead she purchased

Balmoral on the other side of the Cairngorms. I, however, can testify first-hand that you can experience four seasons in one day on that side of the hills too.

We could of course avoid the castle grounds completely, but the alternative route would place us on a twisty section of the A86. This main road link between the Spey Valley and the west of Scotland has frequent, fast traffic with locals, tourists, and convoys of freight vehicles that aren't fun to play with on a pony. I generally try to avoid riding on the roads because I would not describe either of my horses as bombproof in traffic. If truth be told, I'm not sure I would consider any horse to meet this term's criteria. Bombproof is a horsey term used to describe horses that don't spook (get scared) at anything. Many a horse dealer could be heard to exclaim, "You could set a bomb off under that one and they wouldn't blink an eye!" in order to try and secure a sale.

However, horses are flight animals with an initial reaction to run from trouble rather than turn to face it, so even the most docile of creature will meet his or her spooky nemesis at some point. My horses weren't really all that bad in traffic and rarely get spooked, it's just that these days it is the traffic that is bad. A huge number of modern drivers seem to have lost the ability to slow down for either cyclist or animal and somehow expect you to be able to jump out of their way in that blink of an eye. Actually, many think you shouldn't even be using 'their' road in the first place.

There are exceptions of course, and I'm pleased to report that the courteous and understanding still appear to significantly outweigh the rude and rushed. However, many drivers in their impatience have forgotten that horses can be unpredictable beasts that can be spooked by a fast moving, noisy, or bigger vehicle, particularly if driven too close. You see fewer horses using roads on a day-to-day basis and drivers just aren't used to dealing with them. They treat horses like bicycles which are often viewed as an inanimate object anyway, despite the real live person powering it along. They are viewed as a curse too for getting in the way of that faster pace of life and that important meeting the driver is running late for. Some drivers have forgotten that horses appreciate a bit of personal space and would be grateful if you just slowed down a bit so that your vehicle is a little less scary, particularly on wet days when there is the strange noise of the wheels through puddles and the surprise splash of water to contend with.

I'd experienced the 'too close too fast' twice and that was two too many for me. It only takes one idiot a fraction of a second to wipe out your horse, your dreams, and your life. Maybe I was getting soft in my older age, but roads were certainly busier, and drivers appeared to be faster. As a paramedic, I've also experienced first-hand too many times how quickly lives can be changed by the ill-considered actions of others.

So through the castle grounds we crept and, leaving nothing behind other than footprints, we appeared by the A86 at the castle entrance gateway. From here we could scurry a short distance along a verge to converge with a minor road that loops away, runs parallel for a kilometre, then turns back to the main road again. There we could directly cross the main road, walk through some fields, parallel to the road again, cross back over the A86 once more, and weave our way through a long series of fields as we worked our way up behind farms and back into the hills again.

This was a section that took more than its fair share of time to recce! It's also a section where the landowners don't exactly welcome you with open arms, but as long as you responsibly close all the (numerous) gates behind you, stay to the tracks or edges of fields, and don't cause any damage, then you have every right to use it according to Scottish Law. I still felt like I was tiptoeing through the area however, as I didn't feel like I had the energy or eloquence to deal with an edgy encounter with an irate laird. I was still feeling fatigued, rough, and devoid of strength with increasing aches and pains. My thigh bones were pulsing with a deep-seated throb which was particularly uncomfortable and unnerving.

I asked Yvonne for her opinion as to why I might be feeling like this, as one of her useful qualifications is that of a nurse. Hadn't I been pushing myself too hard, in the run up and during this adventure with the many hours in the saddle and the on foot/bike reconnaissance, she queried? Her conclusion - that the amount that I had done, would be likely to cause fatigue and achy legs in anyone - only partially satisfied my concerns.

As I looked back at Yvonne, my concern turned to complete amusement and the moment of unease rapidly vanished. Unbeknown to Yvonne, it seemed that her habitual, cheerful renditions of melodies had lifted her status to that of a type of Pied Piper with the local sheep population. On the track behind her flowed a long flock of at least fifty frolicking sheep, and unusually they seemed to be in somewhat high spirits.

Maybe I'd found the answer to tackle the constant depression of sheep, and all that they require is a singing shepherd to lighten up their lives. We watched, enthralled, as they continued to cheerfully tag along behind us to the very edge of the field, joining in with Yvonne's tunes with random bleating zeal. It seemed such a shame to firmly close the gate on the eager baa baa choir and to abandon the group of happy little faces as we left the farmland behind.

Dropping down through a small woodland (singing "Mary Had a Little Lamb"), we emerged onto the single-track road that led to the west coast of Scotland, only if you were prepared to head over the hills on the rough track of the Corrieyairack Pass. Somewhere a little way along this road, we should find our pile of tents and other required camping gear for the night. That is, of course, if the planning session yesterday had ... well ... gone to plan!

Luckily the best laid plans of mice and men, that often go awry, had not done so this time and we were delighted and relieved to find our kit piled neatly in the correct field, thoughtfully covered by a tarpaulin to fend off any rain. Tonight, we had hired a field so we could simply let the ponies out to graze without expending time and energy to build a corral.

"We are happy with the WHOLE field!" gabbled Katy between huge mouthfuls of grass, "No need at all for any grass limiting corral!"

We didn't even need to play the water bucket filling game as the field had a fresh stream bubbling through it. Had Swift been here, I suspect that she would have been a little disappointed. She always seemed to enjoy the evening ritual of amusing herself at my weary expense at the end of a long day. We popped our tents up in record time, looked at our watches, and within seconds both deduced that two and a half kilometres was no distance at all to walk to the pub. Yvonne's craving for Diet Coke is often as strong as mine for a pint of real ale, so we both thought nothing of agreeing, that this was a very fine idea indeed.

Before we left, we set off in opposite directions around the field to double check the fence strength and to confirm that the field didn't contain anything that might harm a curious and bumbling Highland Pony. We finished our pub preparation by sectioning our tents off from the horses with a short line of electric tape. These ponies will eat anything, and often like to find a comfy bed to lie down on.

Despite anticipation of a long cold drink and a plate of hot food, the two and a half kilometres seemed a long old way to walk. It certainly seemed a long old way when we arrived at the pub only to find it actually wasn't open yet. Thankfully the bar staff took pity on us and let us in for a pre-dinner drink whilst we waited for them to become fully staffed and operational.

Yvonne had left a message for her brother to say that we were in the area, and we'd not long ordered food when he arrived through the door to join us for a meal. A pleasant evening was had all round, with a good feed to help us on our onwards journey. The brotherly lift back to our tents was very much appreciated indeed, and with a quick wave goodnight to the still eating Katy and Skye, we were soon snuggled down in sleeping bags for a good night's sleep.

Day 13:
Laggan to Melgarve
(Distance 16km, Ascent 233m)

We awoke to a day similar to the last, with patches of blue sky interspersed with white fluffy clouds and the feeling that it was going to stay dry. We didn't have all that far to travel today and it would be an easy ride along a tarmac glen road. I generally try to avoid the asphalt, but when it's a traffic free, scenic glen road, I can find it in myself to forgive its monotony.

Unrushed, we had our breakfast and took down the tents. Katy and Skye were happily grazing the grass, flank to flank a little distance away, enjoying the sunny morning in the lee of the craggy ridge that rose out of the field. With the saddle bags packed up, we stored the excess equipment under the tarpaulin where we'd found it. According to the detail in the plan, this would be picked up later by my long-suffering husband and delivered to our next overnight stop at a lovely bothy at the head of the glen.

Turning around to go and collect the ponies, we found them both still flank to flank, not grazing now though, but lying down completely fast asleep. Now I'm aware of the proverb 'let sleeping dogs lie' but I've not heard any advice proposed with respect to the correct procedure for dealing with napping nags. Whilst we decided on the best course of action, we took advantage of their lower and stationary status to slip headcollars gently over their hibernating heads.

Patiently waiting at the respective ends of our lead ropes, not a lot was happening; just the sounds of snores and the birds in the trees and a trail that was eagerly calling. The rhythmic snores were soothing, but we needed to get on our way. The ponies looked snuggled in for the day and waiting a few hours for them to surface from slumbers, wasn't really an option.

I gave Skye's rope a testing tug and, in return, was offered a sigh and a grunt but no movement of any feet at all. I could see that Yvonne was having a similar experience at the end of her lead rope too. In fact, Yvonne had now found herself in a worse predicament than myself, as Katy had flopped flat out and was feigning Requiescat in pace. Playing dead (or thanatosis to give its proper name) is often used as a defence mechanism by a wide variety of animals. When used by an animal as heavy as a Highland Pony, I have to say it is exceedingly effective.

Together we concentrated on encouraging Skye to her feet. Our theory was that Katy, hating to be alone, would also scramble to her feet if we led Skye a short way across the field towards the awaiting saddles. Pulling on her lead rope as Yvonne pushed at Skye's bottom, I enticed her with tales of lush green grass just around the first corner of the trail. With fingers crossed firmly behind my back, I promised I'd let her eat the whole damn lot if she'd just get up on her feet.

I expected the usual 'Make me if you can' type of response, one I'd become accustomed to hearing after every single request I made. Although this was an automatic retort of mischief from Skye, it was a threat she rarely had the dedication to carry through on, and usually did what was requested only a moment later. This time however, with the added encouragement from front and back, I think we took her by surprise as she jumped up rather sharply, giving herself a shake from nose to tail with no impish objection at all.

Yvonne resumed her hopeful watch at the end of Katy's lead rope, and I led Skye away to the fence where our saddles and bags were impatiently waiting. I tied Skye to a tree, which she happily started stripping of anything even remotely green, and turned to see how Yvonne was getting on. The brunt of the matter was that she wasn't getting on at all. The only thing that had changed was that Katy had stretched her head round slightly so she could see where her daughter and pal had gone. The eye that had observed this movement was now fully closed again, back to fulfilling its primary duty of facilitating forty winks.

Highland snoozes

As a team, we again attempted the same technique deployed on Skye, this time me pushing at the rather round and ample bottom of Katy and Yvonne whispering temptations into her ears. The technique, although eventually effective, took more pushing and pulling this time round and involved more sweat and tears in order to achieve the desired results. We did now have a second standing pony, though, and could resume our plans for the day. Soon saddled up and good to go, we set off along the quiet glen road, heading west towards the Corrieyairack Pass.

Katy has always had an opposite passion to me: she loves the feeling of asphalt under her hooves. She prefers this any day to stumbling around tricky trails in the hills. Mostly I think because with the plain and even surface to walk on, she doesn't have to engage her brain on the distracting task of managing ideal feet placement. Instead her brain can be fully deployed on admiring the scenery around her, becoming totally absorbed into her current daydream or identifying the next clump of grass she is going to make a beeline for.

Yvonne and I were both somewhat surprised, therefore, when Katy refused to move forward at all. In fact, worse than merely planting her feet, an action that Yvonne was by now well acquainted with on this trip, she was adamant that turning about was the only thing to do. Back to the field with the lovely grass and that comfy spot upon which to continue her kip.

Skye hadn't exactly attacked the day with exuberance either, but at least she was content to move forward along the road like a teenager dragging her feet. The scuff, scuff, scuff, scuff sounds from all four feet were spoiling the ambiance slightly, but nothing compared to the frustrated expletives currently being emitted from my usually calm and collected trail partner.

Yvonne and Katy were wrapped in a web of ever decreasing circles, but with Katy determined to set off on a tangent, I wasn't sure how to help the rotational pair. If I went back and approached with Skye, then that would give Katy a stronger case for facing the wrong way too ("Are we all going back to the field then?"). I tried continuing along the road to hopefully intensify Katy's monophobia (fear of being left alone) and promote her advancement in the right direction, but this plan didn't prove to be overly effective, and I just found myself further and further ahead.

Doing nothing didn't exactly feel supportive of my struggling friend either. Since I was currently riding one of her ponies and it happened to be the only pony that was doing as it should, I felt particularly guilty. In my indecisiveness I'd come to a halt, but before I could make a choice between the rock and the hard place, Yvonne had jumped off and was making better progress leading Katy from the ground.

Highland ponies, as I've said before, are incredibly strong, particularly in the neck department. For what I would describe as a chunky Highland Pony with strong muscles in all four corners, Katy was also incredibly agile and bendy. Even if you could find the strength to turn her head in the direction you wished to travel, if Katy didn't want to go that way, then her body could completely stay where it was, facing up to 180 degrees in the opposite direction.

I totally felt for Yvonne and knew that she stood no chance at all up on top. The day was hot, but Yvonne's face was redder than any angry emoji I'd ever deployed online. I tentatively suggested that she ride the scuffing Skye while I continued the combat with the cantankerous Katy. My trail partner, however, is nothing if not determined and I was met with a resounding, "No way, I have to win this particular battle!"

We scuffed, huffed, and often halted along in this manner for a while. Skye eventually picked her feet up more and Katy seemed to become resigned to another day on the trail. Yvonne jumped back up and we both held our breath to see what happened. Thankfully, nothing out of the ordinary occurred and Katy finally followed Skye along the road with only the occasional orbiting objection.

It had seemed to take an age to get here, but we were finally passing the nameless loch held in place by the Spey Dam. I'm not sure why it doesn't have a name; maybe mappers just ran out of ideas. It's near Laggan village but a sizeable loch of that name already exists. It is a loch created by slowing the flow of the River Spey, but Loch Spey gives its name to a smaller loch, the true but humble source of the mighty river further west. I'm all out of ideas too, so let's just call it 'Reservoir' as it is so meekly labelled on the map. 'Loch between Loch Spey and Laggan Village' sounds too much of a mouthful to me anyway.

The dam that forms it was built as a later part of the Lochaber scheme, the purpose of which was to provide power to Fort William. The aluminium works there were operating flat out from the beginning of WWII to support the increased deployment of air power in warfare. The dam enabled up to twenty percent of the River Spey's flow to be diverted to Loch Crunachdan and Loch Laggan, then onward to Fort William where it was used to generate the electricity and provide the cooling needed in the manufacturing process.

It might be nameless but the view across it is still one to behold. Looking back from the westerly reaches, its ill-defined edges splatter and splash their way to shore, creating a maze of interconnecting grass for the sheep to graze in amongst its waters. A small island, then a thin stretch of flat land on the far away shore, gives way to the rapid rise of triangular peaks.

Crossing the bridge at the west end of 'Reservoir', it is

strange to be hovering over a clean-sided channel (essentially a canal, stretching both left and right for as far as you can see) in such a remote and rugged landscape. Man's imprint is of course everywhere you look, but this seems somewhat coarse in its indentation in such a naturally pretty place. Also out of place is the thought that, way up here in the tranquil hills, there is an innocent mountain river that contributed so gallantly to the violent and thunderous war effort, fought so far away.

Leaving the views of 'Reservoir' and Loch Crunachdan behind, we emerged from some trees to see the Garvamore Kingshouse up ahead. This Kingshouse (an inn built on a king's highway) would have housed weary travellers in the 1700s of both a military and civilian ilk. The Corrieyairack Pass back then would have been one of Scotland's busier means of travel for the government troops, the resisting Jacobites, and the drovers just trying to make a living in amongst the unrest.

Prior to General Wade making this a road of military importance - enabling him to muster troops from Fort William/Fort Augustus in no time at all to the important Barracks at Ruthven and vice versa - this way through the hills was a historic and important drovers' route. Each year, cattle in their thousands would be walked from Glen Elg on the west coast, via Fort Augustus, over the Corrieyairack through to Dalwhinnie and onwards south to the tryst (or market) at Crieff.

The small black cattle (predecessors to the Highland cattle familiar today) arrived at Glen Elg after swimming across the shortest stretch of sea from Skye at Kylerhea, having been gathered from there and many of the Outer Hebridean Islands. Like us, the drovers put in long days on the hills, stopped wherever they could find grazing, and navigated through the hills in all types of Scottish weather. Whereas we had modern tents to shelter in, they would have had only their plaid (tartan cloth) for poor protection. I can't help but shudder at the thought of cold nights, spent cattle watching, under those meagre garments.

In another similarity, the drovers like me would have had porridge for breakfast and sometimes washed it down with a shot of whisky (never before eleven o'clock, honest!) but this is where the resemblance to my trail diet ends. The rest of their vittles were often limited to onions and black pudding (if they bled their cattle) and very little else.

"Onions?" interrupted Katy, her ears suddenly standing up on end. "I love those in a crisp ring type fashion!" "Are we going to meet any of these lovely drovers up there at the Inn?" she enquired, drooling a little.

I was about to reply with an explanation, but she had already set off eagerly. The thought of onion rings seemed to have perked Katy up a bit and she was striding out well. Nevertheless, we decided to stop near the old inn for a spot of lunch. As there was grass for the horses, we could take a look at the buildings and the pause would give us chance to pay homage to those who had travelled before. Drovers used Garvamore as a 'stance' to rest their cattle overnight as both grass and water were available here. I'm sure this tradition continued after the inn's construction and I like to think that this was one night, at least, where the drovers could find warmth and comfort rather than shivering under their plaids.

The inn would certainly have had a steady trade. Now boarded up and left to slowly perish, I'm sure it misses the hustle and bustle it once felt between its walls and under its roof. There would certainly be little warmth and comfort to find here now. Although that said, I could think of one particular bad weather trek, where Yvonne and I were truly grateful to find overnight shelter behind the stone wall of a crumbling building, away from the driving horizontal rain!

After the 'stance' of our own for lunch at Garvamore, Yvonne suggested we swapped ponies for a while. She wanted to prove to me just how well Katy can go (once you get her going that is) and, I think, wanted to illustrate why it is that she continues to work with such a stubborn mount. Understanding this struggle from working with my own two quirky mounts, especially Swift whose potential has been slow to materialise, I agreed to give her a try.

I'd only ridden Katy on her first ever ride when Yvonne, along with a friend and I, had sat on her for the first time in an arena, a process called 'backing' (or a term I don't like, 'breaking') a horse. Then, like now, she had had the same sticky feet and just didn't understand the process. Not minding a human on her back at all - usually the main challenge of the backing process - she would happily go sideways or backwards no bother, but a forwards motion just didn't seem to be one of her life-time goals.

Katy is an interesting, introverted individual to work with and Yvonne had come a long way with her indeed. Not only in terms of training but actual mileage too. Yvonne was doing a cross-Scotland adventure of her own and was now at approximately mile one hundred. I was interested to see what Katy felt like with more experience under her girth and I hoped it would give me insight into her character, particularly given that our journey onward would continue alone in only a few days' time.

Dreading the thought of stop-start times ahead, I was delighted to discover that this girl had an absolutely lovely stride. Only, of course, when she decides that you are pointing her in the direction of travel that she also wishes to go. She felt strong and safe and extremely comfortable too, a surprisingly long stride for the smaller height of a pony, which I really wasn't expecting.

"I get it," I said to Yvonne, "this one is worth the red face of frustration!"

I've scarcely had similar positive comments about Swift; rare they might be, but when you receive them, they are worth their weight in motivational gold. I hoped my appreciation would wipe the morning struggle just a little from Yvonne's mind and her overall impression of the day. Katy certainly seemed to have the opinion that this morning's battle of sticky feet and spirals had been forgotten.

Actually, she was now getting faster and faster and almost breaking into a trot. I didn't think the slight prospect of drovers carrying onions ring crisps could possibly be so effective, and my suspicions of another cause were soon realised when Katy came to a sudden halt. Her head up high, ears all perky and her nostrils spread out wide, she was pointing with every trembling muscle towards the field on the left. I didn't need to be a mind reader to work this signal out, and sure enough, three sets of similarly perky ears came thundering over the rise, attached to another three Highland ponies.

Katy, it seems, like to investigate every horse she meets, but especially if they are of the same breed as her. Yvonne isn't sure how she can distinguish Highland ponies from the variety of other breeds in the world, but Katy is insistent in stopping for a short conversation with every Highland pony along the trail. Katy used to be a broodmare and I hypothesised that maybe she was double checking whether these were any of her offspring or previous mates. Or perhaps Highland ponies have a specific communication channel and Katy is keen to hear the latest news and hot gossip from her section of society.

Pleasantries exchanged through a series of snorts, huffs, and neighs, and we were back on our way and about to cross the Garva Bridge. This bridge, originally named St George's Bridge (in honour of the King), was built by General Wade in 1732. It's not his usual humpbacked style but is more of a level roadway, perhaps influenced by the need for the bridge to span a wider breadth. It has a central buttress which rests on a rock midriver, but despite its wide girth, it has still suffered over the years from the frequent flood waters of the Spey.

It is a testament to the engineering skills of the time that it is still standing and is perfectly useable by traffic, although it's additionally strengthened by iron braces now. Its name, however, didn't stand the test of time and is more commonly referred to as Garva Bridge by Highlanders so far away from monarch veneration. Although this route was advantageous to both military and Jacobite movements through the hills, tales can be found of natives refusing to use this bridge, instead fording the river alongside. Drovers also complained that the stony construction of the road was hard on their bare feet and the soft feet of their cattle, too.

Skye and Katy didn't give two hoots about the politics

of the bridge's construction, they just knew that they'd rather use a bridge than get their feet wet any day of the week. At another river crossing a while before, when Yvonne and I were out with our team of four, mine had point blank refused to attempt a suspension bridge that swayed slightly. Yvonne's two, on the other hand, had point-blank refused to consider the ford of the river that flowed underneath. It was, after all, almost up to the top of their hooves!

I had watched in a mixture of horror, amusement, and awe as Yvonne calmly lead her staggering ponies over the small, wooden planked bridge as it rocked and swayed with every placement of hoof. Skye and Katy watched with a similar mixture of emotions as I made Swogi dip their toes in the cold, 'frightening' water to re-join them on the other side.

Every horse is different and knowing their strengths and weaknesses is what generally keeps you safe when travelling with them in challenging environments. I reflected again how lucky I was to be able to use these two ponies going forward to complete my trek. At least I knew their characters slightly, and knew a few of their absolute boundaries. The rest of those traits and limits would have to be carefully explored as I continued alone when the final days of the journey unfolded.

From the Garva Bridge it was only another five kilometres to our stance for the night. We soon arrived at the Melgarve bothy, opposite which is a handy field for containing the ponies. It is a rather large field and full of grass, so despite protests from 'starving' ponies we decided to section off a corner to contain them in a smaller area. The fencing in the larger field was also a little broken in places and would take a long time to fully secure.

Ponies all settled and sorted, we shared a laugh at a humorous memory of corralling horses here before. At least, we thought we had corralled them - once, twice, three times over. We were travelling with a friend who was riding a lovable rogue of a cob called Rikki-Roo and he was enormously into human rather than fellow equine company. We'd corralled them in the whole field and had checked and secured the fences well (we thought). Over at the bothy however, every time we turned around, we'd bump into Rikki-Roo standing right behind us as he had released himself from the field yet again and sought out the human company he so craved. It took several attempts to contain him with the others, but I think he would have been happier curling up by the fire in the bothy that night while the circle of conversation and laughter took place around him.

As heavy rain settled in for the night, I totally shared his sentiment. I was grateful for a roof over our heads tonight as a step up in protection and space from my little tent. Again, the exhaustion washed over me in a wave; this was supposed to have been an *easy* ride up the Glen today, but the morning quarrels with Katy had taken its toll on the whole team. The battle scars were soon forgotten with the arrival of Dave with our additional kit and additional friends too. A surprise visit from Sophie and Frankie - friends from our hometown - who thoughtfully brought some wine and Diet Coke was most welcome indeed. The real fire in the bothy, good company, and a tipple or two whiled away the evening in fine fashion as the rain lashed down outside.

I quizzed Dave about things back home - checking that Yogi, Swift and the dogs were all okay. Although Skye was going well for me, I really missed my Team Swogi. I missed the familiarity, the deep connection you feel with your horses from hours on the trail together. You get to know them 'inside out' and can interpret every tiny signal offered: a twitch of an ear, a head gesture, a flick of a tail, the way their bodies move, their likes and dislikes, and their individual personalities. This deep understanding creates predictability, a sense of rhythm and unified oneness. I wasn't there yet with Skye and Katy and was unlikely to achieve such depth in only a few days together. The extent of the relationship with Team Swogi has been slowly built over many years and as a result, the multitude of layers has increased the intensity of our bond - and I missed this dearly.

As I did the final damp night-time check on the ponies, I marvelled at their ability to completely ignore the weather. These Highland ponies were tough, and with thick coats and manes they rarely noticed which of the four seasons was happening around them in one day. Swogi would have been huddled miserably in a corner somewhere and I would probably have had to move them into the lee of the bothy for them to properly rest. Not these hardy gals, though, they were happily munching the grass completely oblivious to the storm.

Day 14:
Melgarve to Fort Augustus
(Distance 22km, Ascent 540m)

We poked our heads out of the bothy in the morning, expecting the worst of weather, but could hardly believe our luck. The rain had completely blown over and we were faced with yet another patchy blue sky and fluffy white clouds type of day. The wind was a little stronger and more cooling, but that was totally fine considering we had the steep climb of the pass to complete today (to approximately 780 metres).

I checked on the ponies and they were lying down. Not wanting a repeat of yesterday's fiasco, I hoped they would get their snoozes over with whilst we ate breakfast and packed the bags. It was a subdued but sociable breakfast with a few sore heads to nurse. The added luxuries brought in by surprise friends to the trail sometimes had their drawbacks.

Gradually the kit made its way either into our saddle bags for the day's climb into the hills, or back to the car for husband-to-husband transfer. Yvonne's husband Adrian would be taking over the logistical support and would meet us later today in Fort Augustus. We were again ready to hit the trail and I tentatively poked my head around the corner of the bothy to see what position the ponies were now parked in.

Breathing a sigh of relief that their pose was perpendicular rather than parallel to the ground, we grabbed the headcollars and hastily caught the twosome before this situation changed. Soon saddled up and ready to go, we paused to admire the view a while longer while the ponies grabbed the last few mouthfuls of grass beside the walls of the bothy. How they found any morsel to munch was a mystery, as the sheep seemed to have done a fine job of mowing this rough land into a meticulous golf-style green.

We jumped on board and rounded the bothy to start the rough track up over the pass. At least, I started slowly up the rough track with Skye, but Katy was back in point blank refusal mode and wasn't going anywhere. Katy and Skye had both walked this track a couple of years before, but I guess that Katy's memory is superior to Skye's. Katy could remember that this track unwinds in an upwards fashion for most of the day and, having seen the view from the top already, she wasn't particularly interested in the effort of climbing to see it again.

So I found myself in the same predicament as yesterday, not knowing the best way to help and feeling rather guilty that I was riding the one pony of Yvonne's who wasn't malfunctioning. Katy was running rings around Yvonne again and a sparring match commenced. Katy had the edge on physicality for sure, and had initially beaten Yvonne to the punch, but by the look on Yvonne's face, I could tell that she had the killer instinct and my bet was straight and on the nose.

I have to admit, I've never before seen a pony try so strongly but passively to get out of a day's work. No matter what Yvonne tried to do, she just couldn't get any hooves to move. It was a kind of sit-in protest; Katy was refusing to come out of the corner for the next round, and I was beginning to wonder if she had hand-cuffed her hooves to the corner stool. Yvonne, not paying any attention to the bell, was bit-by-bit winning the match and I could see that Katy was about to throw in the towel. What none of us expected was for her to spring into action, backwards, up over the bank and into the ditch behind.

I considered, as they all but disappeared from view, that this could possibly have been anticipated, as - even from the start of her ridden career - Katy's preferred direction certainly wasn't forwards. The reaction however was a little extreme, just to get out of walking up a hill. The struggle to get out of the ditch would surely take much more energy than just complying with Yvonne's initial uphill request. I could hear the dark match continuing out of sight, and they finally reappeared still clinched together in a bout. Extraction from the ditch was happening in a forward motion, which was progress of some sort, under explicit, expletive instructions from Yvonne.

It was by no means a clean finish but being against the ropes seemed to shock Katy into compliance, although I wouldn't call it rolling with the punches just yet. Step, by step, with more 'encouragement' than you can ever imagine from Yvonne, she was beginning to edge towards the patiently waiting Skye. Edge is an apt and illustrative term for the action, as it was somewhat crab-like in its presentation. With Katy keeping one eye firmly on the field full of grass that she wished to return to, Yvonne was gaining small amounts of ground in a sideways fashion.

Any ground gained was good, and I was pleased that Yvonne was emerging victorious, but it was going to take forever to proceed in this manner for the rest of the day's ride. After another ten minutes of crustacean scuttles, Yvonne felt she had done enough to prove her point and jumped off once again to lead the belligerent beast from the ground and to try and make some faster progress.

To give Katy her due, the track was in a poor state of repair and was difficult under foot. The stones were loose and rugged, and advancement felt like two steps forward and one step back. It wasn't long before I too felt I needed to help Skye by jumping off myself. Last time here we had ridden the horses all the way to the apex of the pass, but it appeared that this time we were going to spend the majority of the climb walking on our own two feet.

I don't know whether the condition of the trail had been affected by the installation of the controversial Beauly to Denny power lines, or whether this was purely due to erosive weather. Whichever of those two options, it was certainly in a poor old state. The power line construction companies used their own access roads into the hills to assemble the ugly and menacing structures, so close to this historical by-way, but I did wonder what could have destroyed the track so completely if it wasn't vehicular traffic.

General Wade, proud of the quality of his road, would surely be turning in his grave. On the other hand, General Wade may have been impressed and distracted by the feat of engineering the power line involved. The line is around 225 kilometres long, is supported by approximately 600 pylons (some more than sixty metres high), and it runs through extremely inaccessible terrain with the highest point at the apex of the Corrieyairack at 770 metres.

The upgrade was apparently essential to tie renewable electricity projects in the north of Scotland into the National Grid. Protesters, however, felt that other methods of tie-in would be more appropriate in areas of natural beauty, particularly across the National Park and alongside historical structures such as one of the most famous of General Wade's military roads. Underground cables were contemplated, somewhat briefly, but were reportedly too expensive. Considering that the choice of constructing pylons cost around two and a half times the original estimate (totals reaching £820 million so far), the underground option may well have been within monetary scope.

I have to say walking through this beautiful country now, with a peaceful pony on one side and towering pylons on the other, that I agree with a quote I found in the Scottish Herald; "[The power line's] impact on the Highland landscape was compared to taking a razor blade to a Rembrandt." Perhaps, however, the same was felt about General Wade's road at the time and all progress causes scars.

General Wade's construction was no mean feat of engineering either. In 1731, choice of machinery would have been from slim pickings, and protection for working in severe weather conditions at remote locations would have been fairly non-existent. Constructed by 510 Hanoverian soldiers in just one summer, the route crosses the Monadhliath mountains covering forty-five kilometres and reaches heady heights.

The road climbs the steepest section by traversing the hillside in a series of switchbacks. Originally eighteen in number, but later reduced to thirteen, each one was retained or supported by a stone and mortar wall on the outside. It became the highest public road in Britain and was so well constructed that the folks of the time allegedly likened it to the Roman roads of the south. Despite its robust construction, attempted crossings in winter resulted in overturned carriages, blown over by high winds, and deaths of several soldiers. Some deaths were attributed to intoxication after too much whisky at the Garvamore Kingshouse, but I find that hard to believe as, by the time they had staggered up to the top of the pass, they must have surely sobered up. The weather was harsh in those days though and anyone who didn't make it over the top was often only retrieved in spring.

The Corrieyairack (meaning either Corrie of the Short Burn or Red Corrie) is one of the best-known of Wade's roads. It is also the longest surviving stretch of Wade road in Britain and holds the title of a Scheduled Ancient Monument of national importance. How on earth the Beauly to Denny power line was given permission to construct so close to it, I have no idea.

Perhaps if they had looked at General Wade's accounts as inspiration for cost estimates, they may have been able to afford to do something with less unsightly impact. At £90 per mile and only £466 spent on five bridges (totalling around £350,000 in today's money), there is something wrong about the price tag of modern construction methods and certainly something amiss about how they calculate costs in the first instance, always estimating so widely low of the mark.

As we climbed to the higher reaches, the track surface improved and we could jump back up on the ponies to ride. We traversed the steep terrain in a tennis game of back and forth, and the view behind us became spectacular as we looked back down the glen we had ascended. The road we had travelled criss-crossed the countryside, before finding its way directly down the dale and disappearing out of view. The noise of trucks and machinery moving dustily around us during construction somewhat spoilt the atmosphere in more ways than one.

Reaching the peak of the pass, looking over the other side of the mighty Monadhlaiths, we were faced with huge pylons and wind farms on every hillside we could see in the distance. Scatterings of stone cairn stacks were all about the place too, not used for traditional way finding, just idle hands creating clutter. The naturalness of the landscape was destroyed, no sense of beauty or timelessness felt here, despite the wide expanse of view and accounts of historical significance.

At other moments in my journey across the land, I could almost touch and taste the history of the spot in which I stood, as so little had changed over the years; but here all I could witness was a sad future for places of wilderness. Whereas the snow scattered peaks of the Southern Grampians had winked and waved at us from afar in Glen Banchor, the snow sprinkles in the distance here had their eyes firmly closed in disgust.

Saddened and disheartened at the spoiling of the whole panorama, we didn't linger long on the top and started to make our way down the stretched-out descent into Fort Augustus. The descent, less steep on the western side, undulates and winds its way slowly down to the southernmost tip of Loch Ness. The heather and peat make way for grass and ferns and the lower you progress, the greener it becomes. Several of General Wade's bridges on the descent now had modern parallel substitutes made from steel and heavy-duty wooden planks. Large boulders placed at each end of the Wade's bridges, to deter vehicular crossing, gave the impression that the new bridges would be the safer of the two options.   They certainly looked strong enough, especially when compared to the crumbling stone of the older alternatives.

On crossing the second such bridge, from the back end of Katy we heard a load "CRAAACK!" as one of her hind feet disappeared through a patch of rotten wood. Both ponies shot forward to reach the other side in a startled assembly. Luckily, Katy, with the advantage of four-wheel drive, still had three feet firmly secured to propel her forward and hadn't fallen through.

"Is anything built to last these days?" I appealed to the bridge that so nearly let us down, then said to the whole team: "I think we should stick to the original creations, more likely designed with hooves in mind!"

"I totally agree," Katy shakily replied.

"There's grass on Wade's bridges!" said Skye with a cheeky smile.

Yvonne was unusually quiet as she searched in her pocket for a medicinal and shock-relieving Mars Bar.

These bridges were spanning the variety of tributaries that run to the River Tarff to our right. The steep-sided Tarff scores its wandering way through the land at the base of the Glendoe Forest (another area now devoid of the later part of its name), supplying nutrients to feed the narrow and wooded glen that follows the river's path. General Wade's path follows its wandering way too, finally arriving at Fort Augustus with a more direct approach.

Fort Augustus, as you can probably surmise, wasn't the original name of the town. Previously known as Cille Chumein, after St Cummein who built a church there, the new name was imposed during fortifications to deal with the Jacobite uprisings and was renamed in honour of William Augustus, the younger son of King George II.

The fort no longer remains, but part of it was reused when building the Benedictine Abby in 1876. I'm sure St Cummein would find this ironic undertaking of recycling suitably agreeable to him.

Just as the track turns to face Fort Augustus for the final advance, you pass the entrance track to the Blackburn bothy. Tucked away from the main trail, it would be easy to miss, perhaps irritatingly so, when most needed in foul weather with diminished visibility. Possibly a former stalkers' hut, it's a basic shelter of only one room and a simple fireplace but welcome shelter nevertheless when needed by wet or weary travellers.

Looking back up the pass we had descended, the start of the day seemed a huge distance away. On adventures such as these I always marvel at how far you can travel if you just keep going step by step. You don't need to be fast, but it helps not to dawdle and it's beneficial to keep one eye on the horizon.

With the descent complete, we reached our first bit of tarmac and deviated off to the right, to approach Fort Augustus by passing the bunk house we were to stay in that night. We stripped the ponies of bags and saddles there, then continued into the centre of town to meet the canal where it effectively splits the town in two halves, with the staircase of five locks broaching the drop down into Loch Ness.

I'm sure many a foreign tourist leaves Fort Augustus scratching their heads with confusion over the difference between lochs and locks. I'd tell them not to worry as both are pretty in their own right, and it's easy to while away the hours sitting by the side of either word. Just as well really, as that is exactly what Yvonne, the ponies, and I found ourselves doing.

We had arranged to borrow a field not far from the

cascade of locks, but had arrived to find the gate padlocked and had no joy trying to connect with the owner by phone. It was a sunny day, there was grass by the locks to keep the ponies happy, and with an endless supply of ice-cream, Diet Coke, and real ale, the humans were happy too. Waiting here, boat and people-watching in the sunshine, wasn't exactly a hardship and it was a fitting way to celebrate the end of Yvonne's cross-Scotland journey. Like the Caledonian Canal itself, Yvonne had traversed from the Moray coast in the east to Fort Augustus in the west and was ending her trek here before returning to work.

A couple of cruiser boats descended the locks and I contemplated how impressive it must have been to see the tall ships of the day doing the same in the past. The Caledonian Canal was built to fulfil two different objectives. One was to link together the lochs of the Great Glen, providing a safe route for military and merchant ships as the route between the east coast at Inverness and the west coast at Fort William would avoid the perilous seas of the Pentland Firth and Cape Wrath.

Designed by none other than Thomas Telford himself, it opened in 1822 and made use of Loch Dochfour, Loch Ness, Loch Oich, and Loch Lochy with only a third of the sixty-mile distance consisting of man-made canals to link them all together. It has twenty-nine locks, four aqueducts, and ten bridges at various points along its course.

The second motive that helped to secure government funding to instigate this colossal project, was to try and reduce unemployment in the Highlands and reduce migrations following the Highland Clearances. The build took around twelve years to complete and employed over three thousand people during construction. Like General Wade's road, the canal today enjoys the title of a Scheduled Ancient Monument of national importance.

As I sat back, lazily enjoying my sips of beer, my thoughts moved onto the future and the continuation of my journey tomorrow. There's no denying, it was going to be hard work on my own with the Highland Duo with their slower speed and stacks of stubbornness. I watched Katy and Skye, so totally relaxed in the hustle and bustle of mid-town tourism, and accepted that sometimes their pros outweighed their cons. This would have been a sensory overload for Team Swogi and we would have been forced to wait somewhere quiet, further away from the town's luxuries, with an unfortunate absence of ale.

I too was finding the sights and sounds of this small but busy town an insult to my senses. The volume of people and the noise they created was a shock after the peace of the hills. It reminded me of arriving in Kathmandu or Delhi to hectic, street-filled chaos after many days kayaking along the serenity of the Sun Kosi, Brahmaputra, or other Himalayan Rivers. The rivers were serene in their calm setting of nature, but were an exciting course to paddle.

These were adventures of a similar nature to the one currently unfolding. The comparable pack up and move on each day to face challenges unknown, with a heavy reliance on self-resolve to negotiate yourself safely through the rapids. This is also where they differed however, as there was more of a human team to lean on, all looking out for each other to form rescue if or when required.

I'd be alone moving on again tomorrow (in terms of human companions anyway), and whilst Highland ponies might not be my favourite equines to travel with, they do have their plus points. In a sweep of generalisation here, I dislike their slowness of thought and their heaviness of movement, and I'd never be inclined to describe any Highland as 'delicate or precise'. However, in terms of hardiness, durability, and unspookability, you'd be hard pushed to find a superior sort. Putting prejudice and presumption aside, I knew I was lucky to have such steady steeds for company on my onward journey.

They were certainly every child's favourite on the canal side today, and poor Yvonne was doing her bit for the breed's promotion. Answering an excess of questions and succumbing to a queue of doe-eyed kids wanting a short bareback ride on Katy, she was a little swamped. I made my excuses and a rapid retreat on the justification of a clue as to where I could find the code to the field's padlock.

Returning triumphant, half a pony queue later, we both escaped to the quiet of the field and settled the ponies in for the night. Back at the bunkhouse when Yvonne's husband, Adrian, arrived with the additional equipment, I repacked and reorganised to set off alone tomorrow. A hot shower, some wholesome hot pub grub, and a toast to Yvonne's successful completion, and I was more than ready for bed.

Day 15:
Fort Augustus to Invergarry
(Distance 25km, Ascent 269m)

I awoke early to the return of the funny feeling in the pit of my stomach caused by nerves. Would I really be safe continuing along on challenging trails with ponies I didn't know so well? I certainly wasn't looking forward to Katy's morning tantrums, and wondered if I genuinely had enough strength to deal with them. There was only one way to find out about all my worries I suppose. I had to make an attempt, at the very least for my own determined sanity, but also for those who had so generously supported my venture with sponsorship for PFK.

Yvonne helped me to prepare the ponies, giving me last-minute tips on how to handle their individual characteristics, and giving last-minute goodbyes to her little treasures. After a great big hug from me and a solemn promise to look after her ponies better than I would my own, she watched as I set off along the canal side heading south on the Great Glen Way. I had the strong feeling that half of Yvonne didn't want her journey to be over and was wistfully watching me continue mine. The other half, I think, was occupied with curiosity and amusement, wondering how I would cope as I set off with both of her headstrong friends.

The grass by the canal side was beautifully speckled with white, purple, and yellow flowers, but I didn't have long to admire it. Up ahead was a large barge coming our way, and I was faced with my first 'unknown' regarding my new companion's opinions. Swift would have been curious and Yogi a little scared, but between us all we would have proceeded past with minimal fuss. With Katy and Skye I had no idea what was about to happen, so I moved them over to the right of the track, giving more room between ponies and barge. As the large, chugging, water-spurting boat came closer, I talked to the ponies out loud about times gone by when they would have been expected to pull such a barge along this very canal (minus engine of course).

"Horses were especially used during the time of the canal's construction you know, when the barges would be heavy with materials and equipment for the build. It would have been much harder work than anything Yvonne or I ask you to do, you really are very lucky ponies indeed. There's nothing special about the barge on our left though, so it's not even worth a glance..."

I'm pretty sure both ponies completely ignored my ramblings, but it helped to calm *my* nerves at least. They, of course, completely ignored the barge spluttering by as well and were far more interested in the longer vegetation waving in temptation in front of their noses on this side of the trail. Knowing I wouldn't let them drop their heads to the grass to eat, Skye reached up and pulled a large branch down to nibble the leaves of a tree instead.

When Skye finally let go of her wound up sprig, she released it toward her two travelling companions with a flourish. It whacked into me hard and nearly knocked me right off. It then continued its propelled journey directly into Katy's face, and triggered her first hoof moving refusal with me. As Skye continued to bend both rules and branches, I tried to coerce Katy into compliance.

Like Yvonne, nothing I tried would work. No number of tugs to encourage her forward had any effect, as she would effortlessly win any tug-o-war game with her mass. No turns to try sideways had any consequence either, as Katy was agile enough to bend head to tail without moving her feet. In a battle of strength or elasticity, I was always going to lose. I needed to acquire some cunning. I took a deep breath and tried not to think of the tough trails and long way to go ahead. I could walk the rest of the way to the west with a pony in each hand if I had to, but it wasn't exactly what I had planned. I thought back to the struggle yesterday morning at the start of General Wade's Road and had a small light bulb moment. If Katy's preferred option was backwards, then maybe I could unstick her feet using that direction of travel instead - but hopefully without ditch diving this time.

Pulling Skye out of the hedge with one hand, I started waggling the lead rope to Katy with the other. Both heads came up and both looked annoyed, but Katy more so as she lifted her head higher, trying to avoid the rope tickling her chin. Encouraged, I waggled some more and, to avoid the discomfort, Katy lifted her head further then took one step back in disgust. As soon as this foot was unstuck, I asked it to move forward with a firm tug and suddenly we were on the go once more.

I was so pleased that I hadn't needed to dismount, but I did wonder whether this was a permanent solution or just a one trick pony. I decided not to care too much just now, as it was a victory of cunning this time. It was logged as a possible solution and that was all that mattered for the moment. I moved the ponies back over to the flower-filled verge, away from further branch catapults that Skye might shoot, and carried on our way.

Our way (the Great Glen Way) here, was squeezed between the canal on the left and the River Oich on the right. A thin giraffe-like neck of land runs between these two waterways for approximately eight kilometres from Fort Augustus to Aberchalder. Mostly you are oblivious to its modest width, due to trees blocking the view of the river. However, just before and after the locks of Kytra, you feel like you are walking on water, with very little land to either side of the track.

I've always had an affinity to water, so it was a pleasant way to start the day and the third stage of my journey. I was still blessed with warm, dry weather and could hardly believe my luck. Today's route was a long way around to cover a short distance, made necessary due to a main road, a missing bridge, and horse accommodation problems for the night. Shortly, we'd cross a small bridge and almost turn back on ourselves to loop round woodland rather than face fast traffic on the A82.

That is of course, if the gate on the bridge had been left unlocked as promised. The bridge in question is a delightful feature, a double cantilever, lightweight suspension system (apparently) designed by James Dredge built in 1854. It spans around forty-seven metres with its main wrought-iron chains hanging five and a half metres high from granite towers, finished with timber decking over the base. A brewer turned engineer, perhaps cleverly to improve infrastructure for his beer deliveries, Dredge designed this lightweight style of bridge. He enabled huge savings in materials and construction time to bridge many a span in his era. Not understanding the ingenuity of the engineering, myself, and thinking back to our wood-clad bridge experience yesterday, I just hoped it was in a good state of repair.

Replaced by an unsightly concrete construction not far away, this Dredge bridge was now a pedestrian foot bridge and I appreciated its aesthetically pleasing appearance, particularly the shadows created by the suspension chains in the morning sun. As I discovered during recce however, there is a locked gate at the far end that only those on foot or with bike can negotiate. I had knocked on the nearest cottage some weeks ago to luckily find they were key holders and that they would be happy to unlock the gate for my eight hoofed arrival today.

"We don't have to walk through the water, do we?" asked Skye. "I HATE getting my feet wet you know!" she added, shaking her head in her usual 'make-me' objection.

"Me neither," stated Katy in firm hoof-halting agreement.

"Don't worry you two, there's a pretty bridge up ahead we can use!"

"That's fine then," they replied in unison, "bridges, we can do!"

Until you arrive, you never know whether requests from weeks ago have been remembered on the day. I didn't discuss with the Highland Duo that the other option I would consider, if finding the gate still locked, would involve testing a ford of the River Oich to see how deep it might be. I'd still rather do that than tango with tankers on the A82 with two ponies in tow.

I suspected that they would prefer the traffic option themselves, so we could be about to face our first test of 'one for all and all for one' ethics in the newly formed team. Thankfully, however, the request had been duly remembered and the small gate was unlocked when we arrived. We squeezed through the narrow gap ("Some more than others, hey, Katy?") to exit the other side of the bridge.

From here we needed to turn north almost back the way we'd arrived, but this time following the River Oich downstream on its opposite bank. After a couple of kilometres, we'd then turn west before later resuming the southerly direction. Not far up this track, we met a shiny Land Rover trundling towards us, and the driver stopped for a chat. Recognising his voice from a phone conversation we'd had a few weeks before, I realised I was talking to the gamekeeper of the Aberchalder Estate.

All through the estate were locked gates and beside them were very strange pedestrian access options. The side gates opened in an upward and outward direction that I'd struggled to get my bike through, let alone two ponies who might stop for a nibble halfway through. If that happened - and let's face it, there was a strong possibility with these two, the gate might crash down right on top of them. When I originally spoke to the gamekeeper about these gates, it was with Yogi and Swift in mind. The problem then was more Swift's height and whether she'd physically be able to duck underneath. The gamekeeper had kindly provided the code to the padlocks for the main gates instead, to allow for an easier way through.

The other access problem we'd discussed was my proposed exit through a caravan site. The last of the locked estate gates opened onto the tarmac drive running through the site and, although yet again I had a right to use it by law, the owners very much didn't want me to (the sign on this gate clearly states "No Access!"). I'd politely spoken to the owners in person during my recce and their opinion remained the same as the sign. They were concerned that walking through the site with equines in tow, along the wide tarmac drive, would be risky for their clients.

To avoid any unnecessary conflict, my other option was to descend out of the woods along the Aldernaig Burn, but the path there was blocked by a huge fallen tree. The gamekeeper was just this minute assuring me that he had tackled this obstacle and, "The tree is now in at least two pieces with a clear way to get through." This was welcome news to hear, as we were already running behind schedule with the slower pace of the Highland Duo, and I hadn't wanted to take a chance on this track only to have to double back to head through the campsite instead. Now reassured, I cheerily waved the gamekeeper goodbye, thanking him for his help.

As it turned out, the Highland Duo managed the pedestrian gates well, and I didn't have to stop and fiddle with codes for the locks which would have surely slowed us down. To be honest, I wasn't really sure if we could travel any slower than we were anyway. The track was loose with sharp stones and the ponies were feeling their feet. Katy's stationary protests were frequent, and although the rope wiggle technique was proving a successful solution, progress was painfully slow on this track.

We'd emerged from woodland to an expanse of bleak, open moorland, and the bleakness and slow progress were creating a feeling of developing desperation. A little way further on, we were joined in this flat landscape on our right-hand side by the beginnings of a flat expanse of water. Wandering along the side of this loch, distracted momentarily from desolation, I spotted a strange little island with a peculiar lone tree in the centre.

According to local folklore, this small artificial Island (with its cherry on top) is all that is left of a bespoke secret hideout. Commissioned by Ailean na leine ruaidhe, otherwise known as Allan of the Red Shirt, a stone mason under his instruction built a sixty foot diameter hideaway island. The folklore doesn't suggest what it was he was hiding from, but it does mention that he was a prolific reiver (raider) of Glengarry and a heroic chap.

Maybe a Robin Hood of his time, but whatever he was keeping under wraps, he really didn't want to be found. On completion of the job, in praying mantis style he killed the mason outright by one shot with an arrow. As a fellow Scot once said, "To keep your own secrets is wisdom; but to expect others to keep them is folly" (William Scott Downey). Allan was obviously of a similar distrustful opinion.

It was a relief to finally reach the southern end of Loch Lundie where the track had softened to match the less rugged landscape. The isolation of moorland was now replaced with more comforting mixed woodlands, and a swathe of purple rhododendrons lined the loch side. Non-native rhododendrons in the Scottish landscape are a sure sign of a 'big house somewhere nearby'. The big house in question here, was probably the MacDonnell's Invergarry Castle, which suffered from an exciting time during the Jacobite/English monarchy melee. Changing sides under protest numerous times, the castle was burned, repaired, and blown up over the years. Eventually replaced by Invergarry House (now known as the Glengarry Castle Hotel), the site of the castle enjoys a more peaceful era.

Someone along the way, however, dropped the seeds of the then fashionable but destructive rhododendron, causing a war to continue to rage up by the loch. Beautiful its flowers may be, but it is a large threat to native species and the Forestry Commission have invested millions in trying to eradicate it. Dominantly overgrowing virtually everything else, its leaf litter is toxic and it harbours a fungus that damages other trees and plants too.

I have to admit that personally I find rhododendron quite beautiful in bloom. I love that it signifies a stately home nearby that I can try to discover in ruin or restored splendour. It reminds me of childhood holidays in Snowdonia where it thrived in the mild and damp climate. Free of today's red tape and fears, my brother and I enjoyed limitless adventure of the land that lay around the caravan site, with its own shrubbery tunnels and ruins to explore. When I say limitless ... we weren't supposed to go up to the ruined castle alone, but with a Skye-like attitude to rules my whole life, I can only apologise to my parents!

In the Mawddach Valley and Abergwynant Woods, amongst the rhododendron's company, I learnt the art of staying on a lively pony on steep and stony ground. First as a paying customer, then later as casual staff at weekends whilst at university, I spent many idyllic hours at the Abergwynant Trekking Centre just outside Dolgellau. At its peak the trekking centre had a herd of about sixty horses, and it wouldn't be unknown for most of them to go out on a trek carrying customers. Often left with a pony but no saddle for staff, the learning curve was as steep as the ground that traversed the foothills of Cader Idris Mountain. There was the occasional farm work to do as well, and rounding up sheep on a pony who knew her job better than I ever would was a fun and exhilarating experience that I will never forget.

I always found it hard to go home at the end of the day, and would sometimes stay instead in a caravan overlooking the field of horses. I was fascinated to watch how the huge herd interacted, breaking into friendly pairs or groups as they relaxed after a hard day's work. They would seek their best pals out, not caring about size, colour, or creed, with the tiniest pony standing nose to tail (as best it could) with the largest horse in the meadow.

Come morning, they keenly trooped in of their own accord, all knowing the routine and just where they should stand in the barn. Leaving the yard to commence a trek was the most hectic time as the ponies and horses jostled to get into their preferred position in the ride line. Once settled, all was smooth for the rest of the outing, and each horse could be called by name to trot up one by one if falling behind.

The whole herd became firm friends to me and I have to admit that years later, when I returned for a visit, I cried when I learned the trekking part of the farm had shut down and all the horses moved on. I still remember the names of about a third of the herd (Seren, Star, Jack, Tzar, Prince, Gypsy, Beauty, Peddler, Snoopy, Peanuts, Rosie, Pip, Coral, Buster, Duke, Big Duke, Smokey, Penny, Velvet, Porcha, Spotted Sam, Billy, Bella, Sparky), and remember the character and feel of many of the others whose names I can no longer recall.

It was a magical time in my life. If I could have done that job long-term and earned my keep, I'd still be doing it now. The enchantment evidently lives on though, as I still find most of my spare time is spent with equines on hilly trails. Not all dropped seeds are harmful, and I certainly wouldn't be undertaking this journey now if it wasn't for the seeds sown by the welcoming, encouraging and hard-working Jones family (thank you Vernon, Rupert and Doris).

Dropping south from the loch, we were soon at the fork in the path. To head right was to commit to the caravan site route, which was easier and more direct, but may cause upset. To pick left was more of a physical challenge; a nice grassy track to start, finishing in a rough scramble up a steep slope to join a bigger path where the gamekeeper had sliced through the tree.

I don't like to disrupt where I'm not welcome, and the gamekeeper had taken the time to clear my route. I'd also spent a few hours making the rough upwards scramble safer for hooves with a little bit of groundwork myself on the recce. It seemed silly to waste these efforts and appeared that the right option all round was to exit stage left.

The descent was cool through the trees, but I was worried about the steep upwards slope to come. Yogi would simply have looked at the slope, pressed his turbo-boost button, and pulled us all to the top. Once engaged, his turbo-boost worked no matter how rough the ground was under hoof. I just wasn't sure if the Highland Duo would be so obliging but they both took me by surprise. I led rather than rode, but they handled the loose slope well, in their own unique and individual ways.

Skye listened carefully and put her feet where I suggested, following the route I had cleared for an easier controlled course. Katy followed behind and put her feet anywhere she damn well liked as she stomped and slid her way up the hill. It wasn't overly graceful, but it worked for her, and we were now all at the top; all panting a little and all looking at the huge tree that completely blocked our path. I don't know which tree the gamekeeper had cut, but it certainly wasn't the one I had told him about.

In true Victor Meldrew style - "I don't believe it!" - I stood aghast, not knowing quite what to do. To about face down the slippery, tree stump filled, and loose, rocky slope we'd just arrived by, didn't appear the most attractive option. Neither did back-tracking the lengthy trail up to the caravan park, possibly causing distress by passing through.

I looked at the lowest part of the tree, as there was certainly no way round through the thick vegetation at either end. I'd need to cut back some branches, but maybe a step over was worth a try. I was confident that given this situation with Swogi, I'd be able to persuade them over with ease. Looking at the more compact duo by my side now, I wasn't sure their legs were long enough, even if I could coerce and convince their mulish minds into cooperative action.

I keep a small saw in my pack, and so set to work on the upward growing branches. I'd have about eight to work through to make a big enough gap and was already starting to sweat. The job in hand would be much more suited to a chain saw, I thought, as I considered the power tools at the gamekeeper's disposal. How had he managed to mistakenly cut the wrong tree? I thought my emailed map with grid reference had been reasonably clear, but seemingly such clues of clarification hadn't been crystal enough.

While I irately beavered away, Katy and Skye blissfully paid no attention as they were studiously focussed on their own undertaking. In their own version of Highland Clearances, they were busy removing every blade of grass they could find in the glade. Delighted by the pause in proceedings, I wondered how perturbed they would be when presented with the problem pole.

I'd now cut through the branches and was making sure the ones on the top of the trunk were smooth enough not to catch their bellies as they confidently strode over the top. The powers of positive thinking were worth a try I supposed. Swift, with her work-it-out brain, would have been choice to lead the team over this hurdle had she been here, but I wasn't sure which of the Highland team to try first.

In the end I grabbed the nearest (Skye) as my powers of positivity were vanishing fast and I honestly had low expectations for either pony. It wasn't that I had little faith in their abilities, although in terms of relationships we were still building trust, it was more that this trunk was huge. The removal of branches from the section I'd cleared hadn't made it appear any smaller, and I just didn't think it was physically possible for ponies with such short legs. I approached the trunk in trepidation and allowed Skye some time to explore it with her nose.

"It doesn't look or smell very edible," she concluded, pushing the pine needles away in disgust.

"It's not eating it I had in mind," I replied.

"What else could you do with something like this?" she asked, somewhat confused.

"Perhaps just step over it to the lovely long grass on the other side?" I suggested.

"OVER THAT?" she exclaimed.

"The grass Skye ... just look at that grass ... *over* there!"

"The grass *is* always greener on the other side," she agreed as she flared her nostrils to take in the sweet scent.

I stepped over the trunk in a demonstrative manner to see if she would follow suit, and she walked up until her chest met the tree. Stretching her neck over as far as she could, she attempted to grasp the foliage on the far side, but it remained just out of reach. She paused for a moment as I held my breath, and slowly her right leg lifted and up over the trunk it went. Half expecting it to be retracted rapidly, I gave a small tug to encourage the left leg to tag along too and it willingly obliged.

With surprise in her eyes, not quite comprehending how she had found herself in this position, a belly scrape followed - as did two frantic back legs not wanting to be left behind - and she was over in a flash of fur and fir. I couldn't quite believe it myself.

"What a brave little pony you are!" I expressed as I smothered her in nice scratches and praise.

"Whatever," she said as she barged me out of the way on her mission to scoff the sweeter and unquestionably greener grass.

I turned slowly and thought with determination, right then - Katy next! We met eyeball to eyeball over the tree and she clearly proclaimed, "Oh no not me!" Content to see that Skye hadn't gone far, she returned to her undergrowth eradication task. "There's still plenty to do here, it's more efficient to work separately, no need for both of us to head over there." Needless to say, Katy took much more persuasion and cunning to convince. She firstly had to satisfy herself that there really was no other way around, and we were now on the third approach to the cleared gap.

"Third time lucky!" I exclaimed brightly.

"The gap's too small for someone as sturdy as me," she snorted.

"Its wide enough - look." as I again did a step over display.

"The grass over here is good," spluttered Skye

helpfully, with her mouth stuffed to the brim.

"All right," said Katy, "but I want it recorded that I don't think this is a very good idea at all."

Eyeball to eyeball over the tree

And that's how I found myself in the predicament of having a pony stuck over a log, front legs on one side and back legs the other, barely touching the ground. A real-life rocking horse, seesawing back and forth on her rather rounded belly. Thankfully, Katy isn't one to get flustered about the strange and wonderful quandaries she frequently finds herself in, and was hanging there quite content. I imagined there would be many children who would queue up to pay good money for such a seesaw ride in the park, but the surrounding woodland was empty. I, therefore, politely and gently requested that Katy move forward to extract herself from her position.

"I don't think I can," answered Katy.

"Yes, you can, just wriggle a bit in a FORWARDS direction," I said, stressing my preferred direction. "You *definitely* can't go back."

"I told you this wasn't a good idea – it's on record."

"Recorded or not, you do need to *mooooove!*" And I added more pull to her rope.

With her front feet dangling in the air, she looked like a maestro awaiting their cue to begin to play a grand piano. I had a flash back to jazz musician Fats Waller asking himself "Is you all on, Fats?" as he looked down at his large frame encasing his piano stool (I grew up on jazz music thanks to my dad's obsession).

"Who are you calling Fats?" Katy hollered. "It's baby blubber, that's all!"

And with that, she toppled and wriggled towards me and front feet finally contacted the ground. With a slide and a shove and samba like style, she slowly unstuck from suspension.

"Well done," I said, "I knew you could do it!"

"I told you it was a great idea," Katy replied.

"I'm not so sure now," said Skye, realising she now had to share all the greener grass.

Katy was looking rather pleased with herself and rather thrilled with the fresh green grass that I was letting her have as reward. We paused for a while for more Highland Clearances and for me to give myself a necessary pep talk. That whole situation was a little more challenging and stressful than I'd really needed on our first day together as a team. However, we'd pulled through our tight spot united (eventually), and only one of us had more grey hairs as a result. The other two were slightly ruffled but generally unperturbed.

Thank goodness the next part was easy as we dropped down onto a little tarmac side road. I confess, I couldn't contain a grisly glare as we passed the entrance to the forbidden caravan park. Meanwhile, the ponies were happily moving along, oblivious to their veto, and we'd soon be at a point to cross over the A87 - another main road I'd preferred to avoid.

We'd then double back on the other side of the River Garry to a bunkhouse and field in Invergarry. Now, Fort Augustus to Invergarry by road is approximately thirteen kilometres. Using tracks to avoid most of the road adds one kilometre more, but due to a missing bridge on that trail where humans could still pass but not hooves, our diversion would have us complete twenty-four kilometres instead.

This was turning into a long day indeed. With Team Swogi speed, I'd have expected to be snugly ensconced in the hostel by now with slippers on and feet up, but the Highland Duo still had four kilometres to go. I didn't mind too much as their pole vault performance had impressed, and the rest of today's trail should be plain sailing if somewhat slow. Emerging from woods at the White Bridge car park, we crossed first the A87 then the bridge over the gushing River Garry. Here was another place where I'd spent a lot of my time. As a dam released river, the Garry's water levels are guaranteed without reliance on unpredictable Scottish weather. Its mighty rapids and play waves make it popular with kayakers and rafters alike.

It was also incredibly popular with the local midge population, who grew to epic proportions by feasting on the regularly exposed flesh of those getting changed into suitable attire for the water. I hated the mad arm-waving dash to change clothes for kayaking, always ending up with your skin in a lumpy mess. I hated it to such an extent, that one evening here was all that it took to instigate an upgrade in transport from car to a van, so that I had somewhere safe to get changed in (my 'paddle wagon').

Moving away from the midges as fast as the short-legged ponies allowed, we turned east again back to Invergarry. I'd been unable to find any suitable spot to set up a corral in the woods, and the trail we were now taking would be repeated in the opposite direction tomorrow. The short overlap, however, would be worthwhile for all in the party; a large grass-filled field for the ponies and a midge-free bunk house for me.

In about an hour, we were back at the A82 and would have to travel along it for a short section to reach the gate in the fence. Unfortunately, there was no way in from the bunk house side which was adjacent to the field. I waited for a break in the traffic - at least, that was the plan, but as soon as we stepped onto the clear road someone had obviously just waved the starter flag. A concoction suddenly appeared out of thin air of cars, motorhomes, motorbikes, lorries, low loaders, tractors, and even a bus.

For the second time today, "I don't believe it!" escaped my lips. Katy couldn't care less, but Skye was not far from a full flight response with fear. Most of the traffic listed above she could cope with, but due to a prior incident, she had a phobic response to motorhomes. She jumped about as I quickly jumped off, bringing traffic to a complete standstill in shock (and I hoped a little sympathy too). I still had some learning about these two to do, and obviously I could add to Skye's list that cars might be fine but big white motorhomes were over her boundary.

She bounded along beside me as we inched towards the gate. The drivers were very patient, but the short walk of shame seemed to take forever. It didn't help my red cheeks any when I found the gate firmly stuck shut, and it took what felt like another hour, with bouncy Skye still firmly held in one hand, to force it open. Waving appreciative thanks and taking a few bows for performance (no encores requested I noted), I walked across the large grassy field to the bunk house on the far side.

"Is this really ALL ours for the night?" asked Katy with a glazed look in her eyes.

"Well I think you've both earned it, don't you?"

"Absolutely YES!" they replied in a harmonious duet.

I really should have set up a corral to contain the extent of consumption, but the girls had had a long journey so far and still had a long way to go. I figured that a good feed for the night was important as the next two nights grazing would be poor. Besides, I reasoned with myself; I am completely and downright exhausted!

Still not feeling well in myself, I was finding the physicality of the journey more arduous than I really should. Despite reassurance from others that I'd just been doing too much, or I was just feeling the effect of getting older, I knew deep down that something just wasn't as it should be. Yogi wouldn't be the only one getting a health check when I arrived home.

If truth be told, I'd been back and forward to the GP for almost two years now, with a plethora of symptoms that seemed to wax and wane or migrate from one area of body to another. I felt like a complete hypochondriac as no answers so far had been forthcoming. The main symptoms I'd been experiencing were mind-numbing fatigue, migraines, sore joints, and repetitive cold/flu like episodes. These episodes would follow the same set course each time they arrived, unlike the variations found in a series of separate common colds. They would leave me violently coughing and extremely short of breath.

I had been tested for asthma, allergy, COPD (Chronic Obstructive Pulmonary Disease), and rheumatoid arthritis amongst other things, but apart from being slightly iron anaemic, which would explain the fatigue, nothing untoward so far had been found. Although I was currently free from breathing problems, the fatigue I was feeling now, deep down inside, felt worse than ever before. I untacked the girls and dropped the gear gently over the fence. A brief check over from nose to tail, paying meticulous attention to their tree hugging underbellies, doubly confirmed no ill effect from today's adventures. I left them to their frenzied refuelling and staggered my way over the fence and into the bunkhouse.

I barely had the energy to pile the kit in the porch, clean hoof boots, grab a shower, cook some food and eat, let alone deal with the barrage of questions I was now faced with from a fellow roomie. Friendly as this young lad was, his emotional intelligence wasn't currently engaged and he wasn't picking up how much I just wanted to crawl into bed. I rarely enlighten folks to my chosen profession, unless they ask directly, but somehow tonight it had accidentally popped out in tired conversation. I avoid mentioning it if I can (unless flight attendants are asking for help obviously), as it can sometimes get uncomfortable under the collar when you are then faced with fascinated rapture.

I don't know why medical crisis holds such enthrallment, but producers of films, documentaries, and drama do very well out of it. I guess I can't deny my own interest in the subject matter as I otherwise wouldn't do what I do, but some people are truly fanatical. This was one of those moments and the keenly motivated first aider wanted to know everything about the worst job, biggest car accident, driving on blue lights, and anything interesting (i.e. gruesome) that I'd ever witnessed.

I answered as succinctly but politely as I could, used 'a check of the ponies' as an excuse to escape, then shrewdly took cover under my duvet. I had time for a quick reflection before my eyelids began to droop. My first day in the Highland Pony team hadn't gone too badly. Our rhythm together was still in development, but it certainly hadn't been disastrous.

The going was 'heavy' all round compared to travelling with Swogi; heavy to walk, to tow, to move in any direction really, but we had covered some mileage. I'd learnt not to ride under low branches and not to get into any sort of strength battle (I'd lose). I'd learnt to use cunning, was making progress with Katy's stopping habit, and had been less tested by Skye too at the start of the day.

They might be slower than Swogi and a little obsessed with anything green and edible, but they were both very cute and had tried hard. Considering their limited trail experience so far in life, they'd done well with the obstacles today (especially the tree). I was proud of my new compact companions and how amenable they were to accept me as part of their herd.

Day 16:
Invergarry to Tomdoun
(Distance 18km, Ascent 363m)

I woke feeling dreadful and wondered if the Highland Duo had stampeded over my bed in the night. I had a thumping headache and just wanted to go back to sleep. It was tempting indeed, as today would thankfully be a shorter and easier day. In my planning I'd held this easier day in reserve for things that may go wrong. If I'd needed to catch up in place and time for some reason or other, I'd intended to merge yesterday and today into one. Team Swogi, on yesterday's flat trails, would have swallowed the mileage up whole and spat it out just after lunch, and therefore would have managed the doubled-up days by dinner. I was glad I hadn't had to use this option with Katy and Skye however, as I think we'd only be arriving now.

With the easy trail day ahead, I could have lingered in bed a little longer, but I wanted to set out before the morning rush hour on that busy road. I wasn't looking forward to a similar prancing performance of motorhome mechanophobia with Skye. I dragged myself up, munched breakfast on the go, and started to lug all the tack and bags over to the fence. As weary as I was, I wasn't sure whether to welcome unrequested help in this task by my young friend from last night or not.

I decided not to look a gift horse in the mouth and left him to finish the job whilst I attempted to catch the rest of the team. I expected evasion in the expanse of earth they had (about six acres). It was, after all, easy to outrun me and the field was full of sweet tasting grass that would sustain them for at least another day (note normal horses would take a week to eat all that). What I hadn't considered, is how much they had consumed overnight, and as a result neither pony was feeling like running anywhere in any hurry at all.

They waddled, full-bellied beside me, over to the fence and my eagerly awaiting helper, who assisted in preparing the ponies in twice the time it would usually take. This of course was accompanied by medical tales aplenty of incidents he'd handled in the Red Cross. He was lovely, honestly, but he reminded me of an overly helpful first aider I'd once been faced with on an ambulance job – a story I will impart with a smile.

A colleague and I had been called to an overdose patient outside. Initially triaged as a low grade of priority, it didn't sound overly serious. Two minutes into our journey however and it was upgraded with those words that you dread; "Bystander CPR in progress." This essentially means that cardiac arrest has occurred, and someone is being coached over the phone to try to resuscitate them.

The priority shot to the top, we both sat up a little straighter, and I applied more pressure to the pedal under my right foot. We briefly discussed a plan of our immediate individual actions on arrival, as we prepared for the worst. As we arrived on scene and made a quick assessment, we saw several unconcerned young people sunbathing on a grassy bank and, in the midst of this, was an older lady seemingly arguing with a pale-looking lad.

She had her mobile phone on speaker beside her, linked to the ambulance control who were giving out instructions, and was insisting to the youth that she must give him "mouth to mouth" as the ambulance control were telling her to do so. Unsurprisingly, despite his diminished state of health, he was doing his best to fight her off and telling her to, "To leave my mouth well and truly alone!" I've provided a cleaner version of the actual words used at the time.

Much to the lad's surprise, and undeterred by his rejection of life saving breaths, the helpful first aider lady continued the rotation back to thirty chest compressions. Fair play I thought, this lady is certainly up to date with the latest recommendations, to carry out hands-only CPR if unable to provide effective rescue breaths. It took a surprisingly long time to convince her that the poor young lad wasn't in cardiac arrest at all and had merely had a 'whitey' following too many puffs of a spliff. I'm not overly sure, but she may have gone away with the impression that she'd miraculously (single-handedly) saved his life and I suspected would be just as 'helpful' at the next incident she came across.

I'm not knocking first aiders by any means; I train them and work alongside many with huge respect. However, the enthusiasm to carry out aid for common good can sometimes engulf common sense. I'm sure, given time and experience, my youthful friend at the bunk house would ripen into his role, with mundane routine reducing his rapture and thereby relaxing his approach.

Before we parted ways, he admitted that he'd like to join the ambulance service one day. I provided some informative encouragement and set off across the field with a wave and a wonder if he ever applied. The field gate was the same struggle to open, but I discovered that the road was unbelievably deserted.

With my morning blether delaying proceedings, I'd arrived on the tarmac at nine o'clock. The busiest time of day I had thought. However, we retraced our steps without any interruption at all - not even a single car - and thus managed a straighter, less animated procession. Breathing a sigh of relief, we reached the track to the woods and set off to tranquil Tomdoun, our proposed end of day destination. We only had eighteen kilometres to do today and, with the final four kilometres or so being on a quiet glen road and Katy's favourite ground type (tarmac), we should make good time. Just as well really, as I was feeling decidedly under the weather and was dawdling more than Katy would have ever thought possible. I had the distinct feeling that she was genuinely somewhat impressed with my ability to amble.

She was either really impressed or totally bamboozled as she wasn't displaying any of her usual morning stuck-feet tantrums. This was quite a relief given my lack of Highland Pony battle strength this morning. Both ponies were enjoying the relaxed, slower paced start and were mooching along the track edges sampling their delights. I knew Yvonne wouldn't be overly impressed with my introduction of grey in her otherwise black or white grass rules, but I was a little into survival mode here.

Back-tracking the way we'd come yesterday, we arrived at the junction where we'd be back at new territory. Katy took this as her cue and made her opinion quite clear, with hooves firmly planted, that new was not the way she wanted to go. I just didn't have any fight left in me this morning; today was going to require a different approach to this problem. I dismounted from Skye, sat down on the grass, and let the horses do what they liked doing most - eat! Nose down, teeth engaged, Skye looked up at me with her puppy dog eyes in pensive suspicion. I could tell she was wanting to ask a disbelieving question ("We can stop and eat, right?") but was thinking better of drawing my attention to her actions on the off chance it brought them to a catastrophic end.

We had plenty of time. It was a dry, sunny day, and conflict avoidance to preserve energy levels was becoming the main priority. If co-operation could be the consequence of grass consumption, then I was prepared to sit it out for a while, enjoying the warmth of the morning sun and the tweets of the birds in the trees. With my mind in a bit of a stupor, that 'while' had stretched out more than I'd realised. Pulling me back into actuality, my phone was ringing from the depths of my pocket.

This was surprising on two accounts: one, that I must have some sort of signal, and two, that most people who would ring me knew I was away on an adventure and would probably have my hands too full to answer. Glimpsing hastily at the screen as my phone ascended from pocket to ear, I could see that it was Dave (faithful husband) trying to get through. We both connected and spoke with a united, "Is everything okay?"

As the confusion unravelled as to why we'd both think there was an issue to resolve, I realised I'd been sitting still in the middle of the morning for more than my allotted period. As a safety measure before embarking on this excursion, we'd agreed I was only likely to stay perfectly still for twenty minutes at a time, and that if I appeared to be lingering for longer, then things were probably not okay (overnight camps excluded).

In order for this to be monitored, I was carrying a

Garmin inReach satellite device that I would start on tracking mode when I set off in the mornings, with an alert to say that I was on the move. It would track me every twenty minutes, plotting a position on a map that my husband was monitoring as much as he could between work and home commitments. He'd checked in this morning and could see a concentration of twenty-minute plots gathering in an overlapping spot.

This was a hindsight addition to the pile of kit carried with me after the Yogi versus cliff incident. The cliff scramble had taken place in a huge area devoid of mobile phone signal and that had scared me. The possible alternative conclusion to that scenario - of Yogi being injured, and no means to contact help - had caused me to seek out alternative communication channels. This inReach had an emergency locate button and a tracking device, but also the option to send less urgent text messages and I liked its flexibility.

It's amazing where an hour or so can disappear to when you've descended into a decelerated pace of life. I reassured Dave that although energy levels were low, I was still effectively fine and would be presently on my way again. This last statement, I'd particularly projected at Katy! I used the opportunity of the surprise contact with home to check up on the status of Team Swogi. I'd asked after them the last two nights but only by satellite texts. The texts were short and sweet and although it was good to know they were 'okay', this rare phone contact afforded the chance to ask more detailed questions.

The upshot of it all was that they were indeed just fine. Swift was running rings round Dave in her usual manner ("The grumpy minx," he called her) and Yogi - relaxing in his home environment - appeared comfortable and his "normal self." It was nice to know all was well at home as I missed my usual trail companions dearly and I was still worried about what might be wrong with Yogi. It was also nice to know that safety measures to mitigate risk certainly worked well, but I was yet to try the other safety device I'd carried all this way with me and didn't intend to test it out any time soon.

It was a Hit Air Vest, designed to rapidly inflate on unplanned departure from the saddle and cushioning the impact of hitting the ground. With a short strap attaching this lightweight gilet to the saddle, it would inflate airbags (via a small, enclosed gas canister) in all the right places to minimise injury. It was another one of those hindsight purchases, bought after breaking a bone in my back after failing to sit out one of young Swift's floops.

I'd unfortunately made the mistake of expanding her comfort zone too far, too quickly, and discovered that sometimes lessons are hard learnt. At least now I felt that I was gradually getting closer to the light at the end of the tunnel, as far as travelling with my two horses were concerned, and that lessons these days were a little softer in their teachings. The vest may have been a purchase made in hindsight, but it certainly seemed to have done the job so far in its lifespan - I'd not had to sit out a full-on Swift floop since. Murphy's law at play here maybe; if you take a rain jacket with you, you can guarantee some sunshine all day, but the moment you leave it at home the heavens open directly over your head.

The reason I'd gone for this expensive style of vest was to make sure I actually wore it. The more commonly used back protectors were made from foam, and were just too bulky, too heavy, and too hot to wear when heather-bashing in the hills for days on end. I also found they tended to conflict with the higher cantle (back part) of a differently shaped Western saddle. The gilet vest in comparison was so light to wear that you hardly noticed it was there and this was the encouragement I needed to wear it on every horse I rode, not just the historically floopy tall girl Swift.

Jumping back up on Skye and clipping the vest in, I wondered whether the vest technology could be re-designed to suddenly inflate something behind Katy the next time she dug her heels in. The amusing thoughts this concept produced kept me entertained as we began once again to amble along.

Now that I had persuaded Katy to head along in the new direction (or rather waited patiently until she changed her mind), she was striding out surprisingly well. The track was much softer than yesterday's mostly stony affair, and it was flat and compact. This gave Katy less to worry about and she could daydream along without care about where she was placing her hooves.

"See, Katy - it's almost as good as tarmac!" I exclaimed cheerfully.

Ignoring the reference to the track completely, "Is it lunchtime yet?" was the only response she gave. I bit my tongue and refrained from debate as I shook my head in disbelief at the intensity of her grass addiction.

We'd started out enclosed on both sides by tall, dark trees, although the wide track allowed the sunshine through and gave us a view of the bright blue sky. As we emerged from the trees to cleared forestry land, the landscape widened for the first time that day. The hills on the left held a long line of snow just below their summit. It seemed remarkably low in altitude to be hanging there into summer, particularly given the steady warmth felt today. The stiff breeze in the more open space was mild and pleasant. The ponies seemed to enjoy the cooling lift of manes away from sticky necks that the light wind provided.

The rest of the morning passed by at a much better speed and if we weren't careful, despite the added time-out for the satellite device safety drill, we were going to reach our next rendezvous far too early in the day. Spying a little wooden hut at the side of the trail with lush grass all around, I figured a lunch stop was in order. The rendezvous we were casually heading towards was one with my good pal Sal. There was no point in getting there too soon as we'd have no way to proceed without her. There were two cattle grids ahead, with no side gates for those with hooves and Sal was arriving with a system to hopefully solve that problem.

I'd known Sal for many years, but we'd not spent a lot of time in each other's company for a while. We were both passionate about spending time outside but lived too far apart to do this together on a regular basis. Sal was also a paramedic and I was about to start a new job at her ambulance station. To get reacquainted prior to my start date, she'd thought it a good idea to respond to my pre-trip online request.

This request consisted of an appeal for anyone with a van to turn up at a certain grid reference, on a specific date, at a roughly assigned time, with a few planks of wood (which of course I'd happily provide). I'm not sure whether it was the keenness to reacquaint, the eagerness to test her newly purchased van (to be converted to camper), or curiosity to see what on earth I was up to in the woods, but she'd offered her services and I'd gladly accepted.

I was looking forward to catching up with her shortly, but for now I was about to be caught short myself if I didn't disappear behind this hut. The trials of emptying your bladder through the day with two horses in tow is a rapid way to remove all inhibitions. Very much depending on your companion's mood at the exact time, you may not be able to find somewhere to be overly discrete. There may be a requirement to multitask and hold onto two lead ropes at the same time as 'powdering your nose'.

When travelling with a human trail companion added into this mix, your dignity often relies on a certain amount of shut-eyed trust. Once, on the way up a bleak hill with Yvonne, there was no cover in sight and thankfully nobody else in sight either. I did, however, have a very keen Yogi held tightly in one hand and therefore didn't have many private options available to me. Shouting my intentions to Yvonne, I went about my exposed business just as Swift, in an impressive full flow, followed suit. Hearing the flood, Yvonne - with her eyes tightly shut - proclaimed in amazement, "Jeees Claire, you were holding that one in and REALLY needed to go." The fits of giggles that followed nearly had ill-fated consequences, but somehow I stayed on my feet, dignity not quite intact this time.

Smiling at this memory, I slid out from behind the hut to find a large timber truck making its way towards me. Another close call there, I thought to myself. You see not a soul all day then as soon as you need some relief, every man and his dog appears. This man was thankfully five minutes too late and fortunately very friendly. He turned off his lorry and took a Kit-Kat moment to ask me about what I was doing. Mercifully, his interest lay in terms of horse travel and not my previous actions behind the hut.

Hearing that I would be travelling through the woods for the rest of the day, he offered to radio through to all the other timber lorry drivers ahead, to tell them to look out for me on the trail. As grateful as I was to the potential slowing of traffic, I made a mental note that toileting arrangements for the remainder of the afternoon might become somewhat of a challenge with all these drivers on high alert.

With hands washed in the trickling stream at the side of the track, I munched my lunch and tried to calculate my estimated time of arrival at the first cattle grid. It was amazing what difference a compacted, stone free, soft track could do to your average speed. I began to wonder if I'd calculated today's distances wrong, but either way, we were on schedule to arrive too early at the first of the cattle grid obstacles. I gave Sal a quick phone call, and luckily she was on a similarly early schedule.

Meeting at the first of the grids, I was met with a hug followed rapidly by an amused quizzical expression.

"You are going to use those planks to get those ponies over those grids?" her highly raised left eyebrow seemed to ask.

Luckily Sal herself is more solution driven than her eyebrow seemed to be, and she was pulling the planks out of her van with eager enthusiasm. That eyebrow though had seeded some doubts in my mind regarding the part the ponies had to play in the plan. Swogi's actions would be predictable here, and with a small amount of reasoned persuasion I was positive they'd have obliged, particularly since we'd practised walking planks previously at home. The Highland Duo's thoughts on the matter were waiting to be seen. I helped

Sal place the planks carefully side by side to the left of the cattle grid and asked her to stand on the metal grid beside them.

"That way if a pony is silly enough to step onto the grid, you can push them back onto the planks."

This time it was her right eyebrow that rose in a quizzical fashion about the difference in weight ratio between slim Sal and a plump pony, and how the rules of Newton were not in Sal's favour. As I defended my idea to the eyebrow in question, I explained that Yvonne, like me, used a pressure and release training method with her ponies, where the equine is taught to move away from pressure (perceived or physical) in order to do what was asked of them, with the reward of relaxation/safety when they've done what you wanted them to. The reaction to pressure from the Highland Duo I had no doubt, would be more sluggish than with the Swogi team but this plan was perfectly applicable, and Sal shouldn't find herself pushed into the pit.

I approached our makeshift bridge with Skye beside me to see what she thought of it all.

"This isn't like climbing over trees then?" she asked.

"No, Skye –this is really simple, much, much easier than that."

"It won't scrape my belly then?" she enquired.

"No not at all, and look at that lovely grass on the other side."

"I quite like belly scratches," she stated, "but I LOVE grass and right now I'm not eating any and can't reach any at all!"

And with that she lifted her nose from sniffing the end of the plank and strode confidently over to the other side in a perfectly straight line. Katy's line was more peculiar than perfect and Sal's buffer services had to be applied.

"You do know I nearly died falling through that wooden bridge the other day, don't you?" Katy cried, as she twisted to the side halfway across. "I've not quite emotionally recovered."

My emotions had taken a huge leap from my stomach to my throat as Katy's back right foot had come perilously close to falling though the grid. Sal's timely shove to Katy's back end had straightened her up and Sal was staying firmly in place to 'encourage' her to continue to the end of the planks.

"Only one more to go Sal!" I brightly exclaimed as we loaded the planks back in her van. "I'll see you in a wee while at the next one!"

Waving her off, I jumped back on Skye to follow Sal's disappearing van down the road. The next cattle grid would be a different affair entirely as it was situated at the very start of a metal clad bridge spanning the narrows of Loch Garry. The feel and the sound of the metal under the ponies hooves could cause an interesting miniature stampede, but so far, the Highland Duo hadn't let me down. Although they may take persuasion, they usually obliged in the end. I considered that it could be a worse obstacle ahead, as the drovers using this route in times gone by (pre-bridge construction) would have had to ford this narrow. I am sure at times it would have been more of a swim than a wade.

We were soon at the bridge where Sal was patiently waiting with planks in position. Apart from a minor hurried scuffle of feet at the first feel of metal under hoof on the far side of the planks, the Highland Duo tackled the bridge with ease. Maybe they were finally beginning to feel a bit more belief in their new herd leader. I also was feeling a little more belief that I might make it to the end of the day, despite feeling so crook, with only around four kilometres of tarmac on a quiet glen road to go. We'd reached the impressive thirty-five kilometres of single-track road that linked Invergarry to the east with Kinloch Hourn in the west, joining it at roughly a third of the way along it.

The road was originally built by Thomas Telford in the early 19th century when commissioned by the government to construct better networks across the remote Highlands, in order to reduce emigration and increase employment after the Highland Clearances (similar to the Caledonian Canal at Fort Augustus). Little of the initial road remains, but from here to the end of our day, we'd roughly be following its old line.

We'd also be following the western end of Loch Garry, with fern covered slopes running down from the road to its shore. The sun was now hidden behind building clouds, the loch was grey, and the hills beyond a colourless mass. Looking back to the metal bridge crossing the loch, it looked longer than it had felt to cross at the time. Our day would conclude at the Tomdoun Hotel, where Sal and I were going to camp out for the night. Alas, no room at the inn, nor a pint at the bar, as the hotel had been shut down for three years now. Built at the end of the 1800s, the hotel had replaced an earlier drovers' inn and had once stood at the junction of the main road north to Skye (on the A87).

With the coming of hydroelectricity and a road diversion due to the increased size of Loch Lochy to the north, the hotel now sits eighteen kilometres east of Invergarry, on a road to nowhere and on a hiding to nothing in terms of becoming a profitable business (as a standard hotel, anyway). A real shame as its situation and the scenery from the front veranda is something to behold. That is, of course, if you had enough midge spray to smother yourself in whilst trying to enjoy the view. The further west I'd travelled, the bigger and more bitey the midge population had become, and as I arrived at the hotel with the ponies, I felt the wind drop. I knew we were in for a hell of an evening not necessarily in a good way.

Opposite the hotel is a rough patch of grass and fern. Having asked permission, I was to corral the horses there for the night. I chose the patch with the highest rise for any whiff of a breeze, the greenest grass for distraction therapy, and included a circle of ferns for their belly scratching properties. The Highland Duo were still in for an itchy time of it though, and I couldn't help but feel very sorry for them stuck outside all night.

Mind you, these gals were hardy and would cope much better than the Swogi team would have done. Swift, with her sensitive skin, would have gone completely demented here and Yogi wouldn't have been far behind her. They certainly wouldn't have had much rest, pacing back and forth all night to escape the midge clouds. Katy and Skye, on the other hand, dealt with this well, with just the occasional head shake and tail flick. They had no desire to interrupt the industrial production line of grass ingestion too much.

Sal had set up her camping stove on the hotel veranda where a convenient bench and table were parked. The mouth-watering smells of the forthcoming dinner helped to compensate slightly for the midge hell I was experiencing as I battled to pitch my tent. When offering to provide plank support prior to my departure, I'd forgotten that Sal had also offered to pick up a few things along the way for dinner.

Well this was one gal who was certainly to be used as support crew again. It was a completely amazing meal -

freshly caught langoustines no less, served deliciously with a garlic and lemon butter sauce. As I perused for caviar and crackers, she handed me a large glass of champagne. Well okay, maybe getting carried away there; but it was a large, tasty glass of red wine, topped off with a sprinkle of midge.

Sal's van wasn't converted yet, but as we paced up and down the car park for an hour after dinner to enjoy the scenic view (using the Swogi method of midge avoidance), I was eyeing her van with envy each time we turned in its direction. Not only was the inside fairly midge free, it also contained a plethora of enthusiastic cuddles from Millie, her newly rescued dog. It looked considerably cosier than my one-man tent which was hard to locate in the encroaching dark, covered as it was by the swarming black blanket of Scotland's greatest pest.

As I fought my way into my sleeping bag, trying to prevent as many of the blighters from entering my tent as possible, I completely understood the reason for rumours associated with these horrible things: that the midge was the reason for the Romans never conquering Scotland, and that in Scotland's past, people being left tied to a stake in a midge field was used as a horrific form of torture!

Day 17:
Tomdoun to Kinlochhourn
(Distance 25km, Ascent 345m)

As I awoke on my penultimate day, I became aware of the crawling swarm of midges lining the damp inside of my tent's fly sheet. Not only was the day devoid of a breeze, but it was a dank and grey shade of dreich too. A midge's favourite kind of day, but unquestionably not my cup of tea, where a few of them seemed to be holding an Olympic backstroke competition (it seems to be their preferred stroke). As I broke my personal best time to get packed up, breakfasted, and the ponies booted and saddled, I didn't see much of Sal and I really didn't blame her. I was up and away in no time at all, shouting thank you and farewell to the outside of her van. It wasn't that I was in a rush to get going, but the faster I did, the more I could keep moving to avoid becoming the picked clean skeleton of a piranha feast cartoon.

It didn't take long to saunter out of Tomdoun as there really wasn't much to it; just the hotel, a church, and a couple of houses. We were enclosed in midge hell (or heaven from their perspective), with fern-covered verges and breeze sheltering trees lining both sides of the road. The misty conditions may have been atmospheric, but it seemed to have dampened both ponies' enthusiasm for movement this morning.

Considering this was Katy's favourite surface to walk on, and one on which Skye often enjoyed striding out on (so long as it was devoid of large white motorhomes), they weren't exactly making any land speed records. I was feeling slightly better in myself with a little more energy to spare, but it seemed the midge-crowded night and the endless days on the trail were finally taking their toll on the Highland Duo. They appeared to be well and truly exhausted.

"Come on gals, only two more days to go and today is a totally tarmac day!" I said enthusiastically.

"Tired," said Skye.

"Tired and hungry," declared Katy.

"But..." I started, before I was promptly interrupted by a unified:

"Haven't we walked far enough now?"

"Can't we go home yet?"

Their spirits seemed to lift a little as I explained that, at the end of the day, there was a GRASSY field and in it a lovely pair of Highland ponies to meet. Their spirits may have lifted but it did nothing to increase their speed. As we slowly emerged from the trees to experience a splendid view across Poulary Loch, the slightest hint of a midge-relieving breeze elevated the clouds swarming around my head too.

Today we'd be working our way along the remaining twenty-five kilometres of the single-track road to Kinloch Hourn. Here the Atlantic crept shoreward, at the end of one of the most fjord-like sea lochs in Scotland. With the outer waters of the loch protected by the southern reaches of the Isle of Skye, you'd think that the waters twenty-two kilometres inland at the loch head would be tranquil and still. However, the steep sided mountains rising vertically up from the narrow strip of water provided a fierce and erratic funnel effect. Add strong tidal currents to the mix and you'd have to be hardy to fish these waters.

It would be a while before we reached the steep descent down to the edge of the ocean, as first we'd have a climb up to the head of Loch Quoich where the road squeezes past the huge dam. The name 'Quoich', meaning cup or quaich (a traditional Scottish drinking bowl, two-handled and shallow), is hardly fitting now as the loch increased its depth by thirty metres and its surface size by thirteen square kilometres when the dam was completed. Less of a cup and more of a swimming pool these days, but the original name remains.

Loch Quoich Dam was the biggest rockfill dam in Scotland at the time it was built, at thirty-eight metres high and 320 metres long. It was built around 1955 and very much altered the appearance of the glen and the lives in the valley. The Ellice family, who owned most of the surrounding land, lost their estate house (Glenquoich Lodge) which used to stand on the water's edge on the south side of the loch. Now hunkered down towards the middle of the loch, all its gardens and buildings are submerged.

Many settlements and good grazing lands were lost too on the loch fringe, (Camban and Bunchaolie farms for example, which can still be seen outlined on older maps), but power was becoming an important commodity. In the 1940's, the aim of the newly formed North of Scotland Hydro-Electric Board was to bring electricity to the more rural Scottish areas to help with economic regeneration. Few crofts (approximately one in a hundred) in the Highlands had such luxuries, and their lives were about to be changed, enlightened, and brightened with the arrival of a public supply.

This dam holds back the main storage reservoir of the Great Glen hydroelectric scheme, feeding into the Quoich Power Station and onwards to a power station at Invergarry. Many of the dam constructions were a joint affair between engineer and architect to calm objections and opposition from Landowners of the time, who feared ugly structures and over-industrialisation. This may explain the unusual, dressed finish on this dam's face, and also the lengthy time it took to gain constructional consent. The dam only met approval on its fifth planning submission. The four previous attempts took the power to the west, and it seems the objectors preferred it coming to the east. Just goes to show, that the complexity of planning procedures hasn't changed much in the last one hundred years.

As we climbed very steadily up the one hundred metres or so of ascent, up to the top of the dam, I suddenly felt tiny and became aware of a queasy feeling in the pit of my stomach. It was a very different experience approaching this huge structure at a slower pace than in a car. Knowing and sensing the bottled-up power behind it, I couldn't shake the feeling of impending doom. I had, after all, watched the bouncing bomb recreation of Operation Chastise in the Dambuster film, and my unruly imagination was picturing the scenes from water level.

I'm not sure if the ponies felt it too, but they couldn't seem to keep their eyes off the rock-filled mass to the left either. We were proceeding along in a somewhat sideways fashion, with only a small stone wall separating us from the depth of the overflow channel. I'm sure the road doesn't narrow here, but it does seem to suck its tummy in between the dam on one side and the hills on the other. It felt particularly tucked tight when I spied a large white motorhome heading in a wide manner towards us.

Luckily Skye was completely focussed on the channel beside her, and I managed to flag the motorhome driver to pull over by the square of the building at the edge of the dam. There was a momentary hustle and bustle as Skye's eyes opened wide as we approached it and she clattered her way past in surprise. Katy did the same, but in puzzlement, as she couldn't work out what on earth there was for Skye to be so excited about.

The road, now level with the loch, stretched out ahead of us with the mountains rising steeply up to our right. Bright pink rhododendrons gaily speckled the ground on either side, but there was no old stately home here to discover in ruin or restored splendour. That is, unless I was willing to don diving gear and descend into the depths of the cold grey waters of Quoich. The road less travelled here was rougher in texture under hoof, slowing our progress some more, giving plenty of time to soak in the impressive expanse of water we followed. The hills in the distance didn't emerge much from the blanket of mist that encircled them, but the drizzle of the morning had at least cleared.

Plodding along we soon reached the concrete bridge that spans a northern finger-like spur, where the River Quoich and the true Glen of Quoich spilled its waters into the main loch. Just after the bridge there is a tantalising track up to the north which is apparently an old coffin route to Glen Shiel. In times gone by, power struggles of the church often meant that burials could only take place at the 'mother churches' of outlying places, which were often a long way away. Coffin routes or corpse roads were used to move the dead from remote communities to consecrated ground for burial.

It was a brutal process indeed, to task kinsfolk with the duty of carrying their loved ones high over the mountains to be interred by the church that wouldn't delegate its burial rights to somewhere closer by. It would have been a particularly harrowing task in the harsh winters or even the summer storms of a Scottish ilk. Surrounding any passage was a plethora of spiritual superstition, and today many cairns or coffin stones can still be seen where the coffin was placed for a rest and the bearers would toast the deceased. It was strongly believed that if the coffin touched the ground then the ground would be tainted, or worse, the corpse's spirit would return to haunt the living. It was well accepted that coffin roads were deemed as public rights of way and thus many still exist as waymarked trails today.

This route to Glen Sheil, once an important and well-used path (before road connections improved), reportedly becomes indistinct at the top, with a tricky section through the pass of Bealach Duibh Leac to negotiate. As with many a rock, tree, cave, or river crossing, this way through the hills has a claim to fame with Bonny Prince Charlie. In 1746 he is said to have escaped the King's Soldiers by crossing the Bealach Duibh Leac in darkness, arriving at Glen Shiel to find refuge.

This chap sure covered some ground and eluded many infantry patrols with hides, leaps, and brave ascents, but I'm not sure he ever used a horse during his escapes from scrapes. Surely the eaten down grass and regular dung deposits would have given his whereabouts away? I am certain, however, that horses would have been used to undertake the carrying of coffins on at least some of these old routes and this one is one I intend to recce for a possible future adventure.

Following level with the Lochside once more, the road grew moss-covered in the centre, indicating less use by carbon dioxide emitting machines. It became obvious that use of the road was instead being undertaken by those with a smellier and, by the looks of things, a more regular methane production.

"You mean farts don't you?" giggled Skye.

"You mean c ... c ... cows don't you?" Katy said nervously, shivering slightly as she looked over each shoulder in turn.

We all have our nemeses; Skye with big white motorhomes, me with horses in most forms of traffic, Yogi with bogs, Swift with personal space, and Katy with cows. I didn't mention this to her, but the dung deposits looked fresh, there was a lot of it about, and any cows here were likely to be sporting hats made of long and pointy horns. Katy moved up a little closer to Skye and accompanied our progress with regular snorts as she scanned the horizon for any clue of encroaching cattle.

Our gradual ascent now cut regularly through rocky clefts, and the scenery was beginning to change. By the time we'd reached a smaller hydro works just after Loch Coire nan Cnamh, there seemed to be bedrock protruding wherever I looked - as much as the lazy hazy mist, beginning to settle itself down over every available surface, would allow me to see. The mist lay its head on a rock here, its feet up over there, and spread its blanket out over the small valleys in between.

The day was getting late. The girls were worn out and progress had been slow today. I reflected that Katy hadn't once attempted a sit in protest since we started out this morning, but accepted that it probably wasn't a good sign. If she didn't have the energy for that, then she must be completely fatigued. At least any ascent was complete now and the rest of the day would be undertaken in less energy-expending descent.

We were now at a broken-down house at Allt Coire Shubh. There didn't appear to be much human shelter that looked safe, but remembering the midge fest the night before, I considered its potential as an overnight camp. There was a nearby stream and a grassy patch to the right, with a few trees exuding butt scratching potential (for the ponies I might add). The problem was that I hadn't asked for permission to stay here and I didn't want to cause any aggravation. It was only less than two kilometres to go anyway, so wearily I gathered team endorsement to continue onward. Despite her fatigue, Katy was the main advocate within the team for completing the final stretch; for the reasons of gossip gathering and clan reunion that she was anticipating at the farm, I suspected.

We'd been descending for a while now with the rock-scarred landscape setting a mystical scene from the Lord of the Rings. I'm not the only one to consider this a remarkable place to be; in a book by James Hunter (*A Dance Called America*) he described this road: "There are few more scenically spectacular journeys to be made in Britain than the one that takes you from the Great Glen through Glen Garry to the edge of the Atlantic."

I already agreed with Mr J. Hunter about the spectacular scenery, but the best was yet to come. A low stone wall on the right of the road signified that things were about to become much more interesting. Unbelievably steep inclines, rocky overhangs, twists and turns with the river picking up gradient, noise and speed right beside us. It's not for the faint hearted by horseback that's for sure. Emerging from trees, we found ourselves on the precipice of a waterfall, and it felt like the road was going to cascade down with the flow too.

With only a momentary stop for a head held high, wide-eyed check that this wasn't a feet wetting situation and that the trail would still proceed on tarmac, Skye continued to plod on. I gave her a reassuring rub of her neck and thanked her for being so sensible given the extreme circumstances.

"It's okay," she replied, "no motorhomes would dare come down here, so all is safe and well."

"Are those white dots in the distance the Highland ponies we're going to meet?" asked Katy hopefully. "I think I recognise the one on the right."

"Did you even notice the cascading waterfall, Katy?"

"Eh? What?" was the response.

She seemed to have forgotten all about the possibility of cows too.

As the Highland Duo had their steep downhill, backside wiggle going on, it became uncomfortable to sit, so I jumped off Skye for the last section of the day. As I worked out my own leg stiffness with a comedy walk of my own, I kept a close eye on Katy's saddle. Her famous downhill wiggle was legendary for working the saddle (and pack) round, under her belly.

I can't stress enough how important it is to pack light when undertaking an expedition in the dobbineering category. A cumbersome pack balanced on top of a horse would be subject to much wiggles and jiggles, and especially so if Highland ponies were involved. If care wasn't taken over the rough ground travelled, the pack could easily be displaced.

I am certain that others had had this wiggling experience, and none sum it up as well as Dr Samuel Johnson once said in his account of a tour to Scotland (*A Journey to the Western Isles of Scotland*), "for it is not to be imagined without experience, how in climbing crags, and treading bogs, and winding through narrow and obstructed passages, a little bulk will hinder, and a little weight will burthen."

As we wiggled our way down the road we could see that, like Tomdoun, there wasn't much meat to Kinloch Hourn either - just a farm, a basic B&B, and a few houses. There is, however, a thoughtfully added car park for visitors to turn around in, with their curiosity satisfied and the adrenaline of the descent dissolved. Turning around, that is, to embark on the long and exciting climb back to civilisation.

I proceeded over to the farm for introductions and instructions on where to place the girls for the night. Let loose, Katy was delighted to blether with a weathered and wise looking Highland Pony who looked noble enough to be the chief of the clan. Skye, not turned on by idle tittle-tattle, immediately tasked her teeth with trimming every blade of grass in the field.

The midges again were fierce, and motivation to battle with them whilst pitching my still damp tent from last night wasn't strong. I wandered down to the jetty to dip my toes into the Atlantic Ocean, and thought back to doing the same in the North Sea at the very start of my journey. I had in fact now completed my east to west traverse of Scotland. The final day to Glen Elg was really an addition, following the famous drover route to Kylerhea opposite the Isle of Skye, something I had really wanted to do.

This route out of Kinloch Hourn was rocky and so incredibly steep at the start of a long day of boggy ground, dodgy bridges, and river fording trail challenges. It was a distance of thirty kilometres with 828 metres of ascent. I'd considered this the most demanding day of the whole trip, and the nerves I'd closed in the pot after the success of the Mount Keen day were now steadily pushing up the lid.

A feeling had been building all day, but like the midges I'd kept swatting it away; it was the realisation that I didn't think the Highland Duo had enough energy left to do it. They'd already come further than they'd ever travelled in one go before, and faced numerous trail obstacle 'firsts'. They seemed completely exhausted getting here today over easy ground, so was it genuinely fair to push them on?

In the blue-light driving course for my paramedic job, we were taught the avoidance of 'red mist'. This mist descends whilst driving to an emergency call, when you become so focussed on getting to your destination as quickly as possible that your attention to hazards, risks, and safety declines. It was easy to get caught up in red mist on a long-distance ride too. The focus on completion of the distance you'd originally set out to do can push you on regardless of common sense. It was hard to pull out of the mist, but it was the correct and safest thing to do.

If I was totally honest with myself, I think I'd considered the probability that our journey would be cut short when I was feeling so unwell myself at Invergarry. If the gals were lacking energy, I knew I would need more than I had in reserve to rally them safely over the tough pass to Glen Elg. It would have been a long and gruelling finish with the energetic Team Swogi; it seemed an impossible task with the Highland Duo.

I knew I would have unfinished business and regrets in making this call, so it wasn't made with ease. I also understood that this was a well-reasoned decision not based exclusively on nerves. I had nothing to prove, the Highland Duo didn't either, and I didn't want to destroy all that we had achieved by putting us at risk of failure or injury at the last hurdle.

I'd dipped toes in the North Sea and now in the Atlantic and for everyone's sake it was time to call it a day. The ponies were done, I was done, and the aim of the journey was complete too. East to west over the Highlands by saddle, the mission had been absolutely accomplished. We were the winners of the Game of Maps from the initial concept on paper, through to the reality of trail completion by hoof and foot. We would finish our journey here in this beautiful and tranquil place - Kinloch Hourn.

As I swished my toes around in the refreshingly icy waters, the sense of achievement gradually sprouted then flourished. I thought back to the months of planning and preparation, the relentless physicality of the trail, and now the successful completion despite adversity. There was a rapidly growing sense of satisfaction and contentment. The toe-dip in the east seemed like months ago, and as I looked out over the Atlantic waters, the ups and downs of the journey washed over me.

The low times of wet sleeping bags, Yogi worries, the frustration of Swift up front, slow ponies, and of feeling unwell myself were thankfully outweighed by the high times. The highs were as numerous as the beautiful views I'd adored each day and every twist or turn of the trails I'd followed. Those highs I knew would linger most strongly as I returned to the normalities and the mundane of everyday life.

I was reaping the benefits of a slower progression through the landscapes we travelled, able to recall every little detail of the journey from start to finish. Like a sponge slowly absorbing moisture, I'd soaked up the sights, sounds, and emotions sensed. The rhythm of perpetual motion had drummed it all in, deeply imprinting the memories on my mind.

In the past, reward would come from the peak ticked off and the mountain conquered, but this was a different prize. I'd become fascinated with the linking up of the maze of glens and hill-passes that run rings around the peaks. The tops may have their amazing challenge and views, but it's the troughs that contain the hidden secrets, extraordinary delights, and captivating history to unwrap.

Journeying with others provides the added bonus, in the celebration of fellowships formed. The joy in the development of the Swogi team, observing progression in confidence, trust, and a cohesion of unified understanding. A prize that can never be undone, only built upon and explored further next time around. I could also celebrate the bravery and steadfastness of the Highland Duo, without whom I'd never have been able to get over the finish line. Despite bringing that finish line a little closer, I was still feeling fulfilled and immensely impressed by everyone's achievement.

Decision made and with midges amassing, the motivation to pitch camp had not improved. I went and broke the news to the girls that their job was done - who were delighted (I think) as they offered one snort each between snores. Already flat out in slumbers and my judgement underlined, I kicked around for a flat place to pitch.

I had been due to stay in a B&B for my last night at Glen Elg and I felt subconsciously aggrieved that I was not to get my end of trip gift. Too bumpy here, not enough breeze there, sheep poo, a few rocks, too close to the ponies; no campsite lived up to any comfy bed comparison. Feeling dissatisfied, I wandered over to the basic back packers B&B of Kinloch Hourn to see if they had any rooms. Any room would have done, but I had the pick of them all as nobody else was due in that evening.

As I was unexpected, they had no evening food available, but it was of minor concern. The hot shower, the log fire, a seat to sit on, and a comfy bed to look forward to shortly were all that was required. I cooked my last camp food meal on my stove in the woodshed and sitting on the grass outside to eat, I let the peace and quiet of the glen settle over me.

I phoned Dave to arrange pick up for the following day, back up the glen before the road became too steep for the van and trailer. My journey would finish tomorrow, back up the hill as quietly as it began, no fanfare, no fuss, just me and my two furry, four-legged companions.

The tail / tale end

The Journey 'to your horses'

Reflecting on my spectacular journey across Scotland, it hadn't been as self-sufficient as I'd imagined, with various people supporting us along the way. Even so, I certainly finished with more confidence about solo, self-supported travel with horses than when I'd started. Before setting out, I had wondered whether travelling this way for so long would encourage me to do more exploration in this style or whether it would scratch the itch in its entirety due to the hard work it entailed.

With the post-adventure blues kicking in on my return home, I knew resolutely that I hadn't wanted the adventure to end. If there wasn't a need to return to work, I'd have taken a couple of rest days and continued indefinitely. I also realised that it wouldn't be long before I'd be planning my next long-distance dobbineering adventure. There is something so addictive about the rhythmic movement, step after step, felt so deeply in your soul. This continual movement with a sense of purpose; it's no surprise that it becomes almost impossible to stop. Attention to surrounding details are enhanced by the slow pace of travel, prompting enchantment of the smallest of things.

Delight, measured by stimulation of senses alone, is a fundamental and primitive method of gratification. The new sights unfolding around every corner or rise of a hill, mesmerise, excite and promote onward drive. It's a simpler way to enjoy life, away from society's pressures, concentration on the here and now so entirely encompassing with no space left for global concerns. The unpack, repack, and move on, with the reliance on minimal material things and only your own self-resolve and that of your equine companions.

To some, my journeys may seem immense, dangerous, too risky (especially my mother!), but the training, retraining, and the learning from 'Mark Twain experiences' mould into co-ordination and understanding within the team. The deeply developed knowledge of both team capability and the environmental risks in which you move are the factors that keep you safe.

Sometimes you'll look back to a place or situation which, at the time, you moved through with ease. On reflection, however, you feel like you survived by the skin of your teeth. Your mouth goes a little dry, your stomach tightens its grip, and the thoughts of "what if?" arises. The hindsight fear is a useful learning experience too, so long as it doesn't overpower the call to return. Fortunately, if you enjoy adventure, then it presents a strong addiction and before long, you find yourself planning and preparing for the next great challenge with nothing but anticipated success in your sights.

My physical cross-Scotland journey might have come to an end, but the other journey would continue - the one I like to call 'to my horses'. The discoveries made on this journey occur as you explore their hearts and minds. The delights are uncovered as the trust and cohesion evolves and you learn about the capabilities of the team and of yourself. This journey doesn't have an end but it has a start, a road through the middle, and many route choices to make along the way. If you choose the right path, who knows where you'll end up?

Trail riding (or dobbineering) is often viewed as a simple or easy activity in terms of equine-sport, and I sometimes hear the term 'happy hacker' thrown in my direction. This summons up images of plodding along on a steady, shaggy pony on easy, local paths, with loose reins and a smile on your face. On the other hand, I often hear, "Wow, that's brave, I wish I could do that with my horse" and the person then explains how their horse won't cross bridges or gets too excited in open spaces for trail riding to suit them. In response to either view, I probably downplay what we (particularly what my horses) do, by replying, "I am a happy hacker, but I do it in a serious way."

To be a trail rider and to carry out the sport of dobbineering, you need a certain level of fitness, resilience, patience, adaptability, and map reading proficiency. The trail horse ... well they need to be a talented individual indeed, with a wide range of capabilities themselves. They need to be manoeuvrable at the lightest touch from their rider, so that each foot can be positioned accurately where needed and at exactly the right time. However, it is safer for the horse to be able to make choices like this unaided. The horse is often better placed to make judgement than the rider is, by feeling what's safe and what's not through their feet. A sure-footed horse is probably the top trump in terms of essentials for successful trail riding.

They need to be brave to tackle any obstacle in their way; steep gradients (up or down), river crossings, thick vegetation, over or under trees, rattling gates, unsteady bridges, boggy ground, or rock-filled paths. They should be able to face the strange things they might be asked to do: go through tunnels, cross cattle grids, push through herds of cows, squeeze through tight spaces, duck under cable cars (yes, this happened once), and load into any sort of motorised transport, not to mention cope with unfamiliar territory at every twist of the trail and stay overnight in strange places with alien noises through the night. Then there's those other trail users: the motorised traffic (huge logging lorries, quad bikes and tractors), mountain bikers, walkers with large flapping rucksacks, prams, umbrellas, or loose dogs.

A good trail horse will be resilient, able to cope with all kinds of weather, biting insects, and varied (often poor) grazing for weeks at a time. Stamina is important too, as the days are long and the trail can be hard. The best kind of trail horse loves what they do and has an inner drive to carry you through to the end of each day. That best kind of trail horse should be a calm individual, able to work through problems without getting stressed, working together with their rider to get out of a bind.

When you look at my two horses now, you would think they are not far off this description and how lucky I must be to have found them. However, a good trail horse isn't just 'found', it has to be 'made' and that journey is the longest and hardest to take. The rewards do outweigh the graft in the end though, making it a journey that is absolutely worthwhile to take. You just need to find a way to make that very first step.

My first horse Yogi was planned. I spent time searching advertisements, short-listing those that sounded right for me, then travelled long distances to view, before experiencing that 'love at first sight' feeling. He was by no means a perfect match; he was nothing like the ideal, once-in-a-life-time horse I had in mind. He wasn't even the horse I'd originally enquired about in the advert. However, there was just something about him and how he interacted with me, plus a spark of potential that I could glimpse at the end of the tunnel.

I soon realised how extremely long and narrow that tunnel was, when the horse I had purchased to primarily trek in the hills with, wouldn't go out on his own and appeared to fear everything that moved or didn't move. He would buck and bronc when turned for home, his brakes didn't work well, he didn't like to be caught from the field, he wouldn't load into the trailer, and was bargy and aggressive around the stable or food. There was that something about him though that made me persist, although to make this perseverance safe, I needed some help and advice.

That help and advice primarily came from a horse trainer (Leaf), who taught me how to speak and listen to the horse's language. Within the first day of training I'd been guided to curb the barging and could see the way to creating a docile horse, who would be happy to follow me around the yard at the end of a loosely held lead rope and who would seek me out in the field. I also now knew I had a horse whose unpredictable ridden behaviour and insecurities were primarily due to him being in pain.

While I set about establishing the source of Yogi's pain and made attempts to heal him, Leaf made an interesting proposition. Liking, I assume, how quickly I'd lapped up the learning, she offered an exchange. How would I like one of her young horses "completely untouched, so to speak, with no prior issues" in exchange for helping her start to train several other young horses and repair troubled souls in her herd? Those troubled souls were created primarily by poor human-horse interaction that had led to various problems to unpick.

Well I couldn't look a gift horse in the mouth, so my second horse Swift was therefore completely unplanned, but this seemed like a win-win situation to me. Not only would I gain more learning and experience along the way, but I'd have a horse that could be ridden at the end of this process. At the time, it wasn't looking likely that this was going to be an achievable objective with the horse I already had (Yogi).

Little did I realise quite how much I'd have to learn and experience along the way. The young horses and troubled souls were child's play compared to the demon of a filly Leaf had (purposely) picked out for me. It wasn't that Swift was bad, nasty, or aggressive; she was just extremely complicated, mixed-up, and insecure. She bottled everything up inside, and communication - so vital for safety - was challenging at the best of times, let alone during stressful (mainly new) experiences.

The next few years were trying times as I struggled to form a meaningful relationship with Swift, whilst moving forward with her training and watching her grow much taller than anyone had ever anticipated. The game played with her was akin to the board game *Operation* where all the parts were there, but I just needed much care, patience, and a steady hand to pick them out in the correct order. If I slipped up, then the consequences could be alarming and shocking.

I also had to work hard to rehabilitate Yogi with regular back-building muscle exercises and stretches. His mind needed some restoration too, to undo some of his bad habits and unacceptable learnt behaviour, instigated by pain-avoidance. His play was more like a reversed game of *Jenga;* there were pieces already removed, creating an unsteady stack. In this reverse match, I needed to replace the missing blocks to rebuild a strong and secure tower.

With both horses, there were a lot of trials and many more errors but gradually, so gradually, the hard work and stress paid off and migrated into fun, enjoyment, and delightful anticipation. Eventually I could again ride Yogi, and I started leading Swift out behind him when we went out on the trail. As Yogi's fitness improved, those rides increased in length. In Swift's progression towards graduating with a degree in human transportation, she needed to learn how to carry a saddle and some weight on that saddle. She also needed to learn about the big outside world. The rides became longer, the picnics heavier, and before I knew it, we were setting out on our first over-night camp ride in a local glen.

From that moment forward I was addicted to self-supported, overnight equine travel in the hills and glens of the Scottish Highlands. It felt magical to be out in the wilderness, just me and my two companions working as a team, testing our resolve against the elements and the challenge of the route. This was a different concept to backpacking with a rucksack (which I was already so familiar with) and a different dimension to a day out in the saddle. Many cross-over skills could be applied, but there was a whole new level of learning to grasp.

With packhorse in tow, I began to explore the hills and glens in an altered way, revisiting the familiar by unaccustomed means. I discovered new boundaries, new capabilities, new comfort zones, and the new elements that defined the classification of a 'suitable trail' for our unique team. There are pros and cons of travelling with two horses rather than one. It is undoubtedly slower with a large pack on a horse, as the cumbersome burden is deadweight and has more impact at higher speeds, as well as increasing the complexity of manoeuvring skills at every narrowing of the trail. There is twice the work at the start and end of every tiring day, with two horses to groom, prepare and attend to with tender loving care. The two horses also need to have agreeable characters and ideally should be matched at pace. As a combination, this can be tricky to find or create.

However, horses are herd animals and they prefer to travel with another of their kind. It gives confidence, companionship, and someone to keep the flies off their face when they stand nose to tail at night. It also provides a greater carrying capacity for improved self-sufficiency, which creates flexibility about where to camp, further exploration of remote places, and additional comfort (in back-packing terms) for all.

The learning curve was steep and, at many times, hard going. This journey continues yet - no matter how many miles we have done together and although the graph has plateaued slightly, every day firmly remains a school day. After each dobbineering adventure, I still chalk up new learnings. Things are generally easier now, and I take great delight in the ability to observe and appreciate my environment at ease. With less attention required, I can soak in more detail as I am carried along in a soothingly rhythmic fashion, elevated in height, sharing the discerned delights with my companions by unspoken means.

Whether it's the journey to your horses or a journey with your horses, it's amazing how far you can travel if you just keep moving step by step, day after day. Too immersed in the journey itself sometimes, you don't realise how far you've come from the start, until you stop for a while, and take the time to have a detailed look back.

Epilogue

Adventure Statistics

- 17 days (including 2 rest days)
- Approximately 380 kilometres
- Approximately 6000 metres of ascent
- 130 hrs riding/walking
- 4 different horses ridden
- 14 glens explored
- 2 dual carriageways & 5 main roads crossed
- 57 gates opened & closed
- 1 repaired saddle, rein, and saddle bag
- 1 torn finger and 1 sprained thumb
- ZERO blisters (I love my hiking boots)
- 1 surprise radio interview
- 13 (unlucky number) ticks removed from human
- 17 ticks removed from equines
- Lost count but at least 50 midge bites to human
- Unknown quantity of midge bites to equines
- 2 cattle grids with no side gates safely negotiated
- 1 fallen tree across trail safely negotiated
- 4 friends/family who helped with obstacles/logistics
- 4 friends who popped in along the route to say hi
- 1 friend who rode with me for 4 days
- 1 same friend who then lent me her ponies
- Many lovely & generous people met along the way
- 693 photos to process
- Over £1500 raised for Prince Fluffy Kareem
- 1 very cheesy grin
- 1 plan forming for another big trip!

Katy & Skye

Katy recovered well from her ordeal and has gone on to join Yvonne and I on many more adventures. Realising that this is a pony who does not like to be towed has really helped our travel times. Preferring to make her own way, following along as packhorse, she is now unclipped as soon as situations allow. It's rare that we see any sticky feet objections these days, and she reliably follows us wherever we go.

She does, however, have a new partner – Tom Tom the (Sat Nav) black and white cob. Skye finally realised her lifetime ambition to be a pampered princess at a nearby riding school. She loves the kids, the attention she gets, the pony club games, and the mischief making opportunities the activities present.

Yogi & Swift

Swift - as suspected - was truly worth the wait, the blood, the sweat, AND the tears. I finally negotiated my way into her soul, and we enjoy an almost serene relationship now. She seeks out my affections, enjoys cuddles with carefree abandon, and communicates openly her preferences and thoughts.

No bottling up of worries anymore, and her explosive floops as a result are thankfully a fading memory. You do still have to respect her personal space when working with her on the ground, but at least the respect is a two-way phenomenon now.

She is confident up front and those flashes of potential I experienced are now an everyday entity. I find myself riding her more and more on long-distance rides as she thinks through every obstacle carefully in a calm and collected fashion. The only thing we haven't mastered yet is a gate opening technique, as they are a very long way down from up there! I am confident, however, that we will eventually overcome this challenge too.

Yogi is fit and well, and at the age of eighteen this year is still able to outwalk most horses I know. I was right to follow gut feelings regarding his strange symptoms during the trek. After a week at the specialist vet in Edinburgh, he was diagnosed with Cushings disease, unusual for a horse so young (twelve years at the time of this adventure), but I'm glad we were able to catch it early on.

Cushings is a disorder of the pituitary gland which normally controls hormonal output. The excessive production of hormones affects many systems throughout the body, and similar to diabetes in humans, the horse becomes poor at processing any sugar in their diet. Yogi didn't display classic signs, but the excessive urination and the mild laminitis were a hint. I thank my lucky stars that he was barefoot at the time because this, without doubt, led to the early diagnosis through the identification of the mildly sore feet.

On half a tiny tablet a day and a hay only diet, with a track system to keep him moving but reduce his grass intake, he remains fit as a fiddle. Yogi's turbo-boost is still firmly on offer and he never seems to tire. Last summer we completed over 600kms of long-distance treks, not counting the long rides out for fitness in between. Up to two weeks at a time completely self-supported over challenging terrain, with only a kit drop half-way to restock.

Swogi and I went back to finish the unfinished

business of the Kinloch Hourn to Glen Elg section a few years after our cross-Scotland trek (with Yvonne, Katy, and Tom Tom). I wasn't disappointed; it was a long, gruelling way but a wonderfully interesting route. No doubt one I'll do again someday. It was a hot day to start, and even though we were all fresh to the trail, the equines struggled with the uphill out of Kinloch Hourn. The river crossings were tricky and bridges as dodgy as suspected. Other challenges were faced such as a field full of young, excited, and in-your-face horses which was a dangerous experience with back feet flying sometimes near our heads.

The end of the day turned wet, windy, and bitterly cold (even for Scotland in June), and we had to stop early, only reaching Glen Elg the next morning. Not prepared for winter conditions, it was one of the coldest nights in a tent that I can recall ever experiencing in the UK. Yvonne and I agree that my decision to stop at Kinloch Hourn to finish my cross-Scotland adventure was absolutely the correct one to make at the time.

Although I haven't technically gone fully from east to west on my own horses in one go yet, we've done it many times in different ways but in separate sections. Who knows, one day I might stage a repeat performance and get Swogi to the end of the trail this time.

Myself & Lyme

You'd be right to question how it's taken six years to get this all written down! Immediately after the trek, there was Yogi to diagnose. I started a new job a month later and searched for a new home nearby. In December we moved further north, finding a house with a small area of land outside.

There was a lot to do to the land to make it suitable for Swogi, but I finally brought them home in the March of that year. Bringing the horses onto my own land was one of those childhood dreams, and the day it happened should have held great celebration. When I felt no joy or elation - just a flat, exhausted indifference. It was the final straw to signify that I was seriously unwell.

The repetitive flu like episodes had continued, but they lasted longer, were more severe, and appeared almost two weeks out of every four. I'd been making mistakes at work, had struggled to concentrate, and couldn't stay awake during mess room conversations. I basically slept my life away between work so that I could still struggle through shifts.

Since the doctors had failed to come up with any solution, I tried, through my fatigue, to find answers myself. Searching online, I found that most of my symptoms matched those of Lyme disease. I saw a GP at my new practice and, offering my thoughts on a cause, had to insist on a test.

"You can't possibly have Lyme Disease" I was told "but I'll test because you insist."

Lyme disease (LD) is an infectious disease caused by bacteria, transmitted to humans by a bite from an infected tick and is common in the Scottish Highlands.

So damn right I insisted; I'd had many tick bites over the years, I lived in a high-risk area, and had numerous symptoms to match. My blood counts were all over the place too, so something physical was causing this - it wasn't "all in my head" as this GP had taken upon himself to suggest.

I never experienced the classic and diagnostic bullseye rash from the bite, and apparently only sixty percent of sufferers do. I'd been aware of the physical symptoms (fatigue, flu episodes, headaches, joint pain, night sweats, muscle weakness, heart palpitations, allergic reactions, and digestive issues), but the cognitive effects crept on in a more subtle way.

I used to be an incredibly organised person. I could juggle lots of things at the same time and nothing was forgotten or overlooked, but now I could no longer think in a logical way. My computer and paper filing systems became a mess and I struggled to find anything anywhere, if only I could remember what it was that I was looking for anyway. At my worst I couldn't listen to music, watch a film, fill in a form, read a book, make simple decisions, concentrate on any conversation, find words for coherent speech, or look at a computer screen for more than five minutes.

I was irritable, short-tempered (with full on rages aimed at poor Dave over the smallest of things), I was paranoid and emotionally felt numb. I couldn't remember the last time I'd laughed or cried, but I could certainly tell you when I'd last lost my temper and I'd never had a short fuse in my life. I had a lovely new house with my horses right outside and a fantastic new job with great people. Life should have been full of fun and laughter but instead it was flat.

The last bout of 'flu' really scared me, as I was bed

ridden for days and really struggled to breathe. The one time I ventured out of the bedroom, I became lost in my own house. I was so confused that I couldn't work out where I was. As I recovered slightly, I took Dan and Tully to the beach a few days later - a simple ten-minute drive. I didn't have the breath to walk, but Dan and I sat on the sand while Tully burnt off her bounce.

On the way home I realised I'd been driving for twenty-five minutes and didn't recognise my surroundings; I'd missed the turning for home and hadn't even noticed. I didn't drive again for quite some time after that. All these cognitive problems are described in one simple term on the list of LD symptoms - brain fog. It's an accurate description but possibly only if you've ever experienced it.

I waited in anguish for the results of the test, as I didn't know where I would turn next if it was negative. I was begrudgingly diagnosed in March 2015 by the same GP who said it couldn't possibly be that. No apology or recognition for the years that I'd had this and the years I'd been tested for everything but. Despite diagnosis, I had no doubt that the hypochondriac label was still firmly attached to my notes.

The treatment I then received from the NHS for my long-term, misdiagnosed LD is considered ineffective by Lyme specialists around the world. I felt let down, dismissed, and disbelieved by the organisation I give most of my time to. There were no options offered when symptoms persisted after four weeks of oral low-dose antibiotics. In the end, I had to seek out private treatment at my own cost.

After a year of treatment (use of savings) and recovery, I thought I was doing well, but by May 2017 I was again struggling with cardiac symptoms. This time symptoms were more serious, but it still took about fifteen months to eventually be diagnosed with Lyme carditis (I did have an atypical presentation). This means basically that the Lyme bacteria had invaded my heart tissue so I had a month of intravenous antibiotics this time, arguably what I should have had in the first place.

Although this treatment really made a huge difference, I don't think I'll ever regain the physical stamina I once had but most of the cognitive effects have subsided. I still struggle with sensory overload, such as busy/noisy places, and listening to music. I find working at a computer extremely exhausting and often suffer from a complete lack of facial recognition (even if it is someone I know very well). When I'm tired, I still lose words.

Wavering energy levels also remain. Sometimes I'm full of beans and sometimes I'm flat on my back, but I do appreciate how lucky I am to have pulled out of this mess in such a good state. Many people who I converse with through LD support groups are nowhere near as well as I am. They are left to suffer and rot by health care systems who seem disinterested in a disease that is so incredibly sneaky, debilitating, and devastating. It is also very much on the increase worldwide and I wonder when the world is going to sit up and notice?

As rough as this all sounds, you learn a lot about yourself, other people, and the world around you on every journey, and oddly I wouldn't change what has happened. I am, however, a lot more careful about ticks in the hills and spend time doing preventative education as well as time helping others get well.

I refuse to let this change my dobbineering ambitions. I just have a skin searching night-time routine before bed in my tiny tent now, and a repellent application routine in the morning. An ambition I still have is to fulfil the one thousand miles of continual horse powered journey that would make me eligible to join the Long Riders Guild. I'd like to do this exploring the amazing country in which I live, through glens and over hills with as little tarmac as I can, and of course with Team Swogi by my side.

Into the sunset

About a Lyme

Alone in the corner of a crowded room
The centre no more, I've changed my tune
No choice this change that has been made
An unfortunate price that I have paid

Unable to focus on things that matter
Distracted by next table chatter
Noise near and far sounds just as loud
Mental effort now to be in a crowd

Unable to follow a conversation
With such a shortened span of attention
Excess stimulation of colour and sound
An overdose to blur and confound

Do people think I no longer care?
It's much harder now to be *right there*
I try to remember and to focus
My brain turns your words into hocus pocus

The effort fatigues me but I look just fine
If only you knew the struggle inside
The pain, the exhaustion and the brain-fog
Trying to appear normal is a full-time job

The symptoms are hidden so many will say
"You seemed alright the other day"
It's hard to understand what you cannot see
Please listen when I tell you -just believe me

You that stick by me through thick and thin
The gratitude I feel deep within
You help to support me and ease my pain
Giving hope for days that are better again

Unable to enjoy the things that I love
Film, music, reading all too much
No energy left for out and about
Outdoors now indoors, it's like I've checked out

I no longer laugh as nothing seems fun
I hate the monotone that I have become
Nothing inspires and nothing excites
Just what will it take for me to relight

I grapple around to comprehend
Why I'm not fully on the mend
The treatment has been and long gone
But symptoms keep on rolling along

The chronic is a lonely condition
Regret common place in transition
The *who* me? The *new* me? Is this *me* now?
I want the old me back but I don't know how

Too late now to notice the subtle onset
No button to press for a system reset
A gradual change but the new me sticks
No thanks to those couple of nasty ticks

Hindsight of the past a useful tool
I should have sent that doctor back to school
A disease he said *"You can't possibly own"*
Delayed treatment: left frustrated, ailing, alone

Lyme common, but reported so rare
Nobody in power really seems to care
And with it ticks carry other infections
Which harm further and cause confusions

Widespread lack of recognition and education
Poor treatment within this whole damn nation
Those that suffer are left in the lurch
Due to a lack of quality research

A plea to fight these diseases and infestations
To end these horrific life devastations
How long must the thousands endure?
Before funds are secured to find us a cure.

Printed in Great Britain
by Amazon

75193135R00181